RICHARD III
IN THE NORTH

To Arthur and Edward, historians of the future!
Our princes in the Brackenbury Tower.

RICHARD III
IN THE NORTH

M.J. TROW

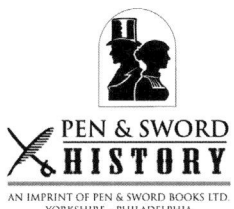

Pen & Sword
HISTORY
AN IMPRINT OF PEN & SWORD BOOKS LTD.
YORKSHIRE – PHILADELPHIA

First published in Great Britain in 2020 by
PEN AND SWORD HISTORY
An imprint of
Pen & Sword Books Ltd
Yorkshire – Philadelphia

Copyright © M.J. Trow, 2020

ISBN 978 1 52677 717 1

The right of M.J. Trow to be identified as Author of
this work has been asserted by him in accordance with the Copyright,
Designs and Patents Act 1988.

A CIP catalogue record for this book is available from the British Library.

All rights reserved. No part of this book may be reproduced or transmitted in
any form or by any means, electronic or mechanical including photocopying,
recording or by any information storage and retrieval system, without permission
from the Publisher in writing.

Typeset in Times New Roman 11/14 by
SJmagic DESIGN SERVICES, India.
Printed and bound in the UK by TJ Books Limited.

Pen & Sword Books Limited incorporates the imprints of Atlas, Archaeology,
Aviation, Discovery, Family History, Fiction, History, Maritime, Military, Military
Classics, Politics, Select, Transport, True Crime, Air World, Frontline Publishing,
Leo Cooper, Remember When, Seaforth Publishing, The Praetorian Press,
Wharncliffe Local History, Wharncliffe Transport, Wharncliffe True Crime and
White Owl.

For a complete list of Pen & Sword titles please contact
PEN & SWORD BOOKS LIMITED
47 Church Street, Barnsley, South Yorkshire, S70 2AS, England
E-mail: enquiries@pen-and-sword.co.uk
Website: www.pen-and-sword.co.uk

Or

PEN AND SWORD BOOKS
1950 Lawrence Rd, Havertown, PA 19083, USA
E-mail: Uspen-and-sword@casematepublishers.com
Website: www.penandswordbooks.com

Contents

Author's Note		vi
Acknowledgements		vii
Prologue:	Looking for Richard	viii
Chronology		xiv
Chapter 1:	Conisbrough	1
Chapter 2:	Raby	6
Chapter 3:	Ludlow	18
Chapter 4:	Wakefield	25
Chapter 5:	Towton	40
Chapter 6:	Middleham and Sheriff Hutton	55
Chapter 7:	Barnet and Tewkesbury	64
Chapter 8:	Lord of the North	77
Chapter 9:	Scotland	93
Chapter 10:	Pontefract	100
Chapter 11:	The Black Deeps	112
Chapter 12:	Royal Progress	123
Chapter 13:	Bosworth	133
Chapter 14:	Beneath Swaledale	144
Epilogue:	The Angel of the North?	149
Appendix I:	Richard's Places in the North	155
Appendix II:	The Murders of Richard III	165
Select Bibliography		170
Index		172

Author's Note

The North

Geographical terms are relative and in a book like this, charting the life of Richard Plantagenet, the story inevitably travels all over the place. In the fifteenth century, the North meant anywhere north of the River Trent which rises in Biddulph Moor, Staffordshire and flows in a broad crescent shape to Alkborough, where it joins the Humber on its way to Hull and the North Sea.

Acknowledgements

I would like to thank everyone who has helped in the creation of this book, from those who have granted permission to use photographs to those who have been unfailing in their kindness, providing coffee and cake at numerous Richard sites across the North and elsewhere.

I must say thank you to Heather Williams and everyone at Pen and Sword – this is a book which I have wanted to write for so long and her enthusiasm on being presented with the project was wonderful.

Above all, and, as always, I want to record my thanks to my wife, Carol. She has always helped with useful critiques of my texts in her capacity as a professional editor, but in this instance has also provided first rate photographs and diagrams and has traipsed with me over some pretty rough terrains in less than kind weather.

Except where otherwise credited, the photographs are copyright Carol Trow. Diagrams of castles and battlefields, maps and heraldic designs are copyright M.J. Trow.

Prologue
Looking for Richard

'Nay, which is more and most of all, where is Plantagenet? They are all entombed in the urns and sepulchres of mortality.'

Sir Ranulph Crow 1625

I first met Richard III when I was six. It was in the old Majestic cinema in Mill Street, Macclesfield and he was played on screen by Laurence Olivier, complete with hunched back, gammy leg, deformed hand, withered arm and black wig. My mother was a huge Shakespeare fan and when Olivier's *Richard* was released, we *had* to go. I can remember the central white tower of the Majestic (still standing) although most of the building has gone, leaving the place in a more ruined state than many of Richard's actual castles in the North!

At six, I did not understand much of the storyline. I knew Richard was evil. He hobbled noiselessly around the sets, throwing long, twisted shadows onto doors and walls. His mood changed from gushing sentimentality to ice-cold psychopathy at the turn of a groat. The most terrifying moment came when, lit from below, he turned with hatred on his little nephew (Richard of York, whom he will later kill). The loud discordant crash of music made me jump out of my skin.

I also knew that Henry Tudor, Earl of Richmond was the good guy. He was played by Stanley Baker, whom my mother knew and was, like me, a Welshman. A halo seemed to surround him in all his scenes on the screen. Other than that, I didn't know who anybody was. Thomas Stanley, one of two brothers who ultimately betrayed Richard, was played by Laurence Naismith who, because he was bald, I took for a bishop!

Re-watching the film now, as I have several times over the years, I am struck by how *old* everybody was. Richard was dead at thirty-three, yet Olivier was forty-eight when he played him. And how could anybody be surprised at the supposedly untimely death of Edward IV when he was played by Cedric Hardwicke, sixty-two? Of all the credited cast, only Stanley Baker, Claire Bloom, as Anne Neville, Richard's queen, and the boys playing the princes in the Tower were the correct ages for the characters they were portraying.

Back in 1956, however, *nothing* could have prepared me for Richard's death at the battle of Bosworth. The setting suddenly changed, from surreal pseudo-Medieval sets at Baynard's Castle and elsewhere, to rural Leicestershire. This was actually shot in Spain and the harsh sunlight looks hopelessly artificial for England. Having had nightmares in his tent before the battle, Richard regains his sangfroid, muttering the un-Shakespearean 'Richard's himself again', and wheels his white horse to charge against Henry Tudor's line. The camera pans with him and Olivier's thunderous 'Victory sits on our helms!' over the galloping hoofs says it all. Music to the ears of a little boy of six!

Then, it all goes horribly wrong. There is a lull in the fighting. Richard yells his completely unhistorical 'A horse! A horse! My kingdom for a horse!' and then he is alone in a hollow, the only sound his breathing as he watches his enemies close in on him. He clashes with Stanley, driving him back with sword and dagger before the Lancastrians surround him, striking and slashing, ripping off his black armour. Then they move back and Olivier, bleeding and in agony, writhes on the ground, that terrible discordant music in effect his death knell.

Rather cornily it seems to me now, the camera focuses on the ribbon of the Garter below his left knee as his body is slung over the back of a horse – *Honi Soit Qui Mal Y Pense* (evil to him who evil thinks) – and the crown, which moments before is seen rolling away under horses' hoofs, is retrieved in a hawthorn bush and raised to be placed on the head of Henry Richmond. The Tudors have arrived.

Today's filmography provides details a six-year-old would not have been interested in. Olivier directed (he had already played Shakespeare's best known villain on stage several times), but he was assisted by an uncredited Alexander Korda, the Hungarian who was more British than the British and made innumerable Empire epics, like *The Drum* and *The Four Feathers*. The music was written by William Walton, who also wrote for Olivier's *Henry V*. *Richard III* was the first film to be premiered simultaneously in theatres and on television in the States, although British audiences had to go 'to the pictures' for the privilege.

For purists, Olivier came in for criticism because he uses large chunks of *Henry VI* for the dialogue, as well as bits from the eighteenth-century rewrites of Colley Cibber and the actor David Garrick. He wanted the redoubtable Orson Welles to play 'princely Buckingham', but in the end, Ralph Richardson insisted on the part. Vivien Leigh wanted to play Anne Neville, but Claire Bloom got that one and apparently, Olivier had an affair with her in the process.

Olivier's makeup took three hours to complete and no doubt the withered fingers idea was taken from the most famous painting of the king (now in the Royal Collection) in which the middle fingers of his right hand, curled around his collar, look as if they have lost their tips. Filming took seventeen weeks and the armies at Bosworth were extras from the Spanish army. There were 500 of them in those nostalgic, halcyon days before CGI!

The film is awash with heraldry that not only resembles a Medieval Book of Hours (Richard's own personal copy has survived), but is surprisingly accurate. That is because one of the cast – Douglas Wilmer, who plays Lord Dorset – was a heraldry buff and Olivier kept pestering him for more information on that score. The fight arranger was the actor Bernard Hepton who went on to become a stalwart of 1980s/'90s television; there is a brief close-up of him as he stabs Richard in the final moments at Bosworth.

The jury is still out on Olivier. Was he the finest actor of his generation? Or a self-centred 'luvvie' who put the 'ham' into Buckingham? Two things are certain. In 1956, he scared a six-year-old boy witless. And, in extending even Shakespeare's villainous nonsense, he put the cause of the real Richard back by centuries.

Fast forward to 1967. The six-year-old boy is now seventeen and he has just passed his driving test (the first time, I am placing it on record!). Richard was part of the A level History course I was undergoing and I had never forgotten my two hours in the Majestic cinema. I wanted to carry out further research into the battle of Bosworth (I still have the artwork to this day) and, since Warwickshire, where I lived, was only a stone's throw from Leicestershire, where Richard died, what could be easier?

I borrowed my father's car, and with a friend set off for Bosworth. There was no visitors' centre then, just anonymous farmland and I realized at once how difficult it is to find your way around an area that held centre stage for only a couple of hours 500 years ago. In true public schoolboy tradition, my friend and I knocked on the door of the farmhouse on Ambion Hill, explained our presence and asked permission to walk the fields.

Public school or not, by the age of seventeen, I had picked up some of the more colourful aspects of the English language, but nothing could have prepared me for the barrage of abuse we got from that farmer. The air turned blue and he frogmarched us to a trough of foul-smelling chemicals where we had to wash our wellies. Why? Because 1967 saw one of the worst outbreaks of Foot and Mouth disease the country has seen. There had been others, in the 1920s and 1950s and this one had begun in Shropshire. A quarantine was set up as standard procedure and all animal movement was banned. Altogether, despite the precautions, 2,364 outbreaks were reported across the UK resulting in the slaughter of 430,000 cows from 2,300 farms. And here were we, completely ignorant, traipsing from one county to another, possibly bringing death and destruction with us. So I did not get to walk the battlefield of Bosworth until I was researching for this book. And when I did, I discovered a little more about the farmer of Ambion Hill. He was not of a naturally friendly disposition, they told me at the battlefield's visitors' centre – to the extent that he used to stand near Dickon's Well with a shotgun under his arm, watching any would-be trespassers. Perhaps my friend and I got off lightly!

Fast forward again, this time to 2008. By that time, I had been teaching History and, latterly, Politics, for thirty-six years and it was time to hang up my chalk. The last school trip I undertook was with a Year Nine (thirteen-year-olds) group to the Richard III Experience at the Tower of London, site of the murder of Henry VI, the execution of William, Lord Hastings and the supposed crime scene of the murders of the princes, Richard's nephews.

I had taught the princes' story as a Medieval whodunnit, using such CSI techniques as were appropriate, a mish-mash of FBI-style offender profiling and, of course, the historical record. But now, we had the chance to meet the king in person and grill him.

We were ushered into an education room somewhere in the White Tower, shown how to bow to the king when he arrived and told to address him as 'Your Grace', not 'Your Majesty', which was a Tudor convention. I was impressed.

The king duly arrived – a tall, broad, good-looking actor in excellent, accurate costume. We bowed and he sat down. The questions started.

'Where are the princes?'

'At their studies,' said the king.

'Can we see them?'

'No, we cannot interrupt their work.'

He waved his hands casually as if they were just across the way. I had already primed the brightest lad in the class to ask the king about Jane Shore, the mistress of Edward IV, Lord Hastings and the Marquis of Dorset. This he did.

'She was a friend of my late brother's,' the king said.

My cleverest lad was not to be fobbed off

'Is she a prostitute?'

Gasps and stifled giggles.

'Yes,' the king said flatly and prepared to move on.

Suddenly, he rounded on the boy, à la Olivier all those years ago.

'Why are you asking me about Jane Shore?' he wanted to know.

My cleverest lad's composure deserted him. He pointed to me and said, 'Mr Trow told me to say it.'

All eyes turned to me, the kids holding their breath, my colleagues trying not to laugh.

'Yes,' said Richard thoughtfully. 'He looks like someone who would know all about Mistress Shore!'

Twelve years before the Tower experience, the Hollywood star Al Pacino made an odd little movie called *Looking For Richard*. He had intended to make a straight film of the play, but realized, having seen Olivier's version, that he could not better it and make a profit, which is, of course, an essential element of film-making today. So, over four years and working around his busy schedule, Pacino produced the movie that has snippets of Shakespeare, re-enactments and chats with the famous and the unknown, probing Richard's character. Pacino eventually produced eighty hours of footage which had to be cut to theatrical length by no less than six editors. The only actor to be paid was Kevin Spacey (as Buckingham), but he ploughed his salary back into the movie to make it work.

Pacino's effort is laudable, though I am not sure about its commercial viability and it illustrates the problem that all historians/researchers have. How do we sweep away 500 years of bias, dogma, bigotry and downright lies to expose the reality of a man who became England's king all that time ago? Perhaps we could start with a bit of luck and a lot of tenacity; we could find Richard's body.

Philippa Langley's own *Looking for Richard* project made everybody else's search look like child's play. Working against the odds, in the teeth of the grim recession post-2008 and wheeling and dealing with a huge variety of powers that be, she organized the impossible, the archaeologist's shibboleth – the search for, and discovery of, a single, named individual. The phrase that went out from the international members of the Richard III Society was as tall an order as it was simple – 'Search for him. Find him. Honour him.'

Philippa is a screen writer who, like many of us, became fascinated by Richard III from an early age. She grew up in Darlington, a less than two-hour horse ride from Richard's fortress of Barnard Castle and his church of St Mary's. When she was a girl, there were no school trips there or to Richard's even greater castle at Middleham. The book that turned her on to Richard was Paul Murray Kendall's biography, published in the year of Olivier's film (I still have my copy which I was given for my eighteenth birthday). Some historians today scoff at Kendall, because he was not, technically, an historian, but his exquisitely written book has stood the test. Kendall made one mistake, however, along with almost everyone else at the time – 'At the dissolution of the monasteries, the "Grey Friars" was plundered; Richard's tomb was destroyed, his body thrown into the River Soar.'

The historian John Ashdown-Hill did not believe that and Philippa liaised with him and a number of key people to set up an archaeological dig in the centre of Leicester, to find the site of the Grey Friars and, more especially, Richard's grave.

The obstacles were huge. A serious financial recession meant that funds usually available were not on the table. The University of Leicester cooperated, however, providing archaeological expertise and an osteo (bone) specialist. Leicester City Council had to be brought on board, so did the owners of the car park underneath which, Philippa believed and various obscure old maps hinted, the body might lie. Philippa herself had something of a Damascus moment when she visited the car park belonging to Leicester Social Services, a tingling, unreal sensation near what may have been the Grey Friars' wall. She wisely kept this to herself – money men are rarely impressed by anything spiritual. The Church had to be brought in too and the deal was that should the bones be found and turn out to be Richard's, they should be re-interred in Leicester Cathedral. As things turned out, there would be serious opposition to that.

As Philippa puts it, 'I would be searching for the mortal remains of an anointed king of England, an unprecedented goal for which no guidelines existed.' Philippa wrote these guidelines herself. The result is one of the most remarkable and important archaeological discoveries of all time. It answers one crucial question about Richard – the extent of his 'deformity' – and for that, we are all grateful. If nothing else, it renders Shakespeare irrelevant.

What it does not do, however, is to give us even the slightest hint of Richard's personality. Christian burials, which Richard's was, do not provide goods for the afterlife. There is no 'time capsule' along with the bare bones to give us clues. We are absolutely no further forward, for example, in the vexed question of Richard's complicity in the murder of his nephews, the princes in the Tower.

And in 2019, my wife and I were wandering Barnard Castle with our two grandsons and a thought occurred to me – why not write a book about Richard III in the North?

Chronology

1452	2 October	Richard born at Fotheringhay Castle, Northamptonshire.
1459	October	Richard and his family under siege at Ludlow Castle, Shropshire. 'Battle' of Ludford Bridge.
1460	30 December	Battle of Wakefield. Richard's father, Richard, Duke of York, and brother, Edmund of Rutland, killed.
1461	February	Richard and his brother, George, Duke of Clarence, sent to the court of Philip, Duke of Burgundy.
	4 March	Edward of York proclaimed King Edward IV in London.
	29 March	Edward defeats Margaret of Anjou's Lancastrian army at Towton, Yorkshire.
	12 June	Richard and George return to England.
	1 November	Richard created Duke of Gloucester.
1465	September	Richard sent to Warwick the Kingmaker's castle at Middleham, Yorkshire.
1469	17 October	Richard created Constable of England.
1470	2 October	Richard goes into exile with Edward to Burgundy.
1471	March	Edward and Richard return to England, landing at Ravenspur.
	14 April	Richard's first battle at Barnet, Hertfordshire. Warwick the Kingmaker killed.
	4 May	Richard's second battle at Tewkesbury, Worcestershire. Edward, Prince of Wales killed. Yorkist victory.
	21 May	Henry VI murdered in the Tower of London, probably on orders from Edward IV.
1472	Spring	Richard marries Anne Neville. Starts to build up a Northern affinity and takes over Neville estates.
1475	29 August	Treaty of Picquiny between Edward and Louis XI of France. Richard disapproves.
1476		Probable birth year of Richard's son, Edward of Middleham.
1478	18 February	George of Clarence convicted of treason by Edward IV's court. Murdered/executed in the Tower of London.
1482	24 August	Richard, as Lieutenant General of the North, invades Scotland. Capture of Berwick and (briefly) Edinburgh.

Chronology

1483	9 April	Death of Edward IV. Succession of Edward, Prince of Wales, as Edward V.
	29-30 April	Richard and Henry, Duke of Buckingham, take possession of the new king at Stony Stratford, Buckinghamshire and arrest the boys' Woodville supporters Rivers, Grey and Vaughan.
	4 May	Richard, Buckingham and Edward V reach London. Coronation postponed. Richard is Lord Protector.
	10 June	Richard writes to Northern earls asking for military support.
	13 June	Council meeting 'coup' in the Tower of London. Rotherham, Archbishop of York and Morton, Bishop of Ely, arrested along with William, Lord Hastings who is executed on Tower Green.
	22 June	Sermon preached at St Paul's Cross, London, claiming Edward IV's children illegitimate and emphasising Richard's claim to the throne.
	6 July	Coronation of Richard III at Westminster Abbey.
	July/August	Royal progress of Richard and Anne ending in York. Probable disappearance of the princes in the Tower.
	10 October	Buckingham's rebellion breaks out.
	2 November	Buckingham executed at Salisbury, Wiltshire.
1484	23 January	Parliament meets at Westminster. Richard's claim to the throne, *Titulus Regius*, unanimously agreed.
	April	Death of Edward of Middleham, possibly from tuberculosis.
	July	Richard sets up the Council of the North.
1485	16 March	Death of Queen Anne, possibly from tuberculosis.
	7 August	Henry Tudor lands at Milford Haven, Pembrokeshire.
	22 August	Battle of Bosworth, Leicestershire. Richard III killed. Henry VII declared king on the battlefield.
	25 August	Richard buried in the Grey Friars, Leicester.
1495		Canopied tomb placed over Richard's grave.
1538		Grey Friars closed and demolished as part of Henry VIII's Dissolution of the Monasteries.
2009	21 February	Phillipa Langley sets up *Looking for Richard* project.
2012	25 August	Human remains found under letter 'R' in Leicester car park.
2013	3 February	DNA match of living Plantagenets with body in car park.
2015	21-29 March	Re-interment of Richard III's body in Leicester Cathedral.

Chapter 1

Conisbrough

The falcon and fetterlock crest of Richard of York. The fetterlock is shown open reflecting the fact that Richard was not going to be shackled by convention.

The odd thing about Richard of York, the future Richard III's father, is that we do not know where he was born. *His* father, also Richard, was made Earl of Cambridge in 1414, but the title carried no lands or income and we know he was strapped for cash. His wife was Anne Mortimer and she gave birth to the future Richard of York on 21 September 1411. Both Anne and Richard of Cambridge were descended from the many sons of Edward III, whose descendants jockeyed for power for nearly 100 years, precipitating the overthrow of Richard II, the rise of the usurper Henry Bolingbroke (Henry IV) and the internecine bloodbath that today we call the Wars of the Roses.

Since the Earl of Cambridge was originally known as Richard of Conisbrough, I believe it is a reasonable supposition that Richard of York was born in the great castle overlooking the Don.

In the time of King Edward (*tempus regni Edwardi*) as the compilers of William the Conqueror's Domesday survey put it in 1086, Conisbrough was already a royal estate, its twenty-eight wattle and daub settlements belonging to the last Saxon king, Harold Godwinson. In Domesday, it is called Cyningsbrough, the king's fortress, but we have no idea what the place actually looked like.

After the Conquest, the ubiquitous William de Warenne was given the fortress and estate by the new king. This was the Norman feudal system, whereby the king ensured loyal support and a plentiful supply of troops by, in effect, renting out parcels of land in exchange for military service. The system had its flaws, but it worked and survived for four centuries. To keep the Saxon population under control, the Normans built castles all over the country, including one at Conisbrough, probably several hundred yards from the earlier Saxon fortress.

Typically, the Norman Conisbrough was a wooden construction, with a keep, an inner and outer bailey, all protected by ditches and wooden palisades on the existing hill spur of magnesium limestone. The castle was intended to protect – or overawe – the Don Valley between Doncaster and Rotherham. The de Warennes continued to hold Conisbrough for the king until the 1170s when Isabel de Warenne married her second husband, Hamelin Plantagenet. Extensive rebuilding took place under his lordship, the entire structure being rebuilt with stone. The keep is unusual for an English castle (although Barnard Castle, further north, is similar) in that it is circular, like most of the examples in Normandy.

The castle which the boy Richard of York would have known, was entered through the outer bailey via a rectangular enclosure containing outbuildings such as barns and stables. A drawbridge (now gone) would have linked this to the inner bailey, which was made by scarping and counter-scarping the hill which formed the motte. The thirteenth-century curtain wall originally had six towers (three of which survive), but there were clearly engineering problems in building this. In places, the wall footings are only 2ft deep. To counter this structural defect, the towers had 'splayed feet', strengthening the stonework at ground level.

In the inner bailey was a large hall where the family and servants entertained and worked. This had two storeys, a huge central hearth, kitchen, pantry and cellar. It also had a chapel. Hamelin Plantagenet's remodelled keep is unique in England. It has six tapering buttresses supporting a hexagonal shape and is 92ft high over four floors. It once had a drawbridge and its own water supply via a well. The place would have been very dark because, unusually, there are no arrow slits in the keep's walls. This means that the keep was intended as a personal *solar* or living quarters for Hamelin Plantagenet rather than the more conventional use as a last-resort defence. There would have been brand torches in iron grilles on walls in various chambers and on the narrow spiral stairs. Only in the great chamber is there a large window and in the bedroom above. The general layout of Conisbrough is not dissimilar to another stronghold held by the family, at Sandal near Wakefield, from which Richard of York would ride to his death on St Egwin's Day, 1460.

We have no information regarding Richard of York's birth. All modern historians describe his lineal descent from both parents and then almost immediately plunge into the tortuous politics of the dynastic squabbles that led to the Wars of the Roses. He would have been brought up in whatever passed for a nursery in Hamelin Plantagenet's keep, suckled by a wet nurse and rocked in his cradle by faithful retainers who either lived in the castle or came from one of the outlying villages.

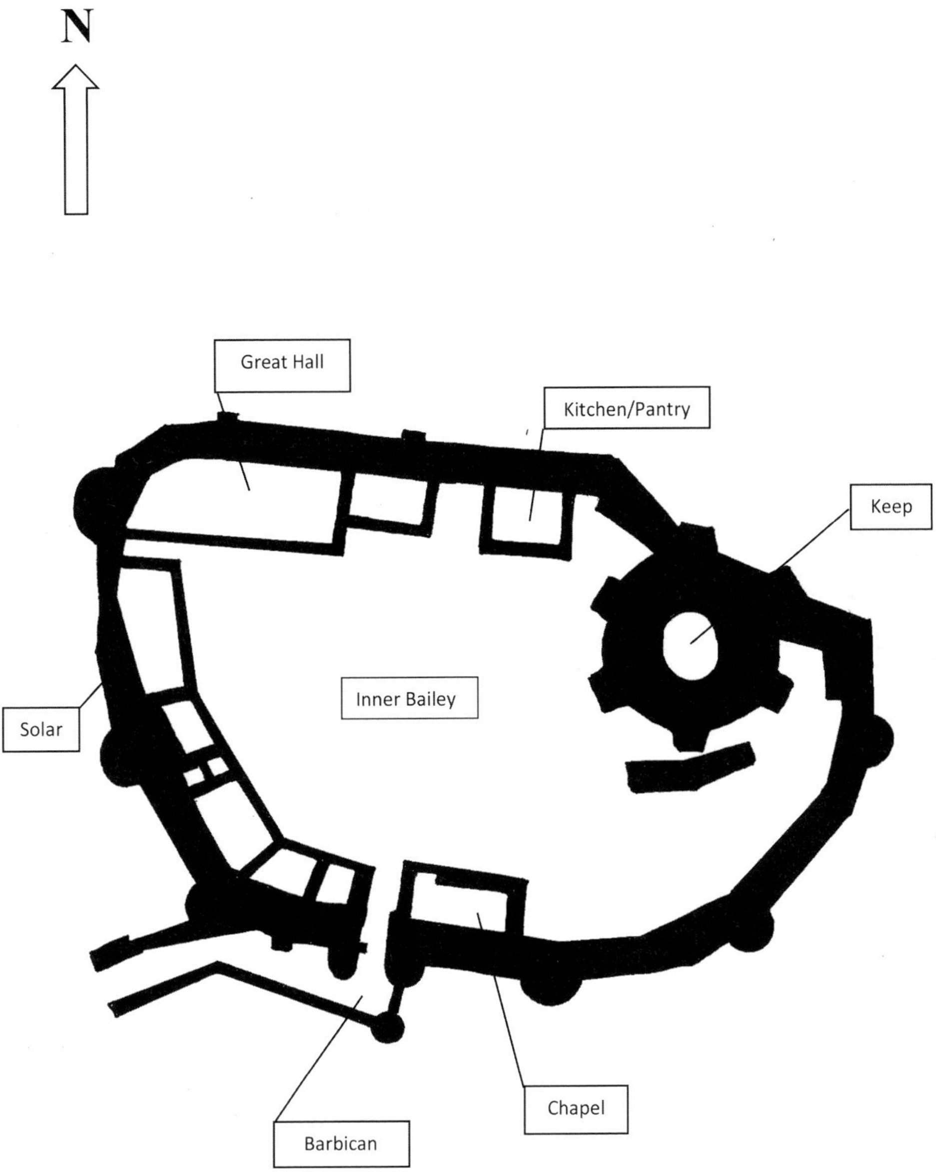

Conisbrough Castle at the time of Richard of York.

His mother, Anne Mortimer, died in that year of natural causes and that, grim as it sounds to a modern readership, would scarcely have impacted on little Richard's life. He may have been expected to attend the funeral, but, brought up by nursemaids as he was, he is unlikely to have been particularly close to his mother.

He was not close to his father either, but in the year of Anne's death, Richard of Cambridge was in trouble. His early life did not change much when Richard was four, but cataclysmic events beyond his control or even knowledge were massing to change the direction of his life forever. As is to be expected, there are no reliable portraits of Richard as a child or even as a man. The contemporary *Talbot Shrewsbury Book*, an illuminated treatise of 1445, has him as clean-shaven, with collar-length blond or auburn hair. Another portrait shows him with longer hair, a centre parting and a splendid forked beard of a type that was fairly common in the early century. Later queries concerning the parentage of his eldest son, Edward, Earl of March, describe Richard as short and dark whereas Edward was auburn/blond and at 6ft 3in, the tallest king in English history. Twelve years before little Richard was born, the anointed king, Richard II, had been overthrown by a rival, Henry Bolingbroke, the son of John of Gaunt, Duke of Lancaster, brother of Edward III. Richard had been held prisoner at Pontefract Castle, perhaps in the extended wine cellar there, which we know was used as a prison in the Civil War of the 1640s and is still open to tourists (see Chapter 10). All reports suggest that it took him ten days to die and the most likely cause was not starvation, as some suggest, but poisoning, perhaps by *amanita phalloides*, death cap mushroom. He was embalmed in Pontefract, wrapped in linen and placed in a lead-lined coffin to be brought by stages south to London.

Henry IV, the first of the Lancastrian kings, was plagued all his life by the single fact of usurpation. It would, of course, be an accusation levelled at Richard III after 1483, but Henry was much more blatant about it. Richard II may have been a weak king; he may even have been a bad one, but Bolingbroke's actions seem to have been carried out with no other motive than malice. There were those among the English nobility who were bitterly unhappy about the state of affairs and the brooding discontent simmered until the summer of 1415, when a knot of conspirators decided to act.

The plot was to replace Henry V, son of the usurper, with Edmund Mortimer, Earl of March, the brother of Richard's mother. Mortimer's descent from Edward III gave him the necessary pedigree, but it is likely that he got cold feet and told the king all about it. Henry was already at Southampton by July 1415, collecting his army to embark on what would become the Agincourt campaign (the city walls around which his men camped are still there). In this situation, the imminent absence of a king, embarking on a venture from which he might not return, was probably grounds enough for the conspirators to move everything forward. Henry acted decisively. Arresting the Earl of Cambridge, Henry, Lord Scrope of Masham and Sir Thomas Grey of Heaton, he tried them in what is today the Red Lion inn and found them guilty of treason. All three were executed a couple of days later on the sloping ground outside Bargate, one of the town's main thoroughfares, which still stands.

Ten weeks later, Henry's bedraggled army, ravaged by dysentery, faced the flower of French chivalry across the muddy fields near Agincourt, a then unknown village near St Pol in the Pas-de-Calais. One of the casualties that day was Edmund,

Duke of York, Richard's uncle, crushed to death, men said, in the desperate, hacking press around the king's standard. Almost overnight, little Richard was not merely the son of an executed traitor – he would become, in 1425, the new Duke of York.

Duke or not, the boy was an infant and an orphan and his wardship was bought, as was the custom, by Ralph Neville, first Earl of Westmoreland, for 3,000 marks. The orphan status meant that technically, the boy was a royal ward, in the care of the crown. In practice, Henry V, king of England and marrying into the royal family of France, had little time for these legalities and sold the York inheritance to the highest bidder, in this case Westmoreland. The boy was brought up with all the military and noble training required for a royal duke, which included swordsmanship, riding and handling a lance. His tutor in these matters was Sir Robert Winterton, a staunch supporter of Henry IV, in his fifties, who was made Constable of Pontefract Castle and was, therefore, Richard II's gaoler at the time of his death. Winterton may have been loyal to the Lancastrian cause, but he was not Henry V's favourite as he had been his father's. From 1416 until 1423 when he came of age, Richard of York was the richest nobleman in the country after the king. His mother's estates alone, from the Mortimer lands of Wales and the Marches, amounted to £3,430 (almost £59 million today).

As a boy, it is likely that Richard lived not at Conisbrough but at Waterton's manor house of Methley Hall and the nearby property of Woodhall and would have been brought up alongside Waterton's own children, Robert and Joan. Before he was eleven, Richard's surrogate mother, Cicely, died and was buried in St Oswald's Church in Methley in what is now the Waterton chapel. Waterton married again and Margaret Clavell brought to the marriage and to Methley her own three children, William, John and Eleanor, making quite a sizeable nursery.

Ralph Neville's duty was to find young Richard a suitable bride, because such relationships ensured the survival of families in an uncertain age. For that, he did not have to look far. Richard's future wife, the mother of both Edward IV and Richard III, lived only a few miles north of Conisbrough, at another of the Neville strongholds, Raby.

Chapter 2

Raby

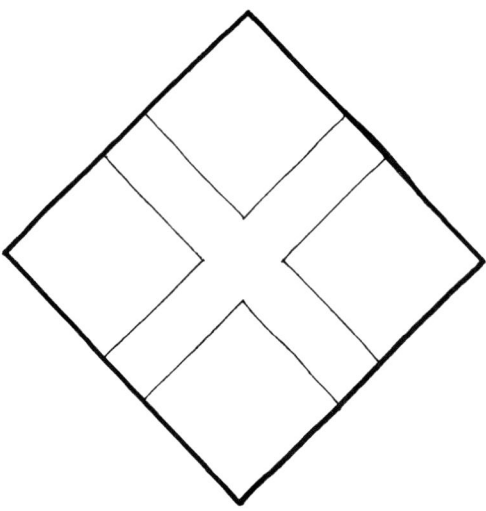

The arms of Cecily Neville of Raby. The lozenge shape as opposed to the conventional shield was used by ladies in the Middle Ages. The saltire (St Andrew's Cross) was part of the Neville family coat of arms. If only all heraldry were that simple!

For centuries, it was fashionable for 'old' families, as opposed to the nouveaux riches of, say, the Tudors or the Industrial Revolution, to claim that their ancestors had 'come over with the Conqueror'. The Nevilles had.

Sources differ over their original home. It was either Calle de Neu Ville or Neuville-sur-Touques, west of Paris. Either way, the name simply meant new town and we find it first recorded in the ninth century. Richard de Novarilla's family provided forty ships for William of Normandy's fleet in October 1066 and his four sons fought at Senlac. These Norman invaders were chancers, thugs descended from the Vikings, who saw limitless opportunities in grabbing English land after the outcome of a single battle. Over time, they morphed into the great baronial families of England, but the concept of warfare and the notion of extending wealth and power by force never quite left them. The Wars of the Roses, in which Richard, his brother and his father were killed, devastated the aristocracy, and a similar casualty list among the landed families would not be found again until the trenches of 1914–18.

Geoffrey de Neville (the spelling that became the norm) was given estates by William as a reward for loyal service and by 1115, the Yorkshire estates of Raby and Brancepeth both belonged to him. Technically, all land in the kingdom was the king's; the Nevilles, along with hundreds of others, were tenants-in-chief, 'holding' their estates on the king's behalf. In normal peacetime conditions, this was a formality, but when internal war threatened, as it did often in the Middle Ages, the king could confiscate lands and titles as well as award them. Similarly, if a family died out, as often happened in an age of high infant mortality, estates were forfeit to the crown for re-disbursement.

Staindrop, on the edge of the Raby estate, was a lead-smelting centre, close to Barnard Castle, the Roman fort at Piercebridge and the Viking stronghold of Gainford. The church contains the alabaster monuments to Ralph Neville, Earl of Westmoreland and his two wives, although neither lady is actually buried there. The font in the church still bears the Neville arms carved on one of its facets. The name Raby is Old Norse – Ra (boundary) and Bry (settlement), a reminder of the ninth and eleventh centuries when the whole of the North was the Danelaw, separated by race, culture and language from the Saxon south. Raby may have belonged to King Knut in the 1020s. The 'Viking thug' who became one of the most powerful of the early Medieval kings, was at pains to square his violent reputation with the church and allegedly gave Staindrop and Raby to the bishops of Durham as a goodwill gesture.

The Danelaw was always prone to attacks from further north. With the removal of the VI legion from York in the early fifth century, Hadrian's Wall was abandoned and the Scots made a whole industry of marauding as far south as they dared. Intermarriage between the Scottish royal family and the local lords was a more permanent way of holding territory and Maldred of Cumberland, the brother of King Duncan of Dunkeld, killed in battle against Macbeth in 1040, was a good example of this. His son Uchtred Fitz Maldred was born at Raby in 1120. His great-grandson Robert married Isabel de Neville, the mother of Geoffrey.

The story of the Nevilles' rise is the story of the North, although the family, by the fifteenth century, had estates in virtually every English county and a large part of Wales. They intermarried with other Northern lords, like the Latimers, the Percys and the Staffords so that the cataclysmic cycle of events we call the Wars of the Roses can be seen as a series of family feuds, the playground spats of little cousins that became nasty, large scale and serious when those cousins grew up.

Ralph Neville (the Norman 'de' had been dropped by now) served in Brittany during the Hundred Years War at a time when English fortunes were slipping. The glory days of Edward III and his son, the Black Prince, had gone and no one of their military stature emerged until Henry V at Agincourt. Ralph was already the fourth Baron Raby and now he was made Earl of Westmoreland too. In the power struggle between Richard II and Henry Bolingbroke, Duke of Lancaster, Neville changed sides and supported the rebels.

Such treachery against an anointed king was technically the most appalling of crimes, but it could, in a harsh and practical world, be well rewarded. Neville was made a Knight of the Garter, a member of the highest order of chivalry, created by Edward III in emulation of the legendary King Arthur's Round Table. He was also made Earl Marshal, which gave him a central position at court, responsible for the organization of all state occasions, keeping records and adjudicating territorial disputes.

Neville married twice. His first wife, Margaret Stafford, bore him eight children and died in 1396. His second, whom he married six months after Margaret's death, was Joan Beaufort, a granddaughter of Edward III. The dynastic tangles of the fifteenth century all stem from the myriad children of Edward, regarded as one of the greatest kings of Medieval England, in that they or their heirs were constantly claiming precedence over the others. As historian Peter A. Hancock puts it, 'I think it is safe to say that Edward III reigned for too long and had too many children.'

Joan was a deeply religious woman who produced another four children for her husband. She appears in the context of an extraordinary book, dictated in the 1430s, but not discovered until 1934 and not published until 1947. It is now regarded as the first autobiography in English and is the work of Margery Kempe, daughter of a King's Lynn merchant, who experienced religious visions. Ridiculed, imprisoned and accused of witchcraft, she went on pilgrimages to Rome and the shrine of St James of Compostella in northern Spain and was invited by Joan Neville, at some point between 1408 and 1413, to stay with her and talk about the scriptures.

Joan was already thirty-six, relatively elderly in terms of child-bearing, when she gave birth to her last daughter, Cecily, at Raby on 3 May 1415. She had been married to her first husband at twelve, then common practice among the aristocracy and within the permitted age range of canon law, and had produced her first child at fourteen. She would have fifteen more over a twenty-two year period, at a time without birth control and virtually no knowledge of post-partum infection and trauma.

The castle where Cecily was born was very different from the current building. Today's Raby looks like a fairy-tale creation, with towers, crenellations and sweeping lawns that any Hollywood epic producer would die for. It is complete with large ponds and a deer park.

Raby, too, was a hit with the Victorians, the first generation of tourists the aristocracy needed to keep their crumbling estates intact. J.M.W. Turner painted the castle in 1817 (he also daubed Barnard Castle) at a time when a new Romanticism was about to burst onto an unsuspecting world, personified by Walter Scott and his Waverley series of Medieval novels. The castle's guide book, from forty years later (by which time the railways had come to Yorkshire) wrote gushingly of the 'noble pile', its nine towers reflected in the lake. Then, as now, most visitors took in the plush state rooms with fussy gilded furniture, and oils by Vermeer and Vandyke.

When Cecily was born, none of this existed. The castle was built in an unusual irregular shape (historian Allen Brown calls it 'rambling and ill-fortified') on the site of a manor house, at first timber and wattle and daub, which a pre-Conquest family would have held against all comers. The dry ditch moat was filled with water in 1415 and the castle's main entrance, the Neville Gateway, had twin towers, three portcullises and a drawbridge. The entrances were always the weakest part of castle walls, hence the need to reinforce them. A raised drawbridge made crossing the moat impossible. Assuming it was lowered, the heavy grille of the portcullis stopped an army in its tracks. It was possible to burn its timbers, but while attackers were lighting fires, they were having to cope with a barrage of arrows from both towers simultaneously.

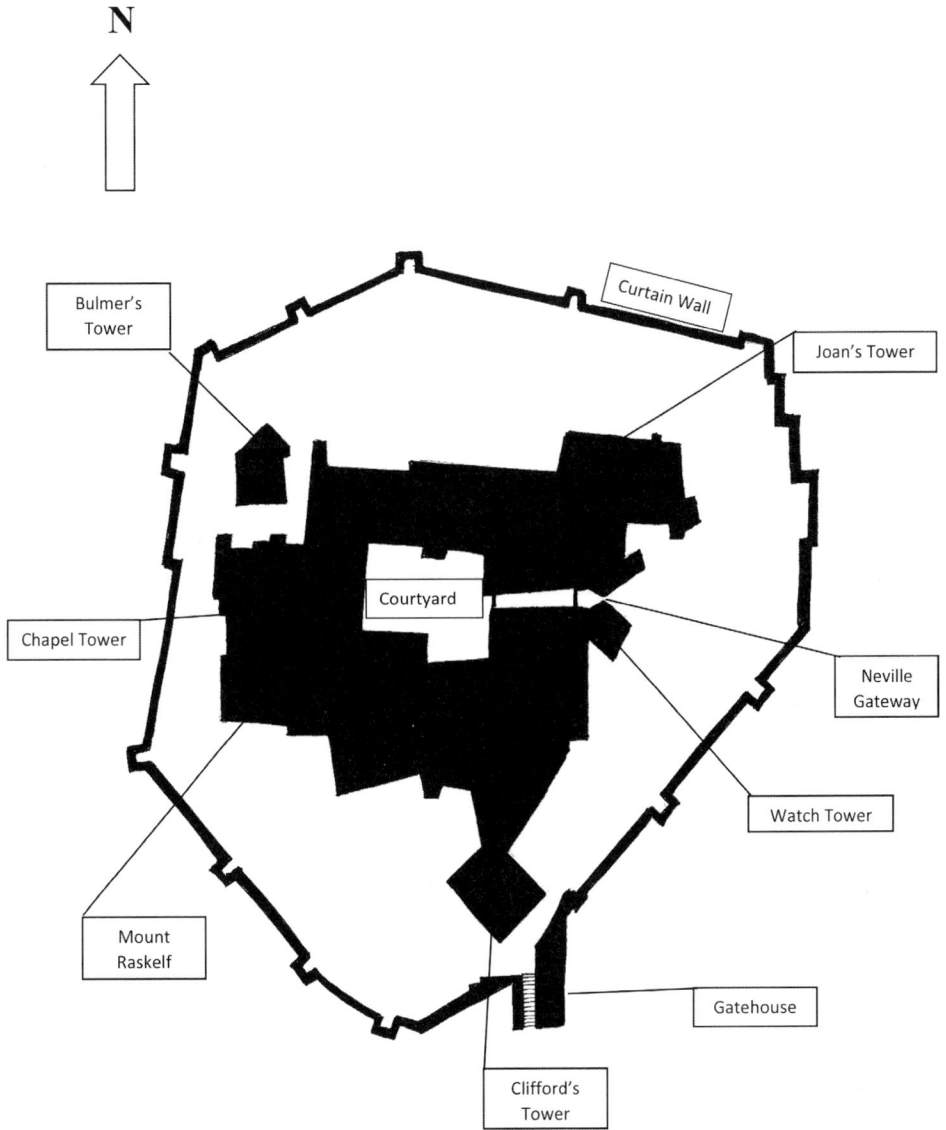

Raby Castle as it would have been in the 1420s.

To the left of the Neville Gateway stood Clifford's Tower, 80ft high with walls 9ft thick even at the top. The Guardroom was behind this (now the Servants' Hall) linked with the Watch Tower, 75ft high. Beyond the main Gateway stood Joan's Tower, named after Cecily's mother, 60ft high. Bulmer's Tower, 76ft, was named after Bertram de Bulmer, grandfather of Isabella Neville. Much of it dates from the fourteenth century and would have been relatively new in Cecily's day. Mount Raskelf, 70ft high and the Kitchen Tower next to it were probably completed in the 1370s.

Cecily's Raby had a huge hall, the central living space of the Nevilles and their army of servants and retainers. It could house 700 guests at a pinch and below the floor, the cellars had storage for wine, grain and salt, as well as ovens and spits for cooking and roasting. It was in this hall, much changed by the Tudor period, that the Catholic plot called the Rising of the North was planned in 1569.

We do not know exactly where the new baby was delivered (is it too simplistic to imagine it may have been Joan's Tower?), but Joan would have been lying in for a month before the due date and would stay in her bed for a further four weeks afterwards. Since she had already had children, the experience was less traumatic than it might have been, though everyone knew that the risks were immense. She would have issued invitations to her 'gossips' (God's siblings), female friends and relatives, who would all be crowded into the birthing chamber for the delivery. The midwife or 'grace-wife', usually an older woman experienced in the procedure, officiated and received a substantial reward – the grace – afterwards. To ward off evil and keep out unwanted Yorkshire draughts, keyholes were blocked, windows were shuttered, candles were lit.

The gossips made caudle, a sweet, spiced drink to balance Joan's humours. Such medical awareness as there was, was based on the translated Latin texts of doctors like Galen, who had himself learned his expertise from the Greeks. Experienced grace-wives could tell whether a pregnancy was male or female by the way the mother presented, but the whole process was overlaid with prayers and superstition that went back centuries.

Cecily's 'navel-string' was cut by the grace-wife and the baby wrapped tightly in swaddling clothes, exactly as it was believed the infant Jesus had been wrapped in the Bethlehem stable centuries before. Once the 'crying-out' was over, the baby was shown to her mother for the first time. 'Upsitting' would take place hours later, when Joan was allowed to sit upright for the first time and everybody present drank the caudle.

Men would have been absent from Cecily's birth. Had she been stillborn, a doctor may have been called to remove the foetus, if necessary, with hooks (there were no forceps in 1415), but in Cecily's case, all was well. Her father was fifty at the time, still an 'old' father today, and he was not expected to be anywhere near the birthing chamber. He would have been central to operations, however, at the baby's baptism. We do not know exactly where this took place. There was a chapel at the castle, originally a separate building within the courtyard, but there was also the church of St Mary in Staindrop, where Nevilles were already buried. Cecily's great-grandfather had set up a collegiate church dedicated to the Virgin (the most popular religious figure of the Middle Ages) to replace the older, smaller building dedicated to St Gregory. The church was a wealthy foundation, with a large body of priests and its vicar in 1412 was William Horne, who may have baptized Cecily.

Cecily would have been dressed in a white 'chrysom' gown and would have been carried to St Mary's by her godparents. At the church door, Horne would have placed salt in the baby's mouth to give her wisdom and to scare away the devil. Oaths were taken, prayers recited and Cecily would have been dunked in the holy water of the font. From there, probably by now screaming her head off, she was carried back to Raby for everybody else to enjoy a good feast.

As the youngest of the Neville children, most of Cecily's half-brothers and sisters were already adults, as the term was understood in the fifteenth century. Of her nine full siblings, two were married and we are unsure of the dates of birth of the others. It is possible that in Raby's nursery, where she would have been suckled by a wet-nurse, there would have been two brothers and a sister. We do not have details of the girl's childhood, but it would have followed closely the similar upbringing of a contemporary family, the Percys, rivals of the Nevilles who dominated the North under the special protection of various kings as long as they played their part in handling the Scots. Servants in the Percy nursery included 'rockers', who spent their time in the monotonous task of rocking the babies' wooden cradles (and presumably getting their children to sleep) and a 'chamberer' who probably carried out the housekeeping and tidied away the toys.

Most of what we know about the education of aristocratic daughters in this period comes from Christine de Pisan, the Frenchwoman born in Italy who was Cicely's contemporary. Christine was ahead of her times in terms of being a poetess in a world of male poets and her views were likewise not the norm for the early fifteenth century. In the *Menagier de Paris*, she writes that girls should be pious, submissive and polite; their almost sole function was to help their husbands. It is a measure of the slowness of marital change that middle-class Victorians felt much the same nearly 400 years later! Cecily would have learned to read from the Bible, to be able to spin and sew (for relaxation, not necessity), to sing and dance and to be able to command a household. When she was married and her husband was absent (which was often) she would need to be able to hire and fire, oversee the work of the estate (which was considerable) and even defend her home against violent attack if need be.

Cecily was born into a rapidly changing world. She was only weeks old when the king, Henry V, set sail from Southampton to begin a campaign to reclaim the lands being lost in the Hundred Years War. It would end in the glorious victory at

Agincourt, on St Crispin's Day (21 October). In the king's absence, the Scots, as usual, went on the rampage and Cecily's father rode north to quell the disturbance. Yeavering was little more than a skirmish, fought near the hamlet of that name in Northumberland, but Ralph Neville stopped the Scots' advance there and for the moment, the crisis had passed.

But a crisis of a different kind blew up on 31 August 1421, when Henry V, the 'lodestar of chivalry', to quote the poet John Lydgate, died of dysentery at Château de Vincennes near Paris. His loss was huge, but the worst aspect of it was that his son, now Henry VI, was only nine months old. There was to be a regency, in which uncles vied with each other for control of the young king and this led to a sense of rudderlessness that bred disorder. Had the boy grown to be a rational and powerful ruler, all would have been well, but he grew to be a 'pious idiot', prone to nervous breakdowns and completely at the mercy of stronger men – and women – who did their best to undermine him. One of these was Richard, Duke of York, who came to Raby in August 1423.

As we have seen, Richard Plantagenet was twelve, an orphan whose wardship had been bought by Ralph Neville. As part of the deal, Neville oversaw the betrothal of the boy to Cecily, then aged nine. This was a classic marriage of convenience – one noble family linking with another, the Nevilles and the Plantagenets – and it happened all the time. Cecily probably already understood that, as a female, she was effectively her father's property until she married, when she became her husband's. The betrothal was one of the last things Ralph Neville did. He died on 12 October 1425 at Raby and was buried under a marble sarcophagus at St Mary's, Staindrop, showing him in his knightly armour with bascinet and aventail on his head and his two wives lying as though asleep, their hands in prayer.

York's wardship had now passed, along with Raby and most of the other Westmoreland estates, to Neville's widow, Joan. She took York and probably Cecily too, to London, to the court of Henry VI, now four. For the next four years, as the girl reached marriageable age and learned the importance of deportment and how to handle powerful people, Cecily moved all over the country and Raby must have seemed like a different world.

The marriage settlement document for York and Cecily has not survived, but it would have contained a dowry, a cash sum given by the bride's family to the groom's and provision for servants, furniture and jewellery. We know from her later life that Cecily spent royally, especially when the situation arose that she almost became a queen, leading to the 'rose of Raby' being called 'proud Cis'. The marriage probably took place in October 1429, but it may have been earlier. Cecily was fourteen and there is every likelihood that the wedding happened either at Raby or perhaps in St Stephen's Chapel in the palace of Westminster.

Among their increasing civic duties, the young couple attended the coronation of Henry VI in the abbey on 6 November 1429. Henry was seventeen with no sign yet of the progressive psychosis which would lead directly to the Wars of the Roses and the deaths of Cecily's husband and three sons. The following year, York was ordered to accompany the new king to France in that, unique among kings of England, Henry was king of France too. York was also created Constable of England which gave him literally the power of life and death over Henry's subjects. Such power can go to a man's head. Cecily stayed with her mother at Windsor Castle, which had been Henry V's favourite residence, while York was at Rouen presiding over the trial of La Pucelle, the Maid of Orleans. Jeanne d'Arc is today a unique enigma; a peasant girl who claimed to have been called by God to rid France of the English. In her own day – and this persisted certainly until Shakespeare's depiction of her in the 1590s – the English saw her as a harlot or the devil incarnate. York watched the girl burn in Rouen marketplace. He then attended Henry's coronation as king of France.

On York's return he was 'living of his estates' which meant that he was now in full possession of his father's lands and hereditary titles. His principal castles were at Fotheringhay in Northamptonshire and Ludlow on the Welsh marches, and the couple spent most of their early marriage at one or the other. As Earl of March, York also owned the lordship of Montgomery in mid-Wales and Wigmore, near Ludlow itself. Much of the domestic life on these estates devolved on Cecily. Still in her teens, she accompanied York to court and to parliament, then still held at various towns all over the country and not yet bolted to Westminster.

The death of John, Duke of Bedford in 1435 changed the direction of the Yorks' lives. Bedford was a brother of Henry V who had acted as regent for his nephew in France during Henry VI's minority. Although a regent was now unnecessary, someone had to govern France in Henry's absence and the job was given to Richard of York. Cecily of course went with him, as did her brother Richard, Earl of Salisbury, William, Lord Fauconberg and the veteran warrior, Sir John Fastolf. Four years later, having played a difficult balancing act with the French, York was replaced by Richard Beauchamp, Earl of Warwick. This was not a condemnation. It was simply that Warwick was a far more experienced politician and now that the French were flexing their nationalist muscles again, such a man was indispensable.

Back at Fotheringhay Castle, Cecily at last conceived and gave birth. Her 'long barreness' was over. The castle, overlooking the River Nene, had belonged to the house of York since the fourteenth century when the first duke, Edward Langley, had taken possession of it. Very little of the castle remains today, but it stood on the edge of the forest of Rockingham, one of the largest in England, guarding the Great North Road that was *the* link between London and the North. Within the strong curtain wall with its massive gatehouse carved with the family's falcon and fetterlock, stood two chapels, a manor house and the usual clutter of offices – barns, stables, brewhouses, kitchens and bakeries. Cecily's only biographer, Amy Licence, reflects for pages on why Richard's birth here was so belated. York and Cecily had been married for nine years, but for nearly half that time had been separated by politics and duty. Whatever the reason, Cecily went through the same procedures as her own mother twenty-four years earlier, perhaps borrowing the holy relics like Aaron's rod, a loaf from the feeding of the five thousand or Christ's swaddling clothes from nearby Peterborough cathedral. The result was a healthy girl, Anne. Alison Weir, in her *Britain's Royal Families* states with certainty that an earlier daughter, Joan, was born and died in 1438, but the details are hazy.

Most noblemen, no doubt Richard of York among them, would have welcomed a male heir in what was a violent, dog-eat-dog patriarchy. We have no information on this. The Yorks' friends, the Pastons of Norfolk, wrote letters that have survived, but that is the luck of the historical draw. Richard of York left nothing in writing expressing his feelings over the births of his children; neither did Cecily. No one kept personal diaries at this time, so we have no idea of the emotions of anyone in the Plantagenet or Neville families.

Cecily was pregnant again in late 1440 and took to her bed at Hatfield, near the church of St Etheldreda. This time it was a boy, Henry, named in honour of the king, but there were complications (perhaps evidenced by the unusual birthplace of Hatfield) and he died at Westminster while only a couple of weeks old.

Fate took the pair to France again, back at Rouen Castle, the following year, when York was reappointed to run the king's council in Normandy. It was here that Edward, later Earl of March and King Edward IV, was born on 28 April 1442, although, as we shall see, there was some doubt about his parentage. The exact time of conception is notoriously difficult to pinpoint and those who contend that Richard of York could not be the boy's father and point to an archer called Blaybourne as Cecily's lover are largely clutching at straws.

Having waited for years to produce children, Cecily now seemed to be pregnant all the time. Her third born, Edmund, later Duke of Rutland, was born in Rouen in May 1443, making him only thirteen months younger than Edward. Eleven months later, again in France, Elizabeth was born. Margaret followed, in May 1446 at Fotheringhay and William, who did not survive, the following July. John was the next born, but he too died young, at one of the Yorks' London residences, La Neyte in Westminster. Depending on the accuracy of the thin records, Cecily had, by 1447, given birth to eight children (perhaps nine) and had lost three (perhaps four). This is not unusual for the time, when childhood ailments, minor in our age of antibiotics, killed babies with ease. The emotional toll on a mother is altogether a more difficult thing to measure. Years later, when Richard III threatened to execute Lord Stanley's son in the event of treason by his father, Stanley is reported to have sent back an answer, 'I have other sons.' But this, if it happened, was propagandistic bravado. Parents loved their children as much in the fifteenth century as we do today and it must have been appallingly difficult for Cecily to cope with this sense of loss, especially at a time when politics was forcing her husband into a dangerous spotlight, centre stage.

York was appointed Lieutenant of Ireland in July 1447, which he took as a personal insult. The king had married the French princess Margaret of Anjou in February 1445 at a peculiar ceremony conducted by proxy by two other people! Margaret and Cecily knew each other and were friends, but the new queen, perhaps sensing that her husband was not fit for purpose on two thrones simultaneously, quickly assumed more responsibility than most men were prepared to accept. York was recalled again from France, his place taken by the Duke of Somerset, Margaret and Henry's favourite. He had been side-lined and Ireland was seen as a dangerous and pestilential backwater way below York's abilities and standing. It was here, in Dublin Castle over the Liffey, that Cecily's next son, George, was born on 21 October, St Crispin's Day, 1449. York now had three healthy sons. What could go wrong?

York carried out his duties with customary efficiency, calling parliaments at Dublin and Drogheda, appointing bishops and putting down rebellions. In his absence, there were allegations of financial misdealings against him and the rebellion led by the low-life Jack Cade in Kent was rumoured to have been instigated by York. So York came home to confront all this and to reassure the king of his utmost loyalty. He had possibly 5,000 men in his retinue, unsure of the reception he would meet and that, to York's enemies, looked suspiciously like an army bent on toppling a monarchy. When he arrived in London on 23 November 1450, a sword was carried ahead of his procession with its blade-tip pointing upwards – symbolic of a king.

While all this was going on, Cecily gave birth again, to a short-lived boy named John, either at Ludlow or Fotheringhay. The family were certainly at Ludlow at Christmas and Cecily conceived again, probably in January 1452. With York squaring up to the king's favourite, the Earl of Somerset, Cecily waited for news at Fotheringhay. Her husband had at least 8,000 men at his back when he reached Blackheath in March. He was conned into an ambush, meeting not, as he had been promised, the king, but Somerset and his cronies. York was forced into a humiliating treaty to behave himself. Many years later, the Tudor chronicler Robert Fabyan contended that Edward, Earl of March, having got wind of this, raised 10,000 men at Ludlow and marched to the defence of his father. It is not impossible but neither is it very likely. Edward would prove himself a precocious and brilliant general at eighteen, but he was now only ten. Who would follow a boy of that age in an all-out clash with authority and go head to head with the Lord's anointed? In the event, there was no rising. York had promised on oath at St Paul's cathedral never to take up arms against his king or the king's advisors. He went back to Ludlow with his tail between his legs and perhaps stopped the cocky little Edward on his way.

Cecily may or may not have been at Ludlow during this stormy time, but she was definitely at Fotheringhay on 2 October because it was then and there that she gave birth to her eleventh or twelfth child, named Richard in honour of his father. 'The owl,' Henry VI tells Richard of Gloucester in Shakespeare's play:

> 'shriek'd at thy birth, an evil sign; the night crow cried, aboding luckless time; dogs howled and hideous tempest shook down trees, chattering [mag]pies in dismal discords sung. Thy mother felt more than a mother's pain and yet brought forth less than a mother's hope, to wit an undigested deformed lump, not like the fruit of such a goodly tree, teeth hadst thou in thy head when thou wast born, to signify thou cam'st to bite the world.'

Sadly, we do not have accurate weather reports for the day of Richard's birth. It was a Monday and probably much like any other 2 October!

John Rous, the chantry priest of Guy's Cliffe, Warwick, who turned spectacularly on Richard after his defeat and death at Bosworth, claims that he was 'retained within his mother's womb for two years'. This means of course that Cecily was carrying him while simultaneously giving birth to John, although a mealy mouthed hypocrite like Rous was probably unaware of the impossibility of that. Celibate churchmen of the Middle Ages were not known for their understanding of pregnancies!

A number of men who should have known better, like Thomas More of Chelsea who eventually became a martyred saint for daring to cross Henry VIII in 1535, slavishly copied Rous and threw in their own nonsense for good measure. Richard was born under the sign of Scorpio, Rous said, and therefore, was associated in the late Medieval mind with a 'smooth front' and a deadly sting in the tail. In fact, Scorpio begins on 5 October, three days after Richard's birth which is written in the king's own handwriting in his Book of Hours. Many babies are born with hair (although the 'to his shoulders' of Rous is ridiculous) and gum irregularities can be mistaken for teeth.

It is noticeable that even Ricardians, supporters of the king, writing before the discovery of his remains under the now famous Leicester car park, cannot fully divorce themselves from the deformity aspect. 'However,' writes A.J. Pollard in his 1991 *Richard III and the Princes in the Tower*, 'it may just be possible that Rous had heard that the birth was unusual.' He may indeed, but that does not mean that such stories have any credence. After 1485, Rous was a man determined to distance himself from his former patron by any means; he never met a good piece of nonsense he did not like.

There is nothing from any contemporary source from the 1450s that refer to any difficulty with Richard's birth. His childhood is a different matter and we will discuss that in the next chapter.

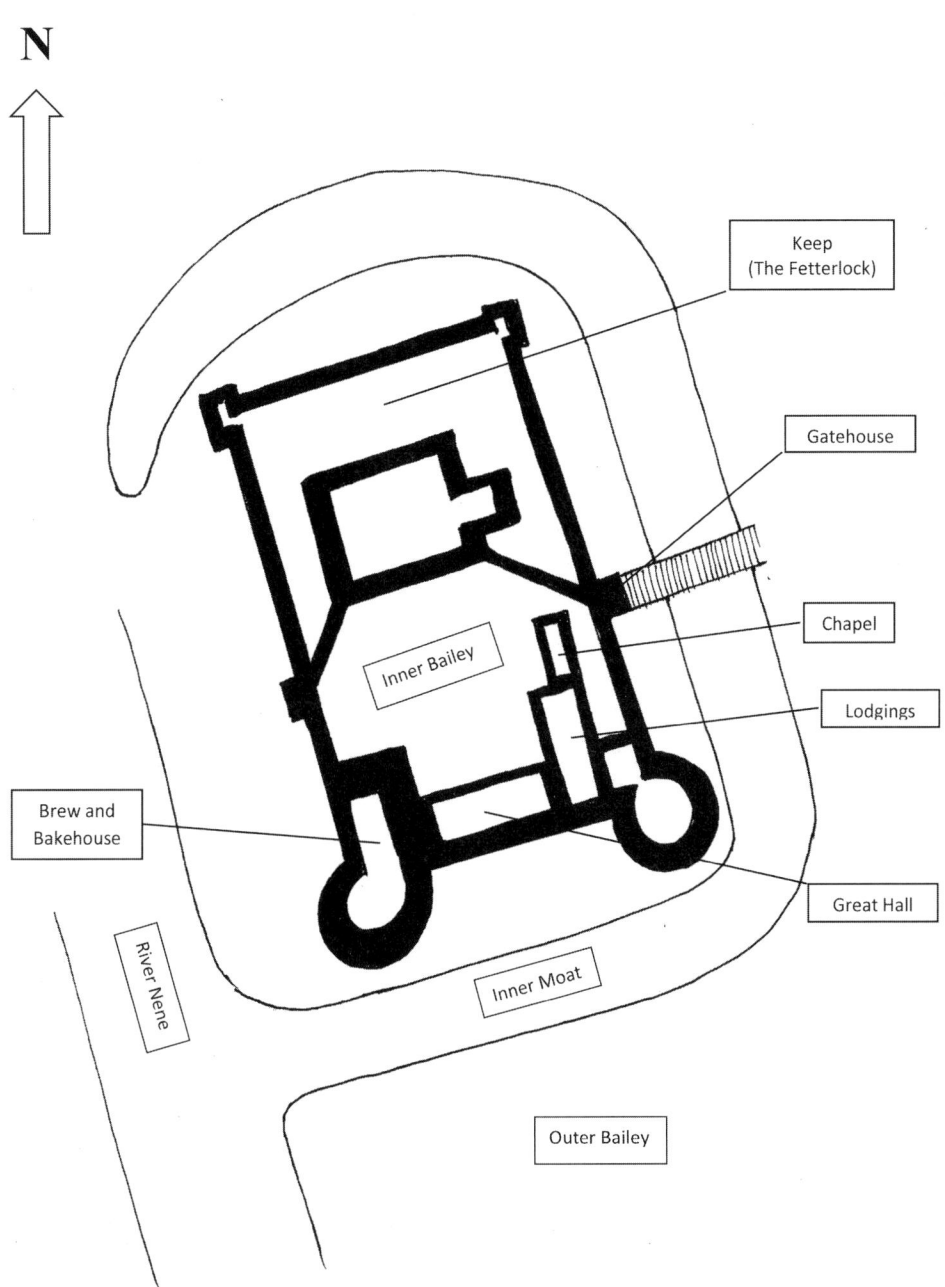

Fotheringhay Castle, the birthplace of Richard III.

Chapter 3

Ludlow

The roses and lion sejant (sitting) of Ludlow with the Plantagenet crown and the white and red roses of York and Lancaster. Although the term 'the Wars of the Roses' is not contemporary, the badges of the flowers themselves were.

For virtually the whole of Richard's childhood, we have only one line that refers to him – the enigmatic 'Richard liveth yet'. It comes from the Clare Roll, a document drawn up in May 1456 to record the links of the de Clare family, earls of Gloucester, with the priory in Suffolk of the same name where the manuscript was probably written. Richard of York was descended from the Clares and his children are listed:

> 'God first sent Anne, which signifyeth grace … Harry, Edward, Edmund, each in his place … and after twin daughters came Elizabeth and Margaret, and afterwards William. John after William next born was; which both he passed to God's grace; George was next and after, Thomas born was, which soon after did pace by the path of death into the heavenly place. Richard liveth yet, but the last of all was Ursula, to Him who God list call.'

There is no mention of Alison Weir's Joan, according to her, the eldest. Harry died young. Edward was fourteen at the time; Edmund thirteen months younger. Elizabeth was twelve, Margaret ten. William and John died as babies. George was seven.

Thomas died within months of his birth and Richard was four. Ursula, the last of the York children, had also died shortly before the Clare Roll was compiled.

Many historians today contend that 'Richard liveth yet' means that Richard is alive, as opposed to the several siblings who were not, but that is not the original interpretation and their argument is weak. Why not say that Edward, Edmund, Elizabeth, George and Margaret 'liveth yet', if that is the correct meaning? To single Richard out simply because he was the youngest would seem an arcane thing to do. Much more likely is the explanation offered by the Victorian historian James Gairdner that Richard's survival was extraordinary, that he was not expected to live. We have already noted the high rate of infant mortality and bearing in mind that five of Cecily's children did not reach the age of one, there may have been some congenital health problem in the York family. If Richard was a sickly child, he showed no sign of it as an adult and we cannot know, in the absence of any evidence, what sort of medical remedies were used on the boy.

All historians agree, again largely because of no evidence to the contrary, that Richard stayed at Fotheringhay with Margaret and George. Cecily must have been with them most of the time, but she could have visited Ludlow or Wigmore on the Welsh marches to support her husband. Today, Fotheringhay is a bleak and depressing ruin, but in Richard's childhood, it was one of the strongest castles in England and the nearby church of St Mary and All Saints with its elaborate replacement tombs of the Plantagenets remains one of the finest in England. The family, including Edward and Edmund, undergoing their education at Ludlow, would probably have met at Christmas, if at no other time, while York enjoyed the status of being the foremost of Henry VI's tenants-in-chief.

But it all fell apart in the summer of 1453, before Richard had even reached his first birthday. The king had 'a sudden and thoughtless fright' and went mad. Insanity ran in the family – Henry's grandfather, Charles VI of France, was known as Charles the Mad and his mother, Catherine de Valois, the widow of Henry V, was less than stable. Whatever psychosis Henry suffered from, it showed itself in long periods (sixteen months in the first instance) of almost catatonic behaviour. He continued to eat and drink (frugally) but could not function as the ruler of a vibrant state the size of England. Even the birth of his son on New Year's Day 1454 failed to elicit any response from him, to the extent that he may have believed that divine intervention was responsible.

In the fifteenth century, the king *was* the government. Parliament was already 200 years old, but it was largely a rubber stamp for royal policy and in the absence of central strength, the baronial families began to jockey for position among themselves. They met as the Great Council and in the spring of 1454, York was appointed Protector and Defender of the Realm. For much of his early reign, Henry had been ordered about by regents who were his uncles. Now, it was York who was giving the orders, but to be fair, he insisted on each member of the Council swearing an oath of allegiance to Henry's infant son, Edward.

Matthew Lewis's biography, *Richard, Duke of York, King By Right*, highlights an important point that illuminates the career of York's son Richard too. Lewis refers to York as 'a plotter, a schemer and a destabilising force of nature consumed by a conviction that he deserved more and who could not settle until his hand grasped that [the crown] which he so desperately wanted'. At the time, however, in the face of a hopelessly weak king and his domineering French wife, Margaret of Anjou, York stood for 'stability, continuity, justice and right'. Is it that our attitudes and concepts of morality have changed over the last 600 years?

The king recovered from his psychosis at Christmas, but since he is supposed to have said that his son was fathered by the Holy Ghost, we have to suspend judgement on that. Queen Margaret lost no time in asserting her husband's new-found sanity and removed York from the Protectorship. This was not done with good grace and a rather bitter York went north to his castle at Sandal Magna to consider his options.

By May 1455, it was obvious that the Yorks would not be allowed to live in their various castles in peace. Richard, by now no doubt toddling, learning his colours and perhaps even letters at the simplest level, was blissfully unaware of the tensions his parents must have felt. The king and Margaret called the Council at Leicester, but York was not invited and the news was leaked that Margaret considered him a rival to the throne. York, the Neville Earl of Salisbury and his son, the Earl of Warwick, marched south with an army, intending to defend himself (again) as a loyal subject in Henry's eyes. This was not the first time that Richard of York was cold-shouldered by Henry's government. Nor was it the first time he had had to assert his loyalty to the king. At least two general pardons for his behaviour (whatever that was is unclear) exist in parliamentary records. The king, meanwhile, marched north and the result was the first of two bloody clashes at St Albans on the 22nd.

The battle was a Yorkist victory but it achieved nothing. Henry was a puppet in the hands of his wife and York could not attack her without attacking him. It is possible to see Richard's father as a tyrant and a bully in all this, but most historians believe that he was acting in good faith to bring stability to a shaky government. The contrived occasion in March 1458 when York and Margaret walked arm-in-arm to a Mass in St Paul's did nothing to change the febrile situation and fooled nobody, except perhaps the ever-smiling Henry VI.

In June of the following year, Margaret, now acting openly as queen without her husband's aid, called the Council to meet at Coventry, an important city in the fifteenth century, in what came to be known as the 'Parliament of Devils'. Again, York, Salisbury and Warwick were not invited, but this time, charges of treason to the crown were brought against them.

This fraught situation may have made York bring his scattered family to his side. George and Richard, the one nine, the other seven, with an armed retinue of mounted knights, travelled across the Midlands along with Margaret and Cecily. They rode through the forest of Rockingham and stayed the night, well-guarded, at Market Harborough. From there, they rode wide of Coventry where the leopards and lilies banner of Henry VI floated over the city walls and spent a day at Warwick Castle, the home of Richard's cousin that would one day be his. They rode on through Shropshire, past Kidderminster, famous for its cloth, and reached Ludlow Castle, high over the River Teme where it joins the Corve.

The town already had a school, founded in the thirteenth century, and the perpendicular-style church of St Lawrence. Today only one of the original four gates, Broad Gate (*just* wide enough for a car!) still stands, leading to Ludford, the

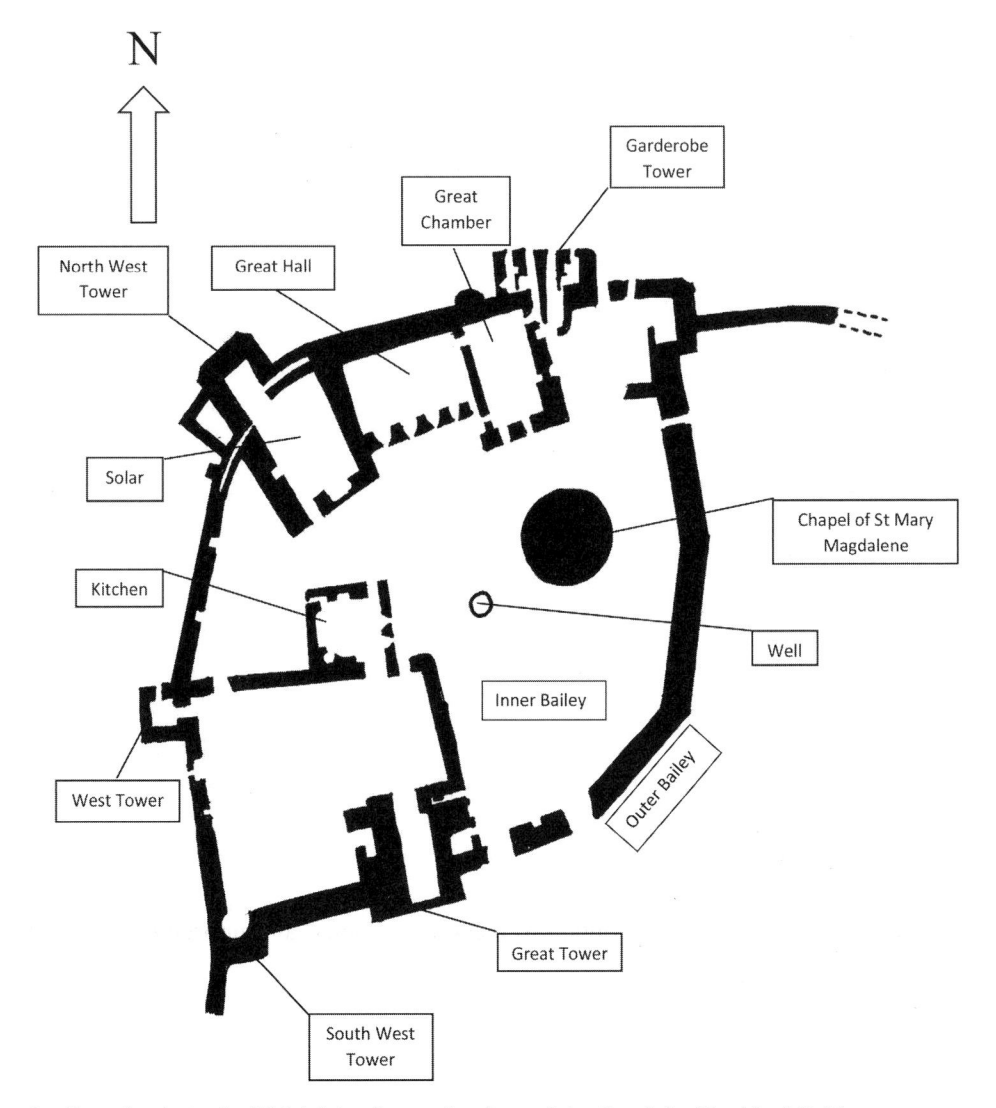

Ludlow Castle in the Welsh Marches at the time of the 'battle' of Ludford Bridge.

original crossing place of the river before a Medieval pack-horse bridge was built. The way in for Richard and his party, then as now, was via the eastern gate, and across the courtyard was the imposing square Norman keep. The outer curtain walls were added to considerably under the Tudors and the Justices' Building, now forming one wing of the keep, had yet to be erected in Richard's day. The circular chapel was there, however, built in Templar style and free-standing in the inner bailey, and it is likely that Richard and his fellow travellers gave thanks there for their safe arrival.

Throughout the summer, the number of residents at Ludlow increased apace. Tents were erected in the bailey and men were billeted in the town that clustered below the walls, the townsfolk doing their best to keep them fed and amused, while no doubt fleecing them if the opportunity arose. York's sons, Edward and Edmund, now in their late teens, were already there. As the Earls of March and Rutland respectively, they had their armed retinues with them. No doubt the days rang to the clash of sword-drill and the clang of the armourer's anvil. Whether Richard was the sickly boy envisaged by Gairdner and Paul Murray Kendall writing fifty years later or whether he was a normal, healthy child, he could have seen nothing like this preparation for war in his young life.

Lord Poins (whose descendants now own the castle) turned up with his Welsh levies. So did Walter Devereux, Lord Ferrers of Chartley. Perhaps more importantly, as August drew on, word came that the ablest of York's supporters, Salisbury and Warwick, were on their way with battle-hardened troops from the garrison at Calais.

When Salisbury arrived, however, on 25 September, his men were already bloodied and exhausted. Although outnumbered perhaps two to one, the earl had clashed with Lord Audley, the king's general, at Blore Heath in Staffordshire two days earlier. He expected to lose, urged his footsoldiers to kiss the ground they stood on and used his supply wagons as a barrier to slow the Lancastrian attack. Salisbury feigned retreat, pulling his central 'battle' back and Audley fell for it. English knights, as opposed to French, usually fought on foot, but in the excitement, Audley's army charged on horseback and were met by a deadly shower of arrows. Salisbury's men surged forward, hammering the fallen and falling into the narrow deep waters of Hemphill Brook.

Audley had promised Queen Margaret that he would send her Salisbury's head. His cavalry had failed to get it so he sent forward his infantry, again to no effect. He himself was caught and killed on the slope above the stream, by then slippery with blood. The Lancastrian army broke into scattered units trying to rally with others. Several men changed sides and turned on their comrades of earlier in the day, a pattern that ran through the whole of the Wars of the Roses.

For three days, the nearby River Tarn was reddened with Lancastrian blood and in the meantime Salisbury had marched on to Ludlow.

We cannot know the effect the sight of wounded men had on little Richard. Even in our 'liberal, caring' twenty-first century, children are still the casualties of war.

In some parts of the world, it is a way of life. No doubt those who believe that Richard grew up to be a homicidal monster would point to Ludlow as the start of it all.

It was days later that a galloper brought the message. The king's army, not the rabble routed at Blore Heath, was marching from Coventry. At Worcester, the great and good of the town did what greedy, selfish citizens always do – they presented a petition to the newly arrived king, offering their loyalty and devotion. Margaret promised a free pardon to all those who supported the Lancastrian cause and no doubt many men fell over themselves, buckling on makeshift armour and grabbing bows. The Royal army reached Leominster and marched north through the October mists and rain on the road that led to Ludford.

Henry and Margaret camped less than a mile from York's castle, in the wooded valley through which the Teme flowed, and built an earth rampart to protect them from any Yorkist attack along the road. It was now 12 October and Richard had just celebrated his seventh birthday. It was now that he perhaps understood treachery for the first time. The Calais garrison that Warwick had brought with him was commanded by Andrew Trollope, Master Porter of the only French city still in English hands. His name was already a legend in England because of his piracy in the Channel. That day, he led his men out of the castle and down the steep slope beyond Broad Gate, going over to the enemy and taking with him an intimate knowledge of York's defences and plans. The Calais men were the most professional that the Yorkists had and now they stood with the Lancastrians across the river.

A council of war was called in the keep's great hall. Cecily would stay with her youngest children, throwing herself on the mercy of the king and her friendship with Margaret of Anjou. York himself, his sons Edward and Edmund, Salisbury and Warwick would get out while they could, slipping away to the west and east under cover of darkness. There is some confusion in the accounts as to exactly where the Yorkist army was. Common sense implies that they stayed locked behind the castle walls, relying on the huge well for water and whatever food provisions they had managed to amass. Various comments, however, suggest that the Yorkists, complete with artillery positioned behind carts as barricades were 'in the field'. Richard Brooks, in his very detailed *Battlefields of Britain and Ireland* envisages the Yorkist position on the rise south of Ludford House, between the road and the river. Today, given the sharp drop of the land from the castle to the river, it is difficult to know where, beyond the walls, the Yorkists could have positioned themselves.

The actions of the senior commanders are appalling by any standards. First, the Yorkists spread a rumour that Henry VI had died suddenly overnight and even suggested that both armies sing a *Te Deum* for him. There is no mention of an actual clash of arms and the 'battle of Ludford' as it is sometimes called, never took place. Cecily must have been part of the discussions but George and Richard were not and at dawn on the 13th, the boys awoke to a Lancastrian army advancing up Ludford Hill, swarming through the Broad Gate and into the castle itself. Their father and their big brothers had gone – the boys, their sister and their mother were suddenly alone.

According to one account, the little family stood by the market cross outside the castle gates and waited to be arrested. They were bundled unceremoniously to Henry's camp while Margaret, as was usual in these situations, unleashed her soldiers on the town. The place was robbed 'to the bare walls', the Lancastrians helping themselves to anything they liked. Anyone who opposed them would, at least, be beaten and probably killed; such was the way of Medieval armies.

As for Cecily, she was 'unmanly and cruelly … entreated and spoiled'. No doubt she protested, furious with Margaret in particular and desperately trying to keep her children safe. Just how roughly she was handled is unknown – some modern historians claim that she was raped – but for Richard, things had changed. His family scattered, his father's cause broken, his mother at best humiliated and embarrassed, the boy's childhood was over.

As prisoners of war, Cecily and her children were taken to Coventry, with its massive cathedral and guild chapels, to face the 'Parliament of Devils'. York and the others were accused 'for their traitorous rearing of war … at Ludford … reputed, taken, declared, adjudged, deemed and attainted of High Treason, as false traitors and enemies' to the king. All their estates were forfeit. Technically, Richard was no longer Duke of York, nor were his sons any longer the Earls of March and Rutland. Neither Salisbury nor Warwick could keep their titles.

Cecily appeared in person before Henry and begged him to reconsider her husband's position, assuring the king of York's loyalty. Out of kindness (and no one denies that Henry VI was a kind man) he awarded her 1,000 marks a year for herself and the three children. She was to be placed under what today we would call house arrest at Tonbridge Castle, in Kent, the home of her sister, Anne, Duchess of Buckingham. How close that relationship was is debatable, because Cecily was 'kept full straight and many a rebuke' was given to her. Whether this was Anne's doing or the work of retainers who got above themselves is not clear.

There could be no more protectorates. Henry remained as weak as water, pushed and pulled in every direction by the queen and her favourites among the Lancastrian nobility. York had reached Ireland with Edmund of Rutland. Edward had got to Calais with Salisbury and Warwick. From their respective eyries, they watched England and waited.

Chapter 4

Wakefield

St Egwin's Day 1460

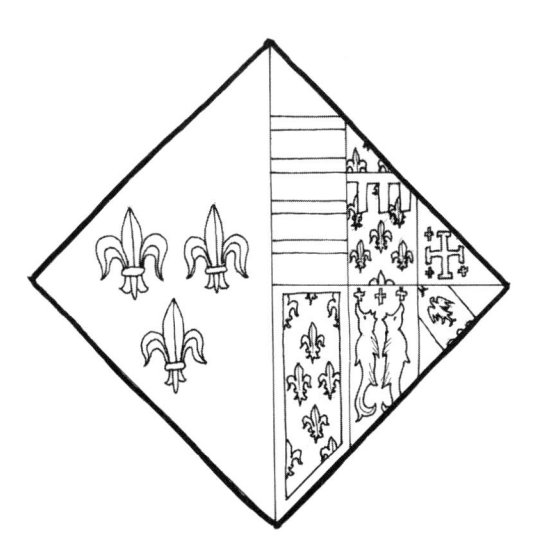

Arms of Margaret of Anjou, wife of Henry VI. I have omitted the 'leopards and lilies' which was the coat of arms of the English royal family and concentrated on the French aspects, hence several fleurs de lys.

Richard was eight when his father was killed somewhere on the open, sloping ground between Sandal Castle and the River Calder. The Victorians, gushingly sentimental and well-meaning, but often wrong, put up a monument on the supposed spot over 400 years later, carved in the Gothic revival style that Richard of York would have known well.

The battle of Wakefield, fought on 30 December 1460, is one of the most poorly documented of all the clashes in the Wars of the Roses. That, of course, did not stop Shakespeare writing about it at length, based largely on the spurious account by Edward Hall, the Tudor apologist, in the 1520s. *The Union of the Two Noble and Illustrious Families York and Lancaster* was a gift for a new dramatist (*King Henry VI* was probably Shakespeare's first play written about 1592), but it was poor history.

In it, at York's Sandal Castle in Act I, Scene II, young Richard is portrayed as a hothead, dreaming perhaps of his own future plans –

> 'And, father, do but think How sweet a thing it is to wear a crown; Within whose circuit is Elysium And all that poets feign of bliss and

joy. Why do we linger thus? I cannot rest Until the white rose that I wear be dyed Even in the lukewarm blood of Henry's heart.'

Not a bad speech for an eight-year-old boy who was not even there!

The events of the past six months had been hectic and frustrating in equal measure. After Ludford Bridge, York and his second son Edmund had sailed for Ireland, beyond the reach of the Lancastrians under their increasingly vengeful queen, Margaret. The York faction's problem was essentially one of communication; trying to coordinate with allies still in England and, even more difficult, with the Nevilles and York's eldest, Edward, who had fled to Calais. A crossing of the Channel, even in good weather, could take two days and the Irish Sea was notoriously temperamental for small ships reliant on the wind. Perhaps unsurprisingly, the Calais contingent got back to England first, landing at Sandwich, Kent on 26 June.

The king's army was effectively caught in a strategic dilemma. Would York arrive first from Ireland, or Edward from France? Accordingly, the Lancastrians kept their options open by roaming the Midlands, ready to march east or west as news arrived. The fastest reliable information was sent by gallopers, men mounted on palfreys, the fast-running horses of the hunt. Roads were notoriously poor all over the country, although in the summer less of a problem than at other times of the year. Maps as we know them did not exist, and sign and mile posts were rare. On the other hand, it was difficult to hide several thousand, or even hundred, armed men in the days before Enclosures provided hedges to edge fields, and any local villager would probably be only too happy to whinge about the depredations of a foraging army in the area, telling their enemies all they wanted to know.

That army was still recruiting early in July and Edward and Warwick had taken London without a shot being fired – not the first or last time the capital would give way to the prevailing wind – and marched northwards, their scouts riding ahead looking for banners and listening for the sounds of horses and cannon wheels on the road.

The king's army was commanded by Humphrey Stafford, Duke of Buckingham, camped beneath his white swan standard with the River Nene to his back. He had chosen his position well and must have been as aware of the Yorkist advance as they were of him. At Northampton, he had ditches and ramparts to his front and flanks, and a preponderance of cannon, taken from the Tower.

The heavy rain had slowed Edward's advance north and the field that lay between the opposing forces was a quagmire. It may have been the 'newe fielde' with banks and ditches between the village of Hardingstone and the abbey of Delapré. Warwick sent his herald forward carrying his bear and ragged staff banner, shortly before two o'clock on the afternoon of 10 July, a Thursday.

Warwick asked to speak to the king. Buckingham refused, sending the rider away with a flea in his ear. This was the last time in the Wars of the Roses that reverence was shown to Henry VI. From now on, he was wheeled out onto the battlefield as a mere token, all decisions being made by somebody else. Edward, younger and more hotheaded perhaps than Warwick, led his 'battle' forward towards Buckingham's position at two o'clock in the afternoon. We do not know the precise formations used at Northampton, but it is likely that Edward, only eighteen at this stage, led the main battle, supported by Warwick on either of the wings and Salisbury (his father) and William, Lord Fauconberg (his father-in-law and a 'knight of great reverence') the other.

Given the situation at Northampton, of one side attacking a fortified and entrenched position, it is unlikely that the cavalry was used. This would be a slog of footsoldiers, bill against bill and halberd against halberd. It was likely to be bloody, but two things counted in the Yorkists' favour. First, the driving rain of the last few days had ruined Buckingham's gunpowder, so his much-vaunted artillery, which should have opened the action, terrified the enemy and chopped down swathes of men, was eerily silent. It would not have been heard above the chink of armour and shouts of psyched-up men, but the artillery merely made a peculiar hissing sound as the fuses went out. The second problem for the Lancastrians was far more damaging. In a move that was sickeningly typical of the loyalty of fifteenth-century armies, the troops of Lord Grey of Ruthin dropped their banners and welcomed the advancing Yorkists into the camp.

This camp was now a death-trap, close-quartered slaughter going on on the muddy revetments, men dying under the sunken wheels of the guns. It was probably all over in half an hour. Buckingham, probably highly visible in his swan tabard, was hacked down and the king of England was once more a Yorkist prisoner.

Most modern historians describe what happened next in a single line, but the emotions involved we can only guess at. News was sent to Cecily that the tide had turned and with it, her fortunes and those of Margaret, George and Richard. She must have felt relieved and triumphant, but on the other hand, her 'captor' was at once her own sister *and* the wife of the suddenly late Duke of Buckingham.

Free and perhaps relaxed for the first time in months, Cecily moved her brood to London in the middle of September and was given quarters at Sir John Fastolf's house in Southwark. The first choice was probably Baynard's Castle, the family home on the north bank near the Fleet River. The building was the second of that name, the first having been destroyed by fire in 1428, and it was a large and imposing fortified manor house fronting the river, with its own jetty and wharf. Cecily and her children may have stayed there for a while, but London was a difficult and unpredictable place. It was nominally Yorkist and not yet the permanent home of the king. All Medieval kings, Henry VI included, were peripatetic, travelling the country from royal castle to royal castle. With such a relatively large population, however, there *had* to be Lancastrian and/or royal sympathisers in the City and perhaps Cecily felt that Baynard's Castle, defendable as it was, was not safe enough. She did not want a repetition of Ludlow.

Fastolf, into whose house they now moved, known today through Shakespeare's distorted lens as Falstaff in *Henry IV*, had died months earlier and was a chequered hero of the Hundred Years War. The man had fought at Harfleur under Henry V in 1415 and was made Knight of the Garter eleven years later. Accused, probably wrongly, of cowardice at the siege of Orleans in 1429, it took him thirteen years to clear his name. Needless to say, it is this image of the cowardly drunk that Shakespeare fastened on. Like many successful warriors in the Middle Ages, Fastolf acquired considerable loot and by the time of his death in 1459 owned four sizeable residences including Fastolf Place south of the Thames.

Excavations carried out in the late 1990s have revealed that the house and grounds were huge, affording Cecily and her children very comfortable accommodation. It was made up of two properties, both acquired by Fastolf in the 1440s, the moated manor house of the Dunley family and the Rosary, a pleasure house built for Edward II. The remains of a mill wheel prove the existence of a tidal mill attached to the property, which had its own fish farm.

Following the death of John Fastolf, the house, with a large staff of servants, was managed by the Paston family of Norfolk, friends of Fastolf, whose surviving letters provide a fascinating insight into fifteenth-century life. Fastolf Place stood opposite the Tower of London, which, in most people's minds today is forever equated with the monstrosity of Richard III. Upriver was the only bridge over the Thames, London Bridge, with its clutter of shops and houses. Just along the river from Fastolf Place was the church of St Mary Overy where Cecily and her children may well have celebrated Mass, and the London palace of the Bishop of Winchester. Southwark was already gaining a reputation as a 'stews', an unsavoury area haunted by prostitutes – the 'Bishop of Winchester's geese' – and would, by Shakespeare's day, be a focus of play-goers at Philip Henslowe's Rose and bear and bull-baiting pits.

The premises where Richard was housed had cost Fastolf £1,650 (over £10 million today) and the moat was a quarter of a mile in circumference. It had a drawbridge and stone causeway, very typical of the transitional homes of the aristocracy and gentry, which were morphing from forbidding defensive castles to welcoming family homes. It had a bakehouse, a larder house (for food), two granaries and a garden studded with elms. There are references to a gallery, a buttery (dining room), kitchen, cellar (for wine), accommodation for Fastolf's servants, a hall and a solar or bedroom for the master of the house. Presumably Cecily slept here during her time in Southwark, but there is no record of the sleeping arrangements of the children. The family were guarded by a German mercenary soldier, Christopher Haussen, about whom virtually nothing is known.

York landed at Chester from Ireland in the middle of September and sent for Cecily to join him at Hereford, a town on the Welsh marches, 144 miles from

London. This would have taken the duchess, assuming reasonable autumn weather, nearly ten days by lumbering fifteenth-century coach. There is little left of the town that Cecily would have known. The cathedral was originally Norman with later additions, barely fifty years old by the time she arrived. Chained securely somewhere inside its vaulted interior was Mappa Mundi, the map of the world, dating from around 1305. There was a castle there, (which may actually have dated from *before* the Norman Conquest) aptly called Richard's Castle. It was presumably here that York and his wife were reunited. Margaret, George and Richard stayed in Southwark where, according to the Paston letters, their ever-loyal big brother Edward visited them every day.

We have no idea what life was like for Richard at this stage in his life, nor what it meant to be the youngest son of the most powerful nobleman in the realm. How much an eight-year-old could really understand of the complex politics that a weak king could engender is debatable, but the *moods* of the time might well have been discernible. Margaret was six years older than Richard, already, in dress and deportment, a young woman. George was only three years older, but almost certainly at this stage, stronger and bigger, thrashing his little brother with wooden swordplay. Edward was a grown man. So, at seventeen, was Edmund. The Fastolf house was more palatial than anywhere Richard would have seen, albeit without the fierce grandeur of castles like Ludlow. Historian David Baldwin conjectures that trips taking the boy across the river into the country's largest city would have been 'eagerly anticipated' and I am sure they were. But little Richard was the son, if only the youngest one, of a man who was about to make himself a king-in-waiting.

Across the river from Fastolf Place, Richard of York astounded everyone in Parliament and beyond when he came to London and asserted his claim to the throne. Given to haughtiness and impulsive actions without consultation, York pushed his own descent from the children of Edward III. While that was genuine, Henry VI's claim, via the male, not female, line, was stronger and his father and grandfather had both been kings. Henry's own performance – he had, after all, ruled for thirty-eight years by this time – counted for little. A lord who failed could be legally removed by the *diffidatio*, a feudal device not unlike the deselection of an MP today. Needless to say, Henry's Lancastrians were outraged; and even some of the Yorkists had misgivings. Henry was the Lord's anointed, argued some. Others reminded everybody that he was the grandson of a usurper, whose grandfather almost certainly had a hand in the murder of Richard II. And do not get started on Henry's foreign wife, Margaret of Anjou, who effectively ran the country during her husband's bouts of insanity.

York had approached London slowly, Cecily and a growing number of lords with him. He had gathered an army as he came, sending Warwick ahead to blacken Henry as a 'dolt and a fool', which, in the absence of any grasp of modern psychiatry, he was. York's banners included the leopards and lilies of England, and a page rode ahead of him with a sword tip pointing to the sky, symbolic of kingship. He had done this before.

He marched in through the monarch's side entrance of Westminster Hall (today St Stephen's) and placed his hand ostentatiously on the marble chair that stood, literally, for the throne. No one cheered. No one backed him, not even loyal lords who had fought with his son at Northampton weeks earlier. York tried again days later and again met silence. In the end, a compromise was reached. Parliament agreed to an Act of Accord whereby Henry VI would continue to rule, but his infant son Edward would not succeed his father. Instead, the crown would pass to York and his heirs.

There was a ceremony held at St Paul's, then the biggest cathedral in the world, to solemnize the decision. Richard of York walked in procession behind the king. The Earl of Warwick carried Henry's sword. Richard's son Edward carried Henry's train. The king, confused and feeble as usual, was literally hemmed in by the Yorks and their entourage.

Margaret of Anjou was in Scotland when she heard the news of the Accord. Furious, she rallied her Lancastrians in the North and marched south. York, Salisbury and Edmund of Rutland left London on 9 December via the Great North Road in search of the enemy. Edward, in the meantime, was sent north-west to Ludlow to scotch any possible trouble from Lancastrians in Wales who might rally to the queen. Warwick stayed in London to watch over things in the capital.

By the end of the month, the North was in chaos. Unlike the seventeenth-century Civil War, there was no general awareness of cause, still less of effect. Neither was there propaganda spread via an increasing literacy. What there *was,* however, was fierce, almost tribal loyalty to lords and feudal family obligations. Nowhere was this more apparent than in Yorkshire, where the Nevilles of Middleham and the Percys, earls of Northumberland since the reign of Richard II, had been jockeying for overall power for decades. This rivalry, more than any altruistic support for rightful kings, may well have urged the Percys to declare for Lancaster and the Nevilles for York. Deaths in battle merely made things worse. The head of the Percy clan, Henry, Earl of Northumberland, had been killed at the first St Albans in May 1455. Much of what happened five years later was about a blood feud every bit as murderous as those carried out by the Vikings in the same area six centuries earlier.

London was 180 miles to the south and whatever compromises were worked out in Parliament's painted chamber, they cut no ice in the North. Meeting at York that month, Northumberland, Clifford and Dacre vowed to destroy the Neville lands throughout Yorkshire. Margaret raised her standard near Hull on the Humber, a town granted royal privileges by Edward I, which was an important port for any attacking army. The Lancastrians Lord Roos, the Baron of Greystoke and Lord Latimer joined the queen there with their troops, perhaps numbering 15,000. The speed of this muster surprised everyone. Traditionally, spring was the start of the campaign season, ending

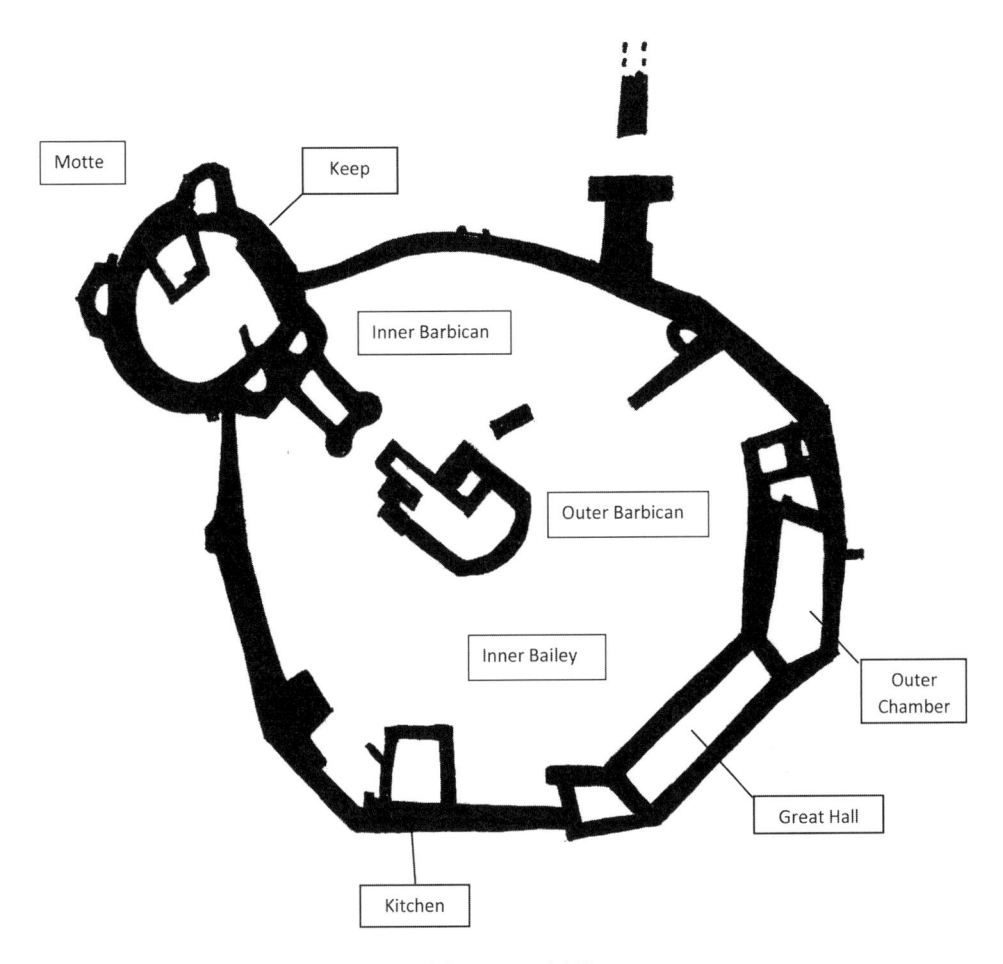

Richard of York's headquarters at Sandal Magna, 1460.

before the harvest needed to be gathered. Yet here, across badly repaired roads at the end of autumn, an unprecedented force was waiting to strike. York had to move fast to consolidate his estates around Wakefield. Sandal Castle was the obvious base, but Pontefract needed to be secured as well, along with York.

The weather was bad and York's progress slow. Heavy rain washed away the flimsy packhorse bridges that crossed rivers. Roads became quagmires and the troops probably abandoned them where they could in favour of firmer ground. We cannot be sure if the Yorkists had an artillery train with them, but the heavy guns were notoriously slow and could cover not much more than twelve miles a day. There is a reference in only one of the chronicles that 'Lovelace, a gentleman of Kent' commanded the artillery 'with great ordnance of guns' and these probably came from the Tower of London.

York's advance guard, almost certainly of cavalry, ran into a Lancastrian patrol near Worksop on the edge of Sherwood Forest. The occupants of the priory of St Mary and St Cuthbert, founded about 1100, may well have watched the action with dread. A marauding army, no matter under whose banner they marched, meant pillaging and, in the case of a fight, wounded to patch and dead to bury. The Church was expected to do it all. York's main battle reached Sandal by 21 December, St Severine's Day. With him were both Nevilles, father and son Thomas and Northern friends Sir James Pickering, Thomas Parre and Thomas Harrington.

We know that Pickering had been with York at Ludford. He came from what is today the East Riding of Yorkshire and had probably fought at Blore Heath in September of the previous year. Both he and Parre, from Kendal in Westmoreland, had been attainted for what was actually treason against their king. Harrington, with estates at Hornby, Lancashire and Brierley near Barnsley, had been a Neville man for years. Attainted by the 'Parliament of Devils' at Coventry for his part in Blore Heath, he had secured his release before York left London.

Some miles away, Sir Edmund Fitzwilliam of Wadworth, near Doncaster, was busy fortifying York's Conisbrough Castle, its strong circular keep capable of bearing the weight of the cannon that he had taken from Sheffield after the Yorkist victory at Northampton. Conisbrough apart, however, much of the countryside around Sandal and its accompanying town of Wakefield, was, in the winter of 1460 at least, staunchly Lancastrian. For reasons that are unclear, the North seems to have been particularly annoyed at York's Act of Accord and his arrival, even at his own castle, with an army, almost certainly made matters worse. There were certainly loyal men inside Sandal with him; the Hull merchant Richard Hanson; William Burton, the bailiff of Wakefield; Sir Henry Radford; the London merchant John Harrow and the ever-faithful Edward Bourchier.

Even so, it was something of a forlorn hope, the ominous name given to the advance guard of an army that has strayed too far and risks being cut off. The Lancastrian army, probably gaining in numbers every day, was ten miles away at Pontefract, one of the strongholds of the Lancastrian regime for the past sixty years.

In a sense, all the Lancastrians had to do was to wait. No castle is impregnable and Sandal's stone structure, replacing the earliest timber version, was centred on a circular shell keep with flanking walls, very thick, a gatehouse and a barbican beyond that. It would have been very difficult for Lancastrian artillery to make much of a dent in that. In the event of a siege, it all depends on the water supply and food provisions of the defenders. Water does not seem to have been a problem, but any advance requests to the people of Wakefield that York may have made had not produced much in the way of food. So, a truce was negotiated between York and the Lancastrian Duke of Somerset that was to last until after the Epiphany (6 January). What we have here in the fifteenth century is a seismic shift of sensibilities. For reasons of weather and communications, the campaigning season across Europe was confined largely to the spring and summer. Beyond that, it was understood that certain points of the Christian calendar were inviolate and no shedding of blood could take place. Christmas, the birth of Christ, was a particular case in point. But things were changing. Blore Heath had been fought on a saint's day and in terms of what happened at Sandal, clearly the truce was not honoured. The sudden overwhelming of the Yorkists may have happened because the Lancastrians broke the truce and Richard's men were unprepared for battle.

The chronicles that describe the events of December 1460 are not all that helpful. Virtually all Medieval chronicles were written by monks, often miles away and years after the events they were describing. This causes two problems. First, the inevitable bias of the writer. Churchmen disapproved of killing, by definition, and their grasp of politics was circumscribed by a moralizing piety. Second, the sheer passage of time renders various comments suspect. *The English Chronicle* which ends in 1461, was written with a Yorkist bias; Margaret of Anjou is the devil incarnate and even worse was John Neville, who went over to the enemy, abandoning York to his fate. The *Annales Rerum Anglicarum* (Annals of English Matters) ends in 1468 and may have been written by William of Worcester. *John Benet's Chronicle* ends in 1462. It too is written in Latin and says very little about Wakefield. Benet was a priest from Bedfordshire and it is not clear why he took up his quill at all.

The *Register of Abbot Whethamstede*, the Bishop of St Albans, compiled before 1465, is of particular relevance. Abbots, as opposed to anonymous monks, were political animals, often the younger sons of noble families with siblings who, in these turbulent years, were often up to their necks in the internecine squabbles of the day. The battle at St Albans, in May 1455, must have had a profound effect on all who served at the abbey and the *Register* includes the second one fought there in February 1461. It is pro-Yorkist, but critical of Richard of York's high-handed demeanour in the December of 1460.

What led to the breaking of the truce and the slaughter of the Yorkists in open country rather than on the battlements of Sandal? According to Jean de Waurin, the whole thing was duplicity on the part of the Lancastrians. De Waurin was a Burgundian chronicler probably in his sixties when he wrote *Recueil des Croniques et anciennes istoires de la Grant Bretagne* (Account of the chronicles and ancient histories of Great Britain). The book traced British history way back and is as unreliable as any other pot boiler of the period. In the years of de Waurin's own lifetime, however, it is more reliable. That said, the chronicler did not visit England

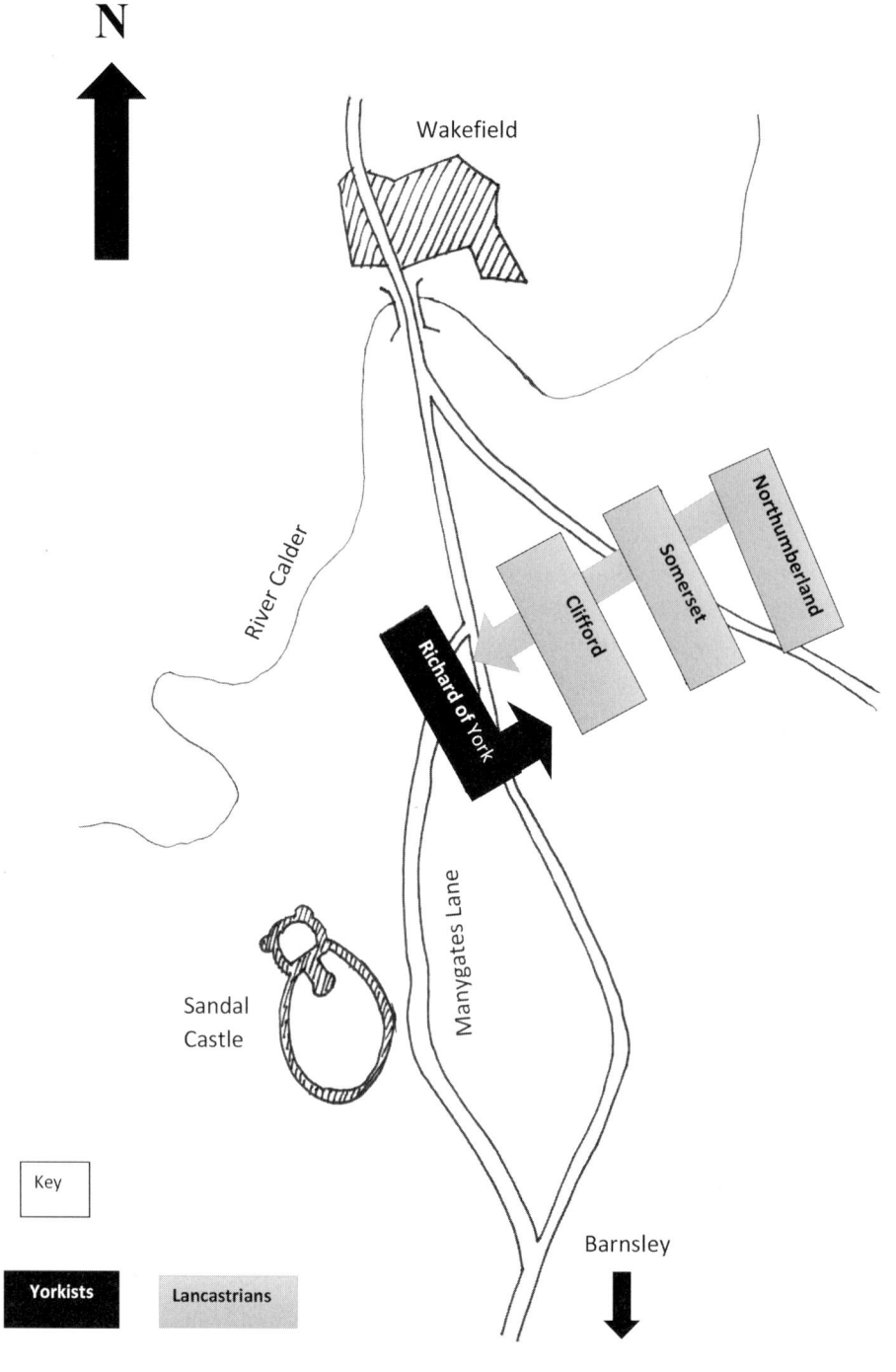

The most likely interpretation of troop movements of the battle of Wakefield, December 1460. Richard of York, trying to rescue a foraging party, was attacked from the right by a superior force of Lancastrians. He could not get back to the safety of Sandal Castle and was killed along with his son, Edmund of Rutland.

until seven years after Wakefield. Bearing in mind his handwritten text was presented as a lavish, illustrated work to Edward IV in 1474 (after de Waurin's death) his slant is inevitably pro-Yorkist. It was not slavishly so, however, because the second edition painted a very unfavourable picture of the Woodville clan, suddenly rocketed to power by Edward's unfortunate marriage to Elizabeth Woodville.

De Waurin's story, unconfirmed by anyone else, is that a number of soldiers, wearing the bear and ragged staff livery of the earls of Warwick, got into the castle in this disguise as a sort of Trojan horse. Their leader was the same Andrew Trollope who had treacherously changed sides at Ludford. All this happened, allegedly, on 29 December, but how could it possibly have happened bearing in mind the gate system at Sandal and the fact that Richard Neville, Earl of Salisbury, was inside the castle and would know at least some of his son's men? Neither does it explain how this sneaky, deceitful lot could persuade York into the open.

Much more likely is that the Sandal garrison was running desperately short of food by the end of December. They had been there for nine days and a foraging party was sent out to grab whatever they could. The lie of the land becomes important here, as it does for all battlefields, but Richard Knowles, in an article for *The Ricardian* in 1992, assumes too much from a deed of 1415 that names an area between the castle and the river as Castlefield, implying that this was one of many enclosed fields in the area. The Enclosure map of Sandal of 1800 does indeed show the exact position of this. The problem is that the two well-documented enclosure eras were the Tudor period, usually to create sheep pasture (especially vital in Yorkshire's wool economy) and the eighteenth century, when the purpose was to create arable fields for the growing of more crops at a time of marked population increase. Both of these periods post-date Wakefield and the 1415 reference to Castlefield is almost meaningless and could refer to the *whole* area between the castle and river at the time. Similarly, in Richard III's last battle in August 1485, there was no such place as Bosworth Field; it is simply a catch-all term for a large area.

I believe the older assumption that the area of battle (now covered by a modern housing estate) was open fields, three or more divided by ditches, with woods beyond that could have formed useful cover for the Lancastrians. This was Wakefield Green. Any foraging party would have been small, perhaps 100 men at most and may have left the castle by a sallyport, a small, inconspicuous gate on a side away from the town, which is no longer visible. There was a deer park nearby in 1545, paled (fenced) and containing about thirty fallow deer. How long this park had been there we do not know, but if it was there – and stocked – in 1460 (which is, after all, eighty-five years earlier) we can be sure the venison supply had already been exhausted, or the Lancastrians got there first.

From Pontefract to the north-west, the Lancastrians would have followed what is today the A645, but which way they went must be open to conjecture. Richard Knowles has them clattering through Crofton and Walton which would have brought them to the east of the castle, skirting Wakefield entirely. If that is correct, then a foraging party, aiming not for the empty (or possibly non-existent) deer park, would have been making for the town of Wakefield itself. The problem with either of these targets is that the Lancastrians were already in place, blocking any sortie in either direction.

The most feasible explanation of the battle itself is that the Lancastrians had positioned themselves to the north of the town while a smaller wing took post somewhere to the east of Sandal church. This was the group that took on York's foraging party, which they clearly outnumbered. Seeing the danger from the ramparts, York ordered his men out of the castle to bail his foragers out and led the attack himself. As dangerous as this was, it was utter folly to take his son, Edmund of Rutland, with him.

Edward Hall was one of the much later Tudor chroniclers who covered the Wars of the Roses. His *Union of the Two Noble and Illustrious Families York and Lancaster* was published posthumously in 1548. He claimed, however, that one of his ancestors, Sir David Hall, died at Wakefield. From Hall to Raphael Holinshed. From Holinshed to William Shakespeare, who writes his own ludicrous version of the battle. A messenger crashes into Sandal with bad news for the Duke of York – 'The queen, with all the northern earls and lords Intend here to besiege you in your castle. She is hard by with twenty thousand men.' Margaret of Anjou was not there, of course. She stayed in Scotland for the whole of the Christmas festival, not venturing south until the battle was well and truly over. The 20,000 is an exaggeration too. Accurate numbers for armies in this period are difficult, but half that number might be more realistic.

Shakespeare was probably right, however, about York's motivation to attack – 'Many a battle have I won in France, When as the enemy hath been ten to one: Why should I not now have the like success?'

Hall's account has York's forces 'environed on every side, like a fish in a net or a deer in a buckstall'. There cannot have been time to manoeuvre as the Yorkists tumbled out of the main gate in defence of the foragers. Conventional battle formations in the fifteenth century had open field movements organized with a screen of archers across the entire front, with one, two or three 'battles' of infantry behind that and cavalry on both wings. Given the situation and the fact that the Lancastrians probably attacked from the east, the Yorkists would have had to run down the hill towards the river with its narrow bridge, scoop up the foragers and turn right to present their formation to the enemy. The speed and size of the Lancastrians probably surprised them (which can be explained if there was a wooded area to the north-east that could have provided shelter) and York found himself cut off from the castle. He would not have had time to use his cannon, either from the walls or in the field and firing from the walls would have risked hitting his own men once the battle was joined.

Hand-to-hand fighting like this was brutal and short. Given the reach of the murderous 18ft pikes and 6ft halberds, many men went down before the crush of bodies took place. A pikeman or halberdier aimed for the face, striking between the cheek-plates of barbuts or under the bottom rims of sallets. At closer quarters still, swords, axes, maces and daggers wrought havoc against partly armoured men, the liveried retainers who had followed their lords across a water-logged winter landscape.

Whatever numbers we accept, whether it is John Benet's (and Shakespeare's) 20,000 or Gregory's 15,000 Lancastrians against York's 5-6,000, there is no doubt that the aristocracy were in heaviest numbers on the Lancastrian side. York only had the Earl of Salisbury and his own son, Edmund of Rutland, to match that.

Polydore Vergil, the Italian 'historian' who got to England in 1503 and wrote unparalleled nonsense about Wakefield (as about much else) places Margaret of Anjou in the thick of it – '… forthwith she made heads against them and gave them the charge … Then the Queen, encouraging her men, vanquished the residue of her enemies in the moment of an hour.'

The queen, who was not there, spurring on her troops from a 120 miles away!

In all probability, the battle of Wakefield was little more than a skirmish, badly executed by all concerned, but one which had grave consequences for the House of York. Again, casualty numbers are notoriously suspect. *Whethamstede's Register* has 700 Yorkist dead, John Benet 'almost a thousand'. Against St Albans and what was to come, that was nothing. The casualty *list,* however, was frightening. It reflects the notion of Shakespeare's Agincourt roll, in which a handful of aristocrats are listed – 'none else of name' – as if the untitled were not somebody's sons, brothers, fathers. William Harrington fell; so did his brother Thomas. Henry Radford, the veteran warrior, James Pickering and probably Thomas Parre.

These men were particularly vulnerable in a fight because they wore their devices sewn onto their tabards and stood or sat their horses beneath their banners. This was vital if they were to act as a rallying point for their own men, but it made them a natural target for the enemy, all of whom would be familiar with the bright heraldry they wore. The days of commanding officers, even when they are in the ranks with their own men, wearing anonymous khaki and camouflage would come five centuries later.

What happened to Richard of York and his son Edmund, as well as Thomas Neville, Earl of Salisbury? Shakespeare's version, as always, has a dramatic but wholly unrealistic side. Lord John Clifford, whose father had been killed at St Albans five years earlier, caught up with Rutland as the seventeen-year-old fought his way to Wakefield bridge, the narrow defile that crossed the Calder and led to the town. In *King Henry VI Part III*, the pair have time for an unlikely exchange of dialogue, during which Rutland pleads for his life. 'Thy father,' Clifford says, on no factual grounds whatsoever, 'slew my father; therefore, die.' And Rutland even has time to talk to God (in Latin) before he breathes his last. As battlefield expert Richard Brooks writes, this is 'sentimental tosh', especially as Shakespeare has seventeen-year-old Rutland as a twelve-year-old!

It is very colourful to have leading characters still alive at the end of battles, so that the full dramatic impact can be felt. In all probability, Rutland died fighting near his father, his tabard and banner of the arms of England, differentiated with a crescent for the second son, marking him out as one of York's heirs. This was possibly in the area called Portobello, due north of the castle.

In the Shakespeare play, York, wandering numbed and bewildered in the ubiquitous 'another part of the field', tells the audience how proud he is of his sons, especially Richard who 'three times did … make a lane to me And thrice cried "Courage, father! Fight it out!" … and when the hardiest warriors did retire, Richard cried "Charge! and give no foot of ground!" and cried "A crown, or else a glorious tomb!"'

The queen, Clifford, Northumberland and the rest catch up with York and make him stand 'upon this molehill here'. *Whethamstede's Register* calls it an anthill, but is probably the source of the story. The queen, bitchy as ever, taunts York with his boys – 'Where are your mess of sons to back you now? The wanton Edward and the lusty George? And where's that valiant crook-back prodigy, Dicky, your boy, that with his grumbling voice Was wont to cheer his dad in mutinies? Or, with the rest, where is your darling Rutland?'

In the *Whethamstede* version, a garland made of reeds, presumably from the Calder, is placed on York's head as a mocking crown. The paper one came later, but Shakespeare has it happening on the battlefield. With curses all round, first Clifford, then Margaret with her 'tiger's heart wrapped in a woman's hide' stabs York, and Clifford hacks off his head. It is unlikely that any of this happened. Richard, remember, was still only eight and living in Fastolf's Place south of the Thames, blissfully unaware of the disaster at Wakefield. George of Clarence was eleven and not at Wakefield; neither was Edward, Earl of March, who was in Shropshire. In all probability, Richard of York was killed somewhere where a monument was placed soon after the battle. It was destroyed in another civil war, in the seventeenth century, but the Victorian replacement is probably not that far from the actual spot, today in a junior school playground.

The Earl of Salisbury got away, but did not get far. He was spotted by a Lancastrian patrol and taken to the Duke of Somerset at Pontefract. The idea was to offer the man for ransom, a common and highly lucrative practice after any battle. The aristocracy had lands and serious cash and their families would pay well for their release. The Pontefract locals, however, did not see it that way – 'the common people of the country [county],' says the *English Chronicle*, 'which loved him not, took him out of the castle by violence and smote off his head.'

According to the *Annales*, a whole ritual of beheadings took place at Pontefract Castle that night, while everybody's blood was still up. York himself, together with

Rutland, Salisbury, Thomas Neville, Thomas Harington, James Pickering, John Harrow, Thomas Parre and Edward Bourchier, were all decapitated and their heads taken, probably in sacks tied to saddle bows, to York, 'to be set', Hall wrote years later, 'upon poles over the gates of the city…'

There were four of those and we have no way of knowing whose head was displayed where. York's, complete now, according to various chroniclers, with a paper crown in lieu of a golden one, ended up on Micklegate Bar. The purpose of this gruesome display was to make it clear to the townsfolk what had happened and also to terrify any would-be rebels into behaving themselves. Rooks and ravens would have pecked out the eyes first, then the tongues and flesh until only bones remained, blackened by the weather.

Exactly who was responsible for this display remains conjecture. They were not the orders of the queen, who was still in Scotland, nor clearly of Henry VI who had no idea that Wakefield had happened. Soon after Edward IV's coronation, however, Salisbury's widow brought a charge of murder against forty-eight men, directly involved or accessories in her husband's death. They were all retainers of the Percy family of Northumberland and that surprised no one.

It was on the morning of Friday, 2 January that Cecily and her children learned of the events in the North. We cannot know, after all this time, how Richard took it. He cannot have known his father well, nor his brother Edmund, because of the – to us, at least – odd lifestyle of the son of a contentious nobleman. One thing was certain; at a stroke, the family fortunes had changed, perhaps for ever and it was time for Cecily to shift for herself and her youngest children.

The she-wolf of France had at last joined her Lancastrians and was marching south across a thirty mile front, bound for London. Rape, murder and pillage were the order of the day and the behaviour of the queen's army was something that would stay in the public mind for a generation. The Bishop of Ely hired thirty-five Burgundian crossbowmen to defend his cathedral, standing tall in the Fenlands.

The York family had lost a father and a son. But there were still three sons left – Edward, George and Richard. And, on a misty morning, 2 February, three suns rose at the same time over the battlefield of Mortimer's Cross in Herefordshire. It was a rare meteorological phenomenon, called today an anthelion. To the edgy soldiers in the army of Edward, Earl of March, it was an omen – and a good one. It was the 'Sunne-in-Splendour' which, henceforward, would be Edward's personal badge.

Chapter 5

Towton

Palm Sunday

Edward IV's Sun in Splendour badge to commemorate his victory at Mortimer's Cross, February 1461, when the curious phenomenon of three suns occurred in the sky.

Queen Margaret's army was coming south as 'locusts swept onwards like a whirlwind' according to the anonymous chronicler of Croyland priory in Lincolnshire. This cleric, extremely well informed for the time, hovers over the story of Richard III like a black cloud. Annoyingly referred to by historians as the 'anonymous Croyland continuator' and his successor as 'the second anonymous Croyland continuator', he has a comment, usually snide, to make about everything. Because his is often the only 'voice' we have in the corridors of power in the period, historians who should know better have taken him at face value.

In London, Margaret's target, there was panic. Yes, Edward of March had routed a Lancastrian army at Mortimer's Cross in early February and had executed Owen Tudor, the Welsh upstart who had the temerity (or bad taste) to marry the unstable widow of a king, Henry V, but that had not stopped Margaret. Richard Neville, Earl of Warwick, still had Henry VI in captivity, almost certainly in the Tower, and could use him as a bargaining chip. Even so, he needed armed men to stop the she-wolf and he called on Parliament to help against 'the misruled and outrageous people in the north parts of this realm, coming towards these parts to the destruction thereof, of you, and subversion of all our land'. This particular line comes from the city records of York, so clearly, Warwick was way past the niceties of not offending Northerners by now!

Ten days after Mortimer's Cross on Shrove Tuesday, 17 February 1461, Warwick sought to block Margaret's advance by holding St Albans. It had been five years since a battle had been fought here and Warwick's forces spanned the Baldock and Sandridge roads at Barnard's Heath north of the town and abbey. There was treachery again as Lovelace, the same 'captain of Kent' who had command of the artillery train at Sandal, sent a message with Warwick's dispositions to the Lancastrians. It was now past St Valentine's day, so Wakefield was only six weeks earlier; yet Lovelace had had time to extricate himself from Sandal, get south and join Warwick's army, probably in London before it set out. Such opportunism – and such unpredictable, feckless behaviour – litters the whole Wars of the Roses period and makes Richard III's later motto *Loyaulté Me Lie* (Loyalty Binds Me) all the more unusual.

The Yorkist advance guard at Dunstable, watching the roads from the north, was routed and Warwick's troops heard no more from them. The first phase of the battle took place in the town of St Albans itself, the Lancastrians attacking from the south-east, pounding up the steep hill to Romeland next to the abbey. They were driven back and Warwick now changed front, beyond St Peter's church along Sandridge Way. He had perhaps 6,000 men, mostly East Anglian retainers of the Duke of Norfolk. His archers were renowned for their steadiness, but the Yorkists had an impressive array of field guns too.

Opposite him, the Duke of Somerset fielded about 9,000 men, mostly Northerners and a smattering of Welsh bowmen. Every man in the Lancastrian army wore stitched to his jack the white feather on black and crimson which was the device of Prince Edward, according to the recent Act of Accord (now presumably defunct with the death of York), out of a job as heir to the throne! There was snow in the wind and Warwick's gunners had trouble with their fuses. The wind itself sent arrows flying wide of the mark, especially at the end of their trajectory.

The second St Albans was not the Yorkists' greatest moment. Somehow their hearts were not in it. Perhaps because York was dead, perhaps because the threat to London seemed unstoppable, Warwick's troops mutinied by turning tail and running. In this situation, a loss of nerve becomes epidemic. Fear is contagious. Men forget their training of how to withdraw under fire and a retreat turns into a rout. Somerset's cavalry chased them as they scattered in all directions, some towards Barnard's Heath, others east to Bow Gate, still more falling back south to the town itself.

Warwick had brought the king with him, suitably guarded, probably as a bargaining tool in just such a situation. Henry was found sitting quietly under a tree (as you do when a battle is raging all around you!) guarded by two Yorkists whose lives he had promised to spare if they protected him. Both men were executed, some said at the insistence of Prince Edward, only a few months older than Richard and, bizarrely for one so young, with his mother's army at St Albans. Edward was knighted on the field by his father once the whole thing was over.

In the soul-searching that always happens after a loss, various theories were put forward. The *Whethamstede Register*, quite happy a thousand years after he wrote to quote the Roman military strategist Vegetius, believed that the sun had dried up the Yorkists' blood, making them softer than Margaret's Northerners who were, according to another account, 'moved and stirred by the spirit of the Devil'.

What now for the sons of York? The grieving Cecily barely had time to wear her widow's weeds. Richard senior and Edmund were gone. Edward was who knew where? That left George, and Richard junior. This is not to say, of course, that Cecily loved her daughters less than her sons, but 'proud Cis' was a practical woman and a child of her times. *Sons* carried on family lines. *Sons* led armies and ruled countries. When women did it, as in the case of Margaret of Anjou, most people believed that there was something unnatural and repellent about that.

Probably as soon as she heard of York's death, Cecily wrote to Philip, Duke of Burgundy, to take the boys and no doubt the girls, into his protection. The Burgundian court was the most glittering and impressive in Europe and they would be far beyond the reach of Margaret and her ineffectual husband there. But time was against all this. It would have taken a minimum of two weeks for a letter to reach Burgundy, even assuming that Cecily's messenger could take a ship straight away from Deptford, along the river from Fastolf Place. Margaret was coming and Warwick had failed to stop her. Cecily had already discounted Baynard's Castle as being too obvious a Yorkist target for any disgruntled Lancastrian Londoner, which is why she had chosen Fastolf Place at all.

Now began the oddest cycle of events in young Richard's life so far. He and George were given into the safekeeping of a widow, Alice Martyn, who is one of the figures, like Edward's later mistress, Jane Shore, who hover around the story of Richard III like ghosts. The only reference to Alice and this period of probably no more than a month, comes from the records of the Privy Seal office and the Exchequer (one is a copy of the other) from 28 March 1463, by which time Richard's big brother Edward was king. Translated from the Latin, it reads:

> '…in consideration of the true heart and faithful service that our wellbeloved Alice Martyn of our City of London, widow, has borne and done unto us heretofore and namely in receiving and keeping of our right entirely beloved brothers, the Dukes of Clarence and Gloucester from danger and peril in their troubles unto the time of their departing out of our realm into the ports of Flanders …'

The sum of 100 shillings was paid by Edward as an annuity (around £33,000 in today's money), but it was cancelled three years later, probably because Edward was strapped for cash. No one has identified Alice Martyn with any certainty. She may have been the wife of Robert Martyn, whose family lived in the Old Exchange in the parish of St Augustine-by-St-Paul's, but that is far from watertight. Alice was probably somebody's lady-in-waiting, known to Cecily already to be dependable and wealthy enough to support two children, should Cecily herself fall into Lancastrian hands.

The York boys would have sailed, probably from Deptford, in a cog, a sea-going unarmed merchantman with a single sail and would have made for Utrecht. Paul Murray Kendall, writing sixty years ago, conjectures that their protector on this voyage was the squire John Skelton, Surveyor of the Port of London. This was probably early March, to have given the Duke of Burgundy time to weight up Cecily's desperate request and to send his answer.

Utrecht had been Trajectum ad Rhenum under the Romans, in reference to the 'crooked Rhine' which branches into the main river twenty-one miles away. Its cathedral, begun in 1254, had just been completed when the boys arrived. Burgundy was the latest of several such territories spanning the Rhine in the centuries before a united Germany. Under Philip the Good, the state rivalled that of France and had been an ally of the English against the French in the Hundred Years War, which explains why Cecily turned to the duke for help. Philip was every inch a Renaissance prince before the Renaissance had truly dawned. He founded the University of Dôle and instituted the Order of the Golden Fleece, later associated with Spain and all things Catholic. Philip knew Richard of York well, if only because the ambitious duke had pestered him on and off for years over potential marriage proposals between their children. There were, broadly speaking, two ways in which a nobleman – or king, come to that – could extend his territory and power. One was by war, but that was expensive and the outcome uncertain. The other was by marriage and, in the case of sons, somebody else's marriageable daughter came complete with a dowry, often in coffers of gold or silver. An alliance *and* money – it was a win-win situation.

Philip had a problem, however. A bitter enemy of the French king, Charles VII, as he was and prone to back the estranged dauphin, Louis, currently already at his court, Philip had to look at the bigger picture. Louis backed York; Charles backed Lancaster; and the whirlwind events of the last few weeks must have given Philip pause for thought. He had his own mighty duchy to protect. Potentially destroying it for the sake of squabbling English families, neither of whom seemed able to gain the upper hand, was, for him, a step too far. Yet, here he was, protecting the youngest sons of the house of York. He hedged and kept the boys in Utrecht, rather than at his sumptuous court in Bruges and carefully watched the events across the Channel.

Margaret of Anjou's attack on London never materialised. She had rescued Henry (again!) and perhaps some sort of new coronation was planned; at least, surely, an elaborate service in Westminster Abbey to give thanks to God for the safe deliverance of His anointed. There again, the queen was all too well aware that Warwick and many of his troops had escaped St Albans and that Edward, Earl of March, now technically Duke of York after his father's death, was still very much at large. She may even have been swung by a delegation led by Jacquetta, Lady Rivers and Anne, the Duchess of Buckingham, which met her on Barnet Heath and begged her not to unleash her Northerners on the City. Whatever the reason, Margaret pulled north to Dunstable, leaving London to a rapturous welcome given to Edward and Warwick, who had met up and were the heroes of the hour; the unbeaten Edward more so than the battered and slightly tarnished Warwick.

Edward waited quietly in Baynard's Castle until he judged the time to be right, then, on Sunday, 1 March, George Neville, his cousin and Bishop of Exeter, preached a sermon in St John's Field. He listed the grievances against Henry VI – and there were many – and reminded everybody of the Act of Accord which Parliament had passed. So it was, not for the first or last time, that a delegation of London burgesses (Yorkists all) went to Baynard's Castle to beg Edward to take the crown.

On Wednesday, 4 March, the new Duke of York heard Mass in St Paul's. In the cross outside, the traditional sounding board of London opinion before Speakers' Corner in Hyde Park took over centuries later, George Neville whipped the crowd into a Yorkist frenzy. Edward rode in procession to Westminster and sat on the throne, the orb in one hand and the sceptre in the other. The crown was placed on his head, not the paper one that had taunted his father, but the golden circlet that was *the* symbol of sovereignty. Edward's claim to the throne, via his father and extending back to Edward III, was read out. Later, it would be enshrined in law by Parliament as *Titulus Regius.*

Across the Channel, the education of George and Richard had been constantly interrupted in the past months, first because of Ludford Bridge, then because of Wakefield and St Albans. Paul Murray Kendall believes that the boys had been educated briefly by the Archbishop of Canterbury, a relative of their father, in the weeks before Wakefield. If this is true, it would have been a continuation of the Latin, French and English, with perhaps a smattering of Greek, which they had already begun under the tutors employed by Cecily. We know from various throwaway asides, that Richard, now nine, was a rather serious, solemn little boy, but bearing in mind the upheavals of the past months, such introversion is hardly surprising.

The Bishop of Utrecht still had the care of the boys when news of Edward's accession came through, and overnight their status changed from acute embarrassments for Duke Philip to princes of the blood royal, brothers of a king. We still have the financial accounts of the council of Utrecht, dated 9 March, for the vast amounts of liquor drunk in honour of 'the two sons of the Duke of York'. It amounted to 489 litres!

But Philip, in Bruges, was still wary. A wily old politician like him knew very well that nothing had been resolved by Edward's succession except that there were now, confusingly, two kings of England. Which of them would prevail?

Queen Margaret had come almost within shouting distance of London. An advance guard of Lancastrian foragers had reached Cripplegate and were repulsed with shouts and insults. Three Lancastrians were killed within sight of the City walls.

The chronicler Gregory wrote, 'Let us walk in a new vineyard and let us make a gay garden in the month of March with this fair white rose and herb, the Earl of March'. All very poetic, but both sides knew that nothing could be settled without a showdown of arms. Unusually for such a complicated political and dynastic tangle, the Wars of the Roses became for a time a south versus north affair, Edward raising troops south of the Thames, and Warwick his Midland contingents with forty men from Coventry and his Burgundian handgunners. Warwick reached the North first, careful to keep away from Margaret until Edward and his Welsh and Kentish levies could join him. They camped near York, probably unaware that the city had already sent 1,000 men to fight for the Lancastrians.

Once again, we are in the realms of the numbers game. A total joint force of 100,000 men may be an exaggeration, but all accounts agree that this was the largest number of fighting men ever assembled at one place in England. It was symbolic of the size of the battle ahead and itself a measure of the stakes involved. By the second week in March, the queen was camped at Tadcaster, eight miles from York, with its church of St Mary and its limestone quarries. Edward got to Pontefract, so near to the disaster at Wakefield the previous year (in fact only four months before) and sent Lord Fitzwalter ahead with a cavalry advance guard, scouts called foreprickers, to take the crossing at Ferrybridge over the River Aire. Waiting for the Lancastrians to attack him at Sandal, the late Richard of York could have seen this crossing place from the castle keep. But now the Yorkists were too late; the bridge had gone.

That night, the vengeful Lord Clifford – Black Face as his enemies called him – who may or may not have killed Edmund Rutland at Wakefield, launched a surprise attack on the town of Pontefract. The first and second St Albans had already seen street-fighting, always more difficult and hazardous than a clash in the open, but a *night* attack was regarded as particularly unchivalrous. In this same decade, Vlad Tepes, known as Dracula, son of the dragon, launched a similar night attack on a Turkish camp when the Ottomans invaded Wallachia (today's Romania), but Tepes was widely regarded as a bloodthirsty madman who did not play by the rules of Christian warfare.

Fitzwalter dashed out into the night in his nightshirt, armed with a poleaxe and was cut down by Clifford's horsemen. So was the Bastard of Salisbury, one of Warwick's brothers. Expecting the whole Lancastrian army to arrive, Warwick himself killed his horse in a gesture to his men that he was going nowhere. 'Let him fly that will,' legend has him saying to Edward, 'for surely I will stay with him who stays with me.' The new king harangued his troops. He gave them permission to kill cowards and promised double wages for all those who stayed.

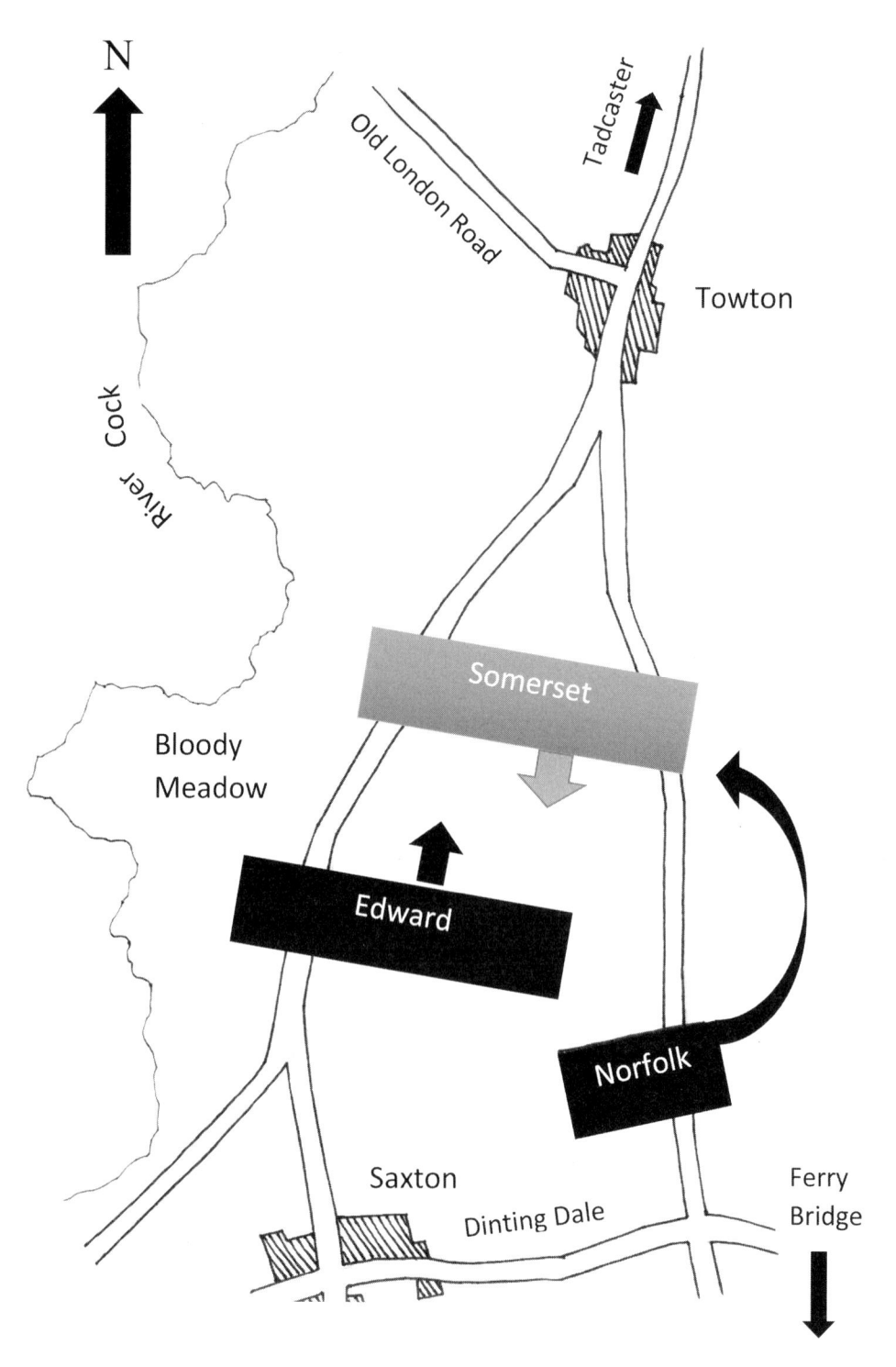

The bloodiest battle of the Wars of the Roses, Towton, March 1461, was fought in a freak snowstorm which limited visibility and made fighting difficult.

But there were no more attacks that night. As a cold dawn crept over the misty Aire, William, Lord Fauconberg crossed the river upstream at Castleford, outflanking Clifford who fell back. He also fell into the trap set for him in the woods near Dintingdale where an arrow split his windpipe and killed him outright. Rutland was avenged. In the Shakespeare version, of course, it is Richard, already described as Duke of Gloucester, who heaps curses on Clifford's head as the blood feud goes on. He does not actually kill him; perhaps because he is still only nine years old and living with the Bishop of Utrecht at the time. Clifford's son Henry ran into Dintingdale and legend has it that he became the 'shepherd lord', given sanctuary by local peasants and not able to reclaim his estates until 1485. Clifford himself was buried in a mass grave of common soldiers.

Edward and Warwick crossed the Aire behind Fauconberg and spent Saturday night, 28 March, in the open as the ground froze around them and men stayed awake to avoid the worst of the frost. Snow was starting to fall at dawn on Palm Sunday, the 29th, something of an aberration, even in the North! The armies faced each other on a high plateau between the villages of Towton and Saxton, straddling the modern roads the A162 and the B1217. There has been much discussion over the timing of the battle of Towton, based largely on the exact concept of time to the men of the fifteenth century. Whereas we measure a day from midnight to midnight, many Medieval people used daylight hours and darkness instead. So whether the clashes at Ferrybridge and Dintingdale took place the day before Towton or were all part of the same coordinated action, begun before daybreak, is now impossible to say. What is certain, however, is that of the three, Towton was the largest and most important.

As had become usual by now, Henry VI, huddled in a cloak and hood and probably only wearing armour for defence against any stray arrows that might come his way, was with the Lancastrians as, until recently, he had been with Warwick's Yorkists. He asked his generals to postpone the fight as it was Palm Sunday. They ignored him. Across the uplands from him, Edward, probably wearing the leopards and lilies tabard as the rightful king of England, roared at his men that no prisoners were to be taken. For all concerned, this was a fight to the death.

It was also contrary to the conventional rules of Medieval warfare. Traditionally, if a knight surrendered on the field, he became the prisoner of a knight of equal or superior rank and would expect his family to pay a sizeable ransom for his release. The numbers of dead and the nature of wounds on their bodies (see below) back up Edward's grim decision. It can probably be explained by the loss of his father at Wakefield, but also by the sheer frustration that Henry VI and his warrior wife were not only still alive but in active contention for the throne. It was a time for a line to be drawn in the Yorkshire earth.

Fauconberg commanded the vanguard and gave orders that his archers should fire once and stand still. In the hard light of a pearly sky and already driving snow, it was not possible to know immediately how successful a volley had been. The Lancastrians fired back, but they were shooting into the wind and their arrows fell short. On his barked commands, Fauconberg's men moved forward, firing again and picking up the fallen shafts of the enemy as they reached them. We know from recent battlefield archaeological finds that at least one cannon exploded at Towton, although there is no mention of guns in any of the earliest encounters. A curved iron tube fragment with a scorched inner face was found recently by a metal detectorist– the barrel had blown apart. This was not uncommon with early fieldpieces, but we have no way of knowing which side owned and fired it. If the explosion happened early in the action, as seems likely, it may be the reason why both sides relied on their archers instead. At the second St Albans, the Burgundian handgunners had had no time to aim and fire their weapons before the Lancastrians were attacking them head on.

Behind Fauconberg, Edward himself commanded the bulk of the army in one large 'battle' rather than breaking up into the more usual smaller formations. He may or may not have had time to have his sun-in-splendour banner woven by this time to commemorate Mortimer's Cross, but if he had, it would have been barely visible through the snow storm as the morning wore on. Behind this mass of armed footsoldiers, bristling with poleaxes, pikes and halberds, the Earl of Norfolk, Sir John Wenlock, and Sir John Denham commanded a cavalry reserve to the right, ready to chivvy the Yorkist stragglers forward and to charge the Lancastrians when they wavered, turning a retreat into a rout.

Before the first arrows flew there was a surreal sound in the silence of the snow; the church bells, from the villages of Towton and Saxton to north and south, summoning the faithful to prayer on Palm Sunday. Did anybody go?

The Lancastrian 'battle', echoing Edward's formation, marched forward first. Its commander was the twenty-four-year-old Duke of Somerset, five years older than Edward, but without his instinctive flair for war. He himself led a second line, leaving the aged Earl of Northumberland and the dodgy Andrew Trollope, known for his elasticity in terms of loyalty, to mount the main attack. The battlefield today has an L-shaped pattern of farm tracks, extending across the B1217. At the road end is Dacre's Cross, once called Towton Cross, and perhaps part of the chantry for the dead set up years later by Richard III. The track running east to west is a little behind the Lancastrian positions. To the west, beyond the Yorkist left wing and the Lancastrian right, the ground falls away sharply in an irregular shape that leads to the River Cock, today no more than a stream. This is private farm land now, but it is where most of the day's slaughter took place.

The archers abandoned their bows at close quarters and hacked at each other with swords, daggers, clubs. Blood spattered the thickening snow and both sides drew apart, exhausted. This phase of the battle probably lasted for about twenty minutes. One of the myths of Towton is that fighting went on for ten hours; physically impossible even for the tough soldiers of the day. Northumberland's troops perhaps numbering 7,000, along with Trollope's 6,000 Welshmen, smashed into Edward's left flank where the ground fell away. In all Medieval battles, the problem was the same; how to hold the ground and to kill as many of the enemy as possible without giving way. The sheer weight of numbers probably drove the Yorkists backwards and the slippery snow made making a stand difficult. In the confusion of noise and panic, communication on a battlefield is difficult. Shakespeare has convenient 'other parts of the field' and lulls in the fighting so that his dialogue can take place. In reality, thousands of men at Towton were standing shoulder to shoulder with their comrades and nose to nose with their enemies. Drums and trumpets were not used to execute commands, so an officer, like Edward or Somerset, would have to send a messenger from one flank to another to give orders. Either that was not tried at Towton or the messenger did not get through, because Northumberland, on the left, had no idea how well Trollope's Welshmen were doing to the right.

Edward dismounted and stood under his banner. This was the traditional English tactic, so scornfully dismissed by the French in the Hundred Years War. At once, it sent a vital message to the men; their new king would die with them.

Most accounts suggest that the battle began a little after nine o'clock and was still going, with appalling slaughter, by early afternoon. By this time, both sides would have been exhausted, cold, yet sweating, bleeding and in pain. This was the key moment in a Medieval battle; which side would crack first? It was now that Norfolk arrived (perfection, some said; others, that he was a tad late) with what one chronicler called 'a fresh band of good men of war', crashing in with his armoured cavalry to reinforce Edward's tottering left wing. As always, the ground dictated tactics. The cavalry would have had to cling to the high ground. Had they ridden further west to outflank the Lancastrians, they would have lost speed and impact on the steep hill that led to the river. This was the last straw for the Lancastrians who broke and ran, most of them hurtling backwards to the north-west towards the lazy meander of the River Cock. Except that the Cock was not so lazy that day. Winter rain had swelled its banks, the snowflakes disappearing as they hit the rushing torrent of water. Men slid down the banks, drowning in the rush, falling over each other in panic. So thick were the numbers of dead here, in the field that would be called Bloody Meadow, that locals were able to cross the river for days without getting their feet wet.

Those who reached Towton found that Somerset had ordered the bridge there destroyed and the river was red. Here and there, knots of Lancastrians tried to stand and fight against Wenlock's and Denham's cavalry, but it was hopeless. The killing went on beyond Tadcaster as men tried to reach York. George Neville wrote later that 'one might have seen the bodies of these unfortunate men lying unburied over a space of nearly six miles in length and three or four furlongs [half a mile] broad.' According to the Gregory chronicle, forty-two Lancastrian knights were taken prisoner and were executed in the field; no trial, no excuses, no mercy.

As night fell on the bloody snow, the Yorkist heralds had the grim job of identifying the dead. They did this largely by the heraldry of the lords and knights and the badges of their retainers. Not everybody wore them and in some cases, the most expensive items had been ripped from corpses by the winning side, anxious for souvenirs and to have something in the way of loot that Edward had promised them. The Earl of Shrewsbury was dead; so was Andrew Trollope. The Earl of Devonshire was taken prisoner and executed later. Eleven barons and forty knights had fallen, among them Lords Dacre, Clifford and Welles. As usual, nobody counted the rest. Northumberland would die within days of his wounds, infected by the frozen soil and germ-encrusted blades. Somerset got away.

The victorious Edward passed bills of attainder in the weeks that followed, condemning the men who had fought against him at Towton and confiscating their lands and titles. Many of them were Yorkshiremen who had not ridden all that far to fight for Henry VI from their local estates. Walter Nuthill came from Rylston; John Smothing, Robert Bolling and Richard Everingham were all from York; John Preston and Richard Lister came from Edward's father's estates at Sandal. Treachery had no friends.

Of the men who fought at Towton – and lived to fight another day – William Hastings of Kirby Muxloe in Leicestershire would become Edward IV's confidant until the king's death in 1483. William Catesby, of Ashby St Legers in Northamptonshire, would remain loyal to the Yorkist cause – and his own – until his own death days after Bosworth. Richard and Thomas Tuddenham were two brothers of a notorious outlaw family who used the war as an excuse to rob and pillage throughout Cambridgeshire. And Thomas Malory, of Newbold Revel in Warwickshire, would spend several years in prison on unspecified charges and go on to write *le Morte d'Arthur* in 1471.

Lord Dacre was buried upright near his horse in Saxton church and mass burial pits were dug there and near the Cock. Henry VIII's historian, John Leland, noted them in his travelogue of the 1540s. Recent excavation of the many bodies buried has proved that some at least were executed by decapitation, the skulls lying in a heap, separated from their bodies. Damage to the heads suggests deliberate mutilation, perhaps the hacking off of ears as grisly mementoes of a ghastly day. As historian David Santiuste puts it, 'God had spoken; Edward had been anointed in the blood of Towton.'

In 1996, chance excavation at Towton Hall revealed part of a large pit which may itself be only a small part of a much larger mass grave. A report by the York Osteoarchaeology Unit in 2004 described in detail the findings of those bodies and others in the previous year. All the individuals were male, between 15 and 50 years of age. Unlike other Medieval burial grounds, the bodies were strong and powerful, indicating a well-fed and well-trained fighting force. Anomalies to some bones suggested years of marching and carrying heavy equipment. Of twenty-eight skulls examined, all but one had cranial wounds, caused by blunt objects like warhammers or maces; or sharp cuts, the work of poleaxe blades. In most cases, the head had been the target of attack; one man (Towton 25) with thirteen cuts to the skull. The shortest body examined was 5ft 2½in and the tallest 5ft 10½in. Only one body showed signs of disease (the vitamin D deficiency illness rickets), and the teeth, in an age before sugar was a de rigueur part of diet, were uniformly good.

Many years later, when he was king, Richard ordered that a chantry be built 'in token of prayer' for those who died at Towton. The present Dacres Cross was erected on its current site in 1939 by Harrogate archaeologist James Ogden, but it was found at the bottom of a hedge and may have been part of Richard's chantry. After the battle, most bodies were given a swift and shallow burial at best and, with winds and scavenging foxes, rotting bodies and bones lay for years exposed to the elements. Edward IV, to atone perhaps for his no-quarter order at Towton, ordered the first chantry to be built, but it was re-edified by Richard in 1483. The new king gave a grant of £40 for the rebuilding and paid for a permanent chaplain, appointed by funds from the Honour of Pontefract. John Leland spent six years touring the country and refers to a 'great chapel' begun by Richard, the foundation stone being laid by Sir John Multon. It remained unfinished at the time of Richard's own death at Bosworth and its whereabouts are unknown today. The number of dead is, as always, disputed. One chronicler gives 26,777. John Paston, he of the family letters, claimed 8,000 for the Yorkists and no doubt many of these were the result of the unchecked slaughter during the rout. Neither Edward nor Warwick was in any mood for restraint. And it was that figure, of 8,000 Yorkist dead, that reached the new king's brothers at Utrecht; that, and the fact that their big brother had won another spectacular victory. They may or may not have been told that among those who escaped, yet again, were Henry VI, his vengeful wife and their heir, another Edward, Prince of Wales.

Edward of York spent the next weeks in the North, chasing the demoralised Lancastrians. At York, he saw his own father's head above Micklegate Bar; it had been rotting there for three months. His brother Edmund's may have been alongside it or perhaps on another of the city's gates. The heads were buried with due solemnity at the priory of St John in Pontefract, reunited with their bodies.

When news of Towton reached Flanders, Philip the Good was relaxed enough to agree that Edward was now, indeed, king of England. Henry and Margaret, it was reported correctly, were hiding in Scotland, always ready to cash in on England's woes. This meant that George and Richard were indeed royal princes and accordingly, they were welcomed by the duke at Bruges. The Milanese ambassador, Prospero Camuglio, wrote to his boss Francesco Sforza, 'Tomorrow, they say, the two younger brothers of March, son of the Duke of York, are coming here and the Duke of Burgundy has given notice for great honours to be shown to them.' Camuglio got Richard's age wrong, assuming he was eleven, but the court and the town pulled out all the stops for the boys. There was a banquet in the alderman's hall and the duke and his entire council were there. Since all the wealthy merchants turned out (Bruges was effectively Europe's financial capital at the time) it was possible, even likely, that one who was there too was William Caxton, not yet famous as a printer, who was the leading English merchant in the town. He may have accompanied the boys on their tour of the duke's library, the finest in the world.

Edward sent word for the princes to come home for his coronation and they were escorted by Philip's horsemen to Calais. They reached Canterbury on Saturday, 30 May, where gifts were presented – two oxen, twenty sheep, three capons and three gallons of wine. The prior of Christ Church met the boys, his priests in green capes, to celebrate Mass on this day of the Vigil of the Holy Trinity. They met up with Edward again at Shene, the royal palace in Richmond. The formal ceremony of kneeling before their king over, it was no doubt hugs and kisses all round. All the evidence we have of Edward is that he was genuinely fond of his siblings, and any formality he would need to acquire as king was still new to him.

On 1 June, the heads of the City Guilds, mayor and aldermen, turned out to meet 'the Lords George and Richard, brothers of the Lord King' at Billingsgate, already a fish market on the banks of the Thames. From there, they almost certainly joined their mother and sisters at Baynard's Castle, now that London was safe from Lancastrian attack. In the forthcoming coronation, George, at eleven, was deemed old enough to have a role to play, but he was guided by Lord Wenlock whose cavalry had routed Margaret's army at Towton. The boys officially welcomed Edward when he rode in procession to London. Anybody who was anybody was there, the crowds no doubt cheering wildly. They made for the Tower, the largest and strongest of London's three castles and the boys, with twenty-six others, were made Knights of the Bath.

The ceremony was elaborate and had developed over time. Richard was taken by two 'governors' and placed, naked, in a bath prepared by three members of the Order. Water was sprinkled over his head as a form of baptism and the precepts of the Order read to him. He was then dried and dressed and spent the rest of the night at prayer in the chapel, probably St John's in the White Tower, before going to confession at dawn, attending Matins and Mass. While all this ritual was probably fairly meaningless to a nine-year-old, for the rest of his life, Richard attended to services and liturgy very closely. More than the mere trappings of a nobleman and later king, he genuinely believed. A short nap was followed by the final ritual. He was taken to Edward and spurs were fastened to his feet. The king strapped a sword belt around Richard's waist and kissed him, 'Be thou a good knight.' We must assume that special suits of armour had been made for Richard and for George, as spurs and a sword would be out of place with the civilian costumes of the day. There was no English armoury at the time (Henry VIII established that at Greenwich years later), but there were enough experts available to recreate the Milanese 'harness' that was popular in England then. It was presents all round: a groom was given Richard's horse; a barber took the bath; the heralds, who would have blasted the occasion with their horns and recorded proceedings afterwards, got an extra twenty marks. Years later, when he was king, Richard would set up the College of Arms in London to formalize the use of heraldry in all official matters.

Edward's Master Cook, in accordance with the ceremony ritual, stopped Richard as he left the royal chamber and claimed the new knight's spurs as his fee, promising to hack them from his heels if ever he broke his knightly oath. Did someone hack the king's spurs from his body at Bosworth and keep them as souvenirs? We will never know. He sat at dinner with the crowd of lords and ladies, but as an initiate, was not allowed to eat or drink himself.

The coronation that followed was a particularly happy one, in that London had been saved from Margaret's savage Northerners. 'The entire kingdom,' wrote an Italian merchant in the capital, 'keeps holiday for the event, which seems a boon from above.' The day after the solemn procession and amid much feasting, drinking and singing, George was made the Duke of Clarence, in honour of an ancestor who was a son of Edward III. The black bull was his crest. At the same time, Sir William Hastings, scion of a noble family that had served the monarchy since Edward III's time, was ennobled. According to Shakespeare, Richard would have both men murdered in the years ahead.

George and Richard lived in the weeks that followed at Placentia, the royal palace at Greenwich, which had once belonged to Humphrey, Duke of Gloucester. The tower they lived in, long demolished, had a hall, a parlour and six rooms. In September 1462, Robert Cousin, the Keeper of the Great Wardrobe, responsible for all royal clothes and armour, sent a range of goodies for Richard's use. They included gowns, tunics, caps, hose, lambskin pelts, more than seventy pairs of boots, a saddle and harness, twelve bowstrings and a sword and scabbard, all things 'necessary for the duke's rank'. Because, by this time, in fact on All Hallows' Day (1 November) 1461, Sir Richard had been created Duke of Gloucester. He took as his badge, *blanc sanglier*, the white boar. There is much speculation as to the heraldic significance of the boar. It was associated with St Anthony, one of the saints for which a much older Richard had a particular fondness. In the Celtic tradition, the animal, still in Richard's day roaming the Northern wildernesses, stood for leadership and direction, the warrior spirit. The Romans held a similar belief, the boar being the sign of several legions throughout the Empire. If nine-year-old Richard knew any of this, it must have been advice from somebody much older.

On the one hand, the rapid elevation of the York boys to ducal status smacks of nepotism. Edward, now IV, was merely giving hand-outs to family and friends. On the other hand, it was important that there was a structure around which the new king could build his power base and rule his kingdom. Edward was still only nineteen, unmarried and without a son and heir. George Clarence filled that role now. In February 1462, Clarence and Richard were made knights of the Garter, the elite group of twenty-five created by Edward III 120 years earlier in homage to King Arthur's legendary round table. Richard went through yet another ceremony, this time in St George's Chapel at Windsor, at which he received a helmet with the boar crest welded to it and a sword. He sat in Stall Nine, his coat of arms stamped in brass at the back of his seat and his banner, with the differenced device of the third son, embroidered on it.

But he was expected to work for it. Two weeks after his creation as Duke of Gloucester, Richard, George, the Earl of Warwick and Warwick's brother, Lord Montagu, were given power to raise troops (the commissions of array) for defence of the North against the Lancastrians, in that Henry VI, useless as he was, was still in Scotland and his wife might force him south at any minute.

Clarence did not leave the environs of London, but Richard did. Paul Murray Kendall refers to him as a 'small, frail boy', but the truth is we have no idea about Richard's health or physique at this point in his life. There are no records of his father's height or his mother's, but Edward was 6ft 3in (his tomb was opened and the body measured in 1789) and stood a full head taller than most of his contemporaries. It was agreed now that Richard, like most noble children all over Europe at this period, should serve his formative years in the household of a great lord. Who greater than Richard Neville, the Earl of Warwick, whom men were beginning to call the kingmaker? And that meant, for the first time in his life, Richard was going North.

Chapter 6
Middleham and Sheriff Hutton

Arms of Richard Neville, Earl of Warwick, known as the Kingmaker. Legend has it that the muzzle on the bear crest was placed there by order of Edward III to shut the Nevilles up!

Richard Neville, Earl of Warwick, was the most powerful nobleman in the land. He loved adulation and expected it from everyone. The Neville estates were everywhere. His bear and ragged staff device floated over castles and manor houses; it was sewn onto the shoulders and chests of countless retainers. In 1466, when Edward IV entertained visitors from Bohemia (today's Czechoslovakia), fifty courses were provided for dinner. Warwick went one better with a banquet of sixty courses. He was a personal friend of the French king Louis XI and people were paid to cheer him as he rode through London streets, shouting, 'Warwick! Warwick!' In Milan, they joked, 'there are at present two chiefs of England, of which Signor de Warwick is one; we forget the name of the other.'

But there were cracks in the shining armour. Warwick was not the general Edward was. He had been outflanked by the Lancastrians at St Albans and did not impress at Towton. He took reversals badly and did not bounce back from them as readily as Edward. There were rumours in France that he was a coward, but that seems unjust and unwarranted.

Above all, Warwick needed the support of the king, for all he was known as the kingmaker in the 1460s. And Edward, in the eyes of Warwick and most of the Plantagenets, had done a rather silly and disturbing thing; he had married into the

Woodville clan. On 1 May 1464, the king went through a marriage ceremony at the manor of Grafton Regis in Northamptonshire to the daughter of Richard Woodville, Earl Rivers. Her first husband, Sir John Grey of Groby, by whom she had two children, was killed at Towton. She also had a lot of relatives and it was not long before they were all pressing the king to extend their titles and estates. It was an unedifying spectacle, but it was no more than every noble family was doing at the time. To the old order, though, it left a nasty taste in the mouth. The Woodvilles were nouveaux riches, with no real pedigree. To make Elizabeth the mother of future kings was abhorrent.

It meant that, while Edward was single, George of Clarence was his heir. Now, all would shift and any issue of Edward and Elizabeth would take precedence. Temporarily blinded by the sensuous, dazzling Elizabeth Edward may have been, but Warwick was under no such illusions. To keep himself in royal favour, assuming his control of the king was slipping, he would have to work on Clarence and Richard of Gloucester.

Richard was still only eleven, already a duke, constable of Corfe Castle and Admiral of England, Ireland and Aquitaine. At this stage of course, these titles and honours were almost meaningless, but they are symbolic of Edward's governmental plan. He would come to rely heavily on Richard in the years ahead, especially as Clarence was so flaky.

Middleham Castle, Warwick's favourite residence in the North, was built by Robert Fitzrandolph in 1190 near the site of an older motte and bailey construction. Building separately, hundreds of yards from the Norman original of Alan Rufus (the Red) was unusual. Most Medieval castles were built of stone to replace the earlier timber versions, but at Middleham, they were separate entities and the Norman motte can still clearly be seen to the south-east. Middleham stands above Coverdale at the edge of the Yorkshire Dales, on the banks of the River Ure and has one of the largest keeps in England. The square-towered rectangle is 105ft north to south and 78 east to west. There are towers at each corner and halfway along the four walls. In Richard's time, there would have been two large ground floor areas, each with a vaulted roof, which would have served as kitchens and storerooms. Above were two great halls, side by side and, soon after Richard's arrival, the ceiling was raised, perhaps to add a clerestory which provided extra air and light. In common with other Medieval castles, Middleham was undergoing a remodelling in the mid-fifteenth century, converting the grim fortresses of the Normans and Angevins to the comfortable family homes of the Plantagenets and their subjects. The move continued under the Tudors, especially since the high, relatively thin walls of Medieval architecture stood no chance against the increasing power of heavy artillery.

The curtain wall, originally thirteenth century, was also modified by the Nevilles, who had acquired the place as early as 1270. A series of chambers, halls and apartments, hung with tapestries and warmed by fireplaces, linked this wall to the concentric keep. There was a chapel, a solar (family room), a bakehouse

Middleham and Sheriff Hutton 57

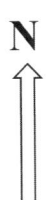

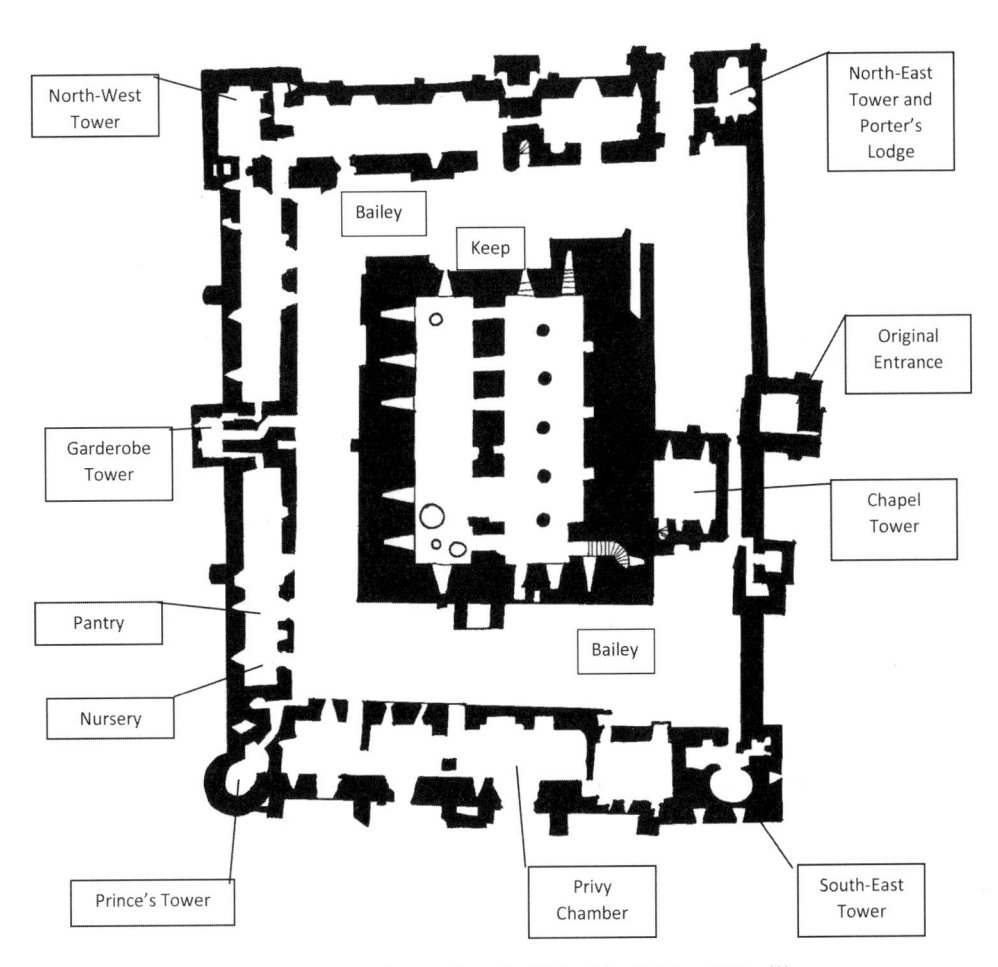

Middleham, the Wensleydale castle much embellished by Richard Neville.

and a nursery. The gateway, which once led to an outer bailey, now gone, had diagonal towers and no doubt a portcullis and perhaps drawbridge. There were stables here, slaughterhouses and a smithy. What appear to be put-log holes are actually bow and gun emplacements; the irony being that, at a time when noble architecture was becoming less military, a civil war raged in England.

Richard had got to Middleham by way of Warwick Castle, over the Avon, another Neville stronghold. We know that in 1465 he attended a service at the church of St Mary's in the town, where the tombs of the Nevilles and earlier earls, the Beauchamps, lay in gilded splendour. The king was still paying for his little brother's wardrobe at this stage, including tapestries, falconry gloves, arrowheads, bowstrings and riding equipment.

We do not know exactly when Richard first reached Middleham and he moved throughout his teenaged years to nearby Sheriff Hutton and south again to Warwick. In his first stay in the North, he met the nobility who had fought with his brother at Towton – the Dacres and Greystokes, the Fitzhughs and the Scropes. He carried out minor ceremonial duties while attending to his ongoing training as a knight and general. As the third son and with two older, perfectly healthy, brothers, Richard was never going to take the throne, but even as a teenager, he may have decided to carve out a mini-realm for himself elsewhere, perhaps here in the North.

Richard was not the only ward looked after by Warwick in those years. Another was Francis Lovell, who would remain fiercely loyal to Richard long after the future king's death. Yet another was Robert Percy, scion of the Nevilles' rivals whose power in the North Warwick was determined to control. They prayed together, studied, practised with swords, bows and poleaxes under the watchful eye of the steward, the controller of the household. Younger brothers, like George and Richard, never knew privacy. They mixed with Warwick's family, both close and extended. They were constantly working with experts like the bowman Thomas Yonge, and priests who taught them scripture and heard their confessions. They got up early and went to Mass. Then they took breakfast – ale, bread, cheese and meat. They sat in one of Middleham's chambers to increase their knowledge of Latin, French, a little law and mathematics. If they learned history at all, it would have been the ancient sort, the Greeks and Romans, still, even in this new age of the Renaissance, held in awe by scholars throughout Europe.

The surviving *Book of Hours* of Ralph Neville, the first Earl of Westmoreland, shows the family at prayer in the generation before Richard and the fashions would have changed little in those years. All devotions were held either in the Chapel Tower or the chapel itself, which would become the home of Richard's own chantry priests in the years to come. This part of Middleham was the province of the dean who cared for the sacristy containing vestments, missals and any relics used in the Mass. The piscina, a basin for holy water in services, still remains in the chapel.

The boys read the *Romances*, tales of chivalry and knightly conduct, even as the real knights around them were killing each other in anything but a chivalric fashion! By this time, Richard would have been given his own 'harness', a suit of armour probably imported from Milan and certainly made to measure. He, George and the other boys would have learned to mount a horse wearing this and to ride at the quintain, driving a wooden lance into a shield that was bolted to a swinging arm holding a morning star (a mace on a chain). The trick was to hit the shield and gallop away before the mace swung round to thud into the rider's back. The horse-training and riding tradition at Middleham is of recent origin, but it may well be that it is based on a now lost riding school in the castle precincts where horse management and equitation still goes on today.

The royal wards hunted together over the Dales, the unenclosed fields of the moorlands looking not very different from today, hawking, and hunting stags and boars, although their numbers were declining fast. Ten miles away was the manor house of Nappa Hall, owned by an Agincourt hero, James Metcalfe. His sons would later serve Richard faithfully. Bolton Castle was the home of Lord Scrope, another famous warrior. And, dotted around the moors and dales, a dozen impressive monasteries stood in perpendicular splendour – Fountains, Rievaulx and, nearest of all, Jervaulx. Middleham itself had enclosed parklands nearby – Sunskar to the south west and Cotescue to the west. There were summerhouses, rabbit warrens known as pillow mounds, kennels, stables and fishponds. Cattle, deer and sheep would have grazed beyond the walls, a ready source of meat for the castles' banquets and feasts.

At religious festivals like Christmas and Corpus Christi, the York and Neville families would ride to York, staying in one of the great city's many religious houses and eating with the mayor and corporation. In 1465, it had only been five years since Richard of York's head had been hoisted above Micklegate Bar; and only four since Edward IV had hauled it down again. In September of that year, Richard, now nearly thirteen, attended a ceremony at York's archbishop's palace to see Warwick's brother, George, enthroned as Georgius Eboracum. There were 2,000 guests including fifteen members of the aristocracy, eighteen knights, eighty-nine squires, eighteen abbots and priors and thirty-three judges. Historian Chris Skidmore describes it as a 'northern coronation' and it is difficult to argue with that. The menu has survived. Five hundred deer were hunted to provide the venison, as were 1,000 egrets, 400 woodcocks, 500 partridges, balanced with high fish content: pike and bream from Yorkshire's rivers and lakes; porpoises and eels from the sea. There were tarts, jellies and custards, spices and wafers. And we haven't started on the wine and ale yet! Thirteen tables had been set up in two chambers waited on by over 400 servants, all in the livery of the two great families spearheaded by the Nevilles.

In the strict hierarchy of sitting at such events, Richard was still too young to sit with the men and instead, sat with Anne, Richard Neville's countess and his sister Elizabeth, now Duchess of Suffolk. The Countesses of Northumberland and Westmoreland were there too, as were Warwick's daughters, Isobel (Richard's age) and Anne, four years younger.

In the years ahead, Anne and Richard would be betrothed and finally, married. Shakespeare has a brutal and ludicrous 'courtship' in which a totally unscrupulous Gloucester promises to kill himself unless Anne marries him (she is having her first husband's body transferred to a new tomb at the time and, according to Shakespeare, it was Richard who put him there). According to some recent novelists, their relationship was a love match and the young couple could almost have graced the

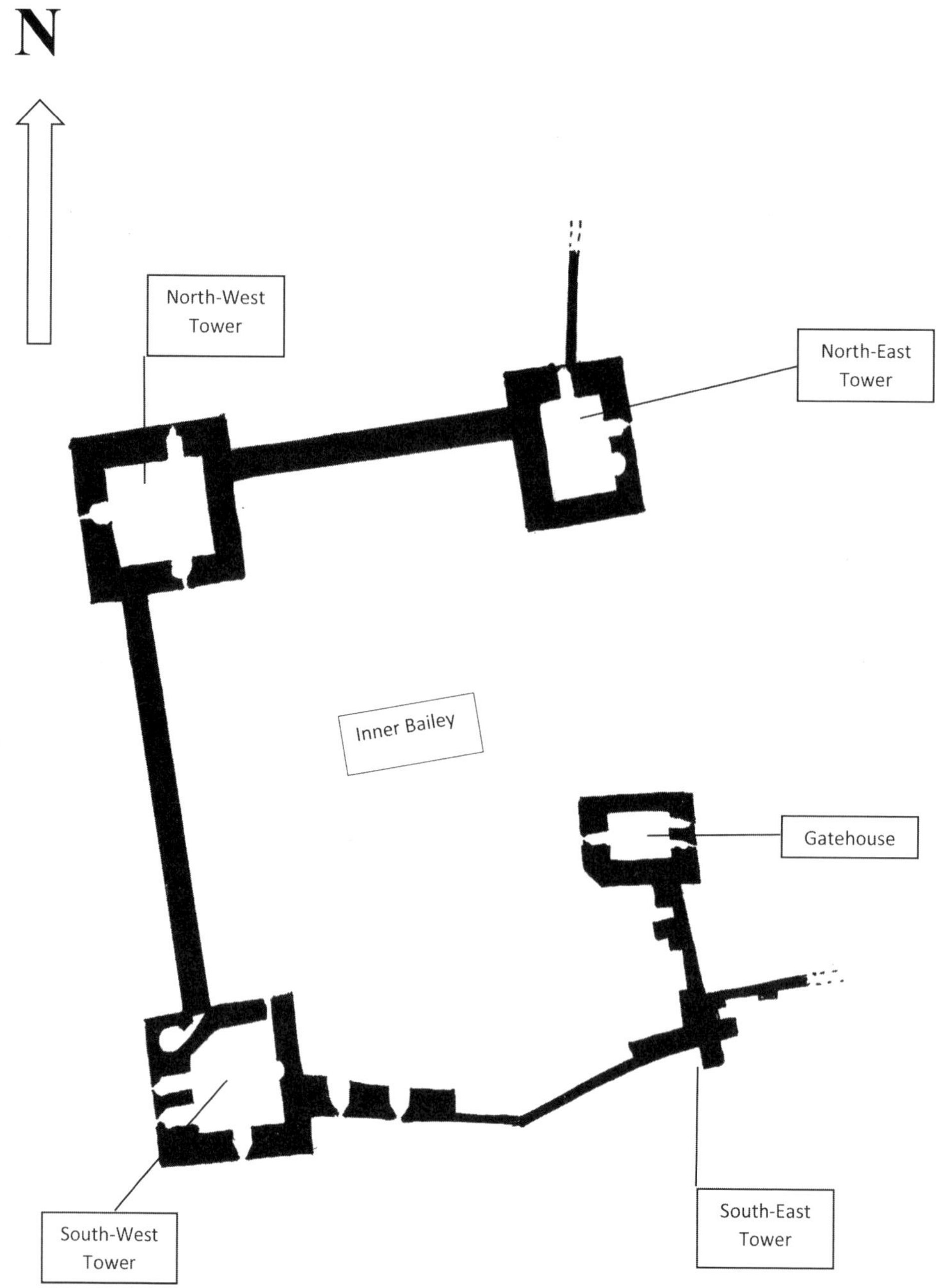
N
North-West Tower
North-East Tower
Inner Bailey
Gatehouse
South-West Tower
South-East Tower

The kingmaker's other castle in Yorkshire, Sheriff Hutton was intended to be the headquarters of the Council of the North.

cover of *Hello!* magazine. In fact, we have no idea of their actual relationship. The marriage was one of political expediency – Warwick could manipulate the Plantagenets via his daughter and son-in-law; the Plantagenets could add vast wealth and essential castles to their demesnes. That said, it is of course possible that Richard and Anne fell in love.

Whereas the castle of Middleham is well documented and open to the public via English Heritage who have produced an excellent guide book, Sheriff Hutton is on private land and remains a ruin, glimpsed only from a distance. Under Richard as king and his heir John de la Pole, the Earl of Lincoln, the castle became a potential headquarters of the Council of the North, so it was altogether a more formal and business-like place than the more family oriented Middleham.

Sheriff Hutton is called Hotun in Domesday and was, in 1086, in the Burford Hundred, split between several owners. Under William of Normandy, it became the holding of Robert of Mortain, who put Sir Nigel Fossard in as lord of the castle. It passed through various hands until the Nevilles acquired it in 1331. As at Middleham, there are actually two castles at Sheriff Hutton (the sheriff in question is reputed to be Bertram de Bulwer, High Sheriff of York in 1166). The first was a timber motte and bailey fortification, the remains of which can still be seen south of the churchyard. The second, of stone, was begun by John, Lord Neville, in 1382.

This lord obtained a royal charter for an annual fair in the town that grew up around the castle, on 14 September, the eve of the Exaltation of the Holy Cross. His son was the First Lord of Westmoreland who owned Middleham too.

Sheriff Hutton's architect, like Middleham's, was John Lewyn of Durham, who had also worked on a number of priories for the Durham See. He also built new kitchens at Raby and Bolton Castle for Lord Scrope. His distinctive style, of turrets and cinquefoil windows, is common to all his buildings.

The castle has a quadrangular keep, with four rectangular towers connected by buildings enclosing an inner bailey. The gatehouse entrance lies to the east, but the original middle and outer wards have now gone. We have no information about young Richard's time spent here in the 1460s.

But, as well as meeting his future bride at Middleham, in that decade something altogether more serious occurred. Richard, probably in his early teens, developed scoliosis. Any historian writing before the discovery of the king's body in the Leicester car park spent a great deal of angst trying to evaluate the origin of the hunchbacked monster as depicted by the Tudors. Surely, it could not come from nowhere? And yet, every single mention of deformity postdates Richard's death and therefore must be suspect. A level-headed writer like Paul Murray Kendall came to a compromise sixty years ago:

> The sickly child who had become a thin, undersized lad, drove himself to grow strong, to wield weapons skilfully. Fiercely, grimly, he worked at the trade of war. His vitality was forced inward to feed his will … Probably as a result of this rigorous training, his right arm and shoulder grew to be somewhat bigger than his left.

The 'sickly child' idea comes, as we have seen, from James Gairdner and the 'Richard liveth yet' line. It may not be true. The Bohemian knight Nicholas von Poppelau is unique in giving us a physical thumbnail sketch of Richard. This was in 1484 when the Duke of Gloucester was king and von Poppelau, probably a spy for the future Holy Roman Emperor, Maximilian I, was touring various courts of Europe. He was impressed with Richard, to whom he spoke through an interpreter (although both men could speak Latin) and ate at least two meals in the king's personal company. He refers to his slim arms and legs so Kendall's surmise is probably not very wide of the mark. Von Poppelau also, infuriatingly, tells us that Richard was 'three fingers' (about two inches) taller than he was; 'infuriatingly' because the Bohemian does not give us his own height! On the basis of the Leicester bones (see Chapter 14) Richard III was 5ft 8in tall when he was killed, which makes von Poppelau about 5ft 6in. Two inches more than this was tall for the time, although of course, compared with brother Edward's massive 6ft 3in, would have been less impressive. On the other hand, Dr Jo Appleby, lecturer in bio-archaeology at Leicester University who carried out extensive research on the car park bones said that scoliosis could reduce the sufferer's height by up to two inches. This would make Richard 5ft 6in and von Poppelau 5ft 4. One website article that appeared shortly after the Leicester analysis took place claims that scoliosis can reduce a person's height by up to a foot! This would have made Richard 4ft 8in and the Bohemian 4ft 6in, which is not only ludicrous but adds to the Tudor-engendered nonsense about deformity long after it should have been consigned to the scrapheap.

From the appearance of Richard's skeleton once it had been cleaned and laid out in a laboratory, the king's spine had a 'C' shaped curve in the upper torso, not the 'S' shape that can mean kyphosis or spinal curvature often called hunchbacked. This would have given Richard a right shoulder slightly higher than his left, but in carefully tailored clothes, such as the king would always have worn, this would not be obvious. In armour, this was even more true. The Milanese suits of Richard's teenaged years and the Augsburg suits more popular in his twenties were usually made with larger shoulder and elbow defences on the left arm because this was the shield-bearing side of the body that took the impact of lances in the lists. Scoliosis is quite common today, as it probably was in the fifteenth century and is idiopathic – that is, the cause remains unknown. Probably at some time around his twelfth birthday, in other words, as Richard arrived at Middleham, the curvature would have begun. Did it cause pain or shortness of breath? Possibly, but such things are relative. A number of conditions, including asthma and tuberculosis show breathing symptoms and, as there was no effective pain relief in the fifteenth century, everybody just got on with their lives as best they could. Richard as a teenager may have adopted a certain way of sitting or standing to alleviate any pressure he felt on his back and legs. On the other hand, there is no mention whatever of the duke or king experiencing any physical problems at all.

Dominic Smee, who took part in a BBC documentary on Richard soon after the discovery of the bones, has a similar condition to Richard's and is of a similar age.

Not only could he ride and use a sword from the saddle (he was trained in this role-play for the documentary), but he felt no ill effects whatever from exertion.

It is likely that only a handful of people would have seen Richard naked. With all due respect to *Poldark* and various recent Jane Austen offerings on television, people in the past rarely stripped, even to the waist, so the sight of Richard's condition would be known to only a few. His wife, his mistresses, a handful of servants; they alone could testify. But one of them must have leaked the information and the gossip grew. It is even possible that the coronation ceremony (see Chapter 11) gave somebody the idea as early as 1486. It must have reached the Welsh bard Dafydd Llywd who was probably the first to impugn Richard with stories that his deformed and twisted body matched his morals. Shakespeare built on all this a hundred years later, inventing a withered arm and shrunken leg which we now know Richard did not possess.

In the meantime, the North was not a safe place. Three of the largest castles, Alnwick, Dunstanburgh and Bamburgh were held by Lancastrians. Margaret of Anjou smarmed her way around Louis of France, offering him Calais in exchange for troops and money. She landed at Bamburgh, the magnificent castle towering over the Northumbrian beaches, in October 1462 and Warwick was already in Yorkshire to beat her back. Edward was marching north too. Ten-year-old Richard, at Middleham, was watching armed men marching again, as he had at Ludlow, but this time there was no battle, not even the glimmer of one. Margaret ran and her fleet was hit by a massive storm in the North Sea. She and her son Edward got to Berwick and Edward IV was stopped at Durham, not by the Lancastrians, but an attack of measles, probably a more virulent strain than we know today.

All three of the Lancastrian castles had surrendered by January 1463, and Paul Murray Kendall conjectures that Richard may have accompanied the armies that took them. No other historian refers to this and it comes from the need to fill in the all too obvious gaps in our knowledge of the young duke's life.

Before February 1466, when Edward IV's first child, Elizabeth, was born, Clarence was still the king's heir and Clarence got all the perks. In terms of the North, he was given forfeited Percy lands and the Honour of Richmond in Yorkshire, along with the county and lordship of Chester. There were others elsewhere and by 1467 the annual income of Clarence's estates was 5,000 marks a year, nearly as much as the new queen owned.

Richard, as the younger brother, got less. In the North all he had was Richmond, which Clarence grabbed back after whining jealously to Edward. Even so, the duke did not complain. He may have been growing up in the household of the Earl of Warwick. He may have been to an extent sidelined by his older brother. But he was already fiercely loyal to Edward, determined to support him no matter what. And he was, perhaps, already falling in love with the North.

Chapter 7

Barnet and Tewkesbury
Easter Sunday and St Godehard's Day

Arms of Edward, Prince of Wales. The royal coat of arms was for many centuries the quartered leopards and lilies (actually lions and fleurs de lys). The label (horizontal bar) at the top of the shield is a symbol of 'differencing' to distinguish the coat of arms of the eldest son from his father.

On 30 January 1462, Richard came south to take part in a solemn ceremony. He was commemorating, along with the king, the two years since their father, Richard of York, had been killed at Wakefield. This took place at Fotheringhay, Richard's birthplace. The hearse was covered in a beautiful cloth with the roses and suns of York, kings and angels in cloth of gold. The focus was not the castle, but the nearby sumptuous church of St Mary and All Saints begun by the second duke of York in 1411. In the 1430s, the original church was doubled in size, with a college cloister, quire and lady chapel for the use of the chantry priests who lived and worked there. The pulpit in the church, still there today, was a gift from Edward IV and may have been created to commemorate the re-interment of the bodies.

A fortnight later, determined not to be outdone, the Nevilles – the kingmaker, Chancellor as well as Archbishop George and John, Lord Montagu – buried the Countess of Salisbury with her husband and son in Bisham Abbey, Buckinghamshire.

The ongoing tension in the North between the Nevilles, representing the king in this instance, and the Scots, simmered down by early December 1463, and Edward, probably with Richard in his retinue, signed a ten-month truce at Pontefract. That year, we know that the king gave his brothers two tuns of Gascon wine each for Christmas.

It was as early as this that the difference in ability and personality of the king's brothers became ever more obvious. Early in 1464, Edward decided to settle the wild North permanently by eradicating the various pockets of Lancastrian support. This meant raising money and troops all over the country. Richard, still only thirteen, was given control of nine counties in the commissions of array, responsible for raising troops. Clarence, at sixteen, was not given one. We have already noted the sudden flood of posts and favours that Richard received, from the honour of Richmond to the admiral's chain of office and the constableship of Corfe Castle in Dorset. Edward wanted to keep at least one brother sweet.

After various skirmishes across the North, which did not involve the Duke of Gloucester, by the summer of 1465, Edward was undisputed master of the country. Wales and the annoying town of Berwick-on-Tweed near the Scots' border still held out for the Lancastrians. But it was the king's clandestine marriage that led to the unravelling of it all and led to an end of stability. Edward's links with Elizabeth Woodville came as a surprise to the Earl of Warwick who was, in line with his kingmaker status, trying to negotiate a French marriage for what he assumed was an unmarried king of England. It was humiliating for Warwick, but any rift between him and Edward seems to have been glossed over, at least for the time being.

Richard's mid to late teens, a time when his scoliosis must have been worsening, is almost a closed book. We know that in the spring of 1465 he left Middleham and the wardship of Warwick and joined his brother's court at Greenwich, the palace of Placentia. As everybody, the teenaged duke probably included, looked on in horror, the vast Woodville clan was granted title after title and estates all over the country. Edward enjoyed his lavish spending, on banquets and feasting – the sort of over-indulgence which may have led to his death at the age of forty. His wife was even more extravagant. Paul Murray Kendall paints a picture of Edward's court as one gilded by the sun beams of the Renaissance, but if so, it was a weak light by comparison with almost any other court in Europe. After the hard, bleak moors of Yorkshire, however, it must have seemed a different world to Richard.

The following year, Warwick renewed his bid to win George of Clarence and Richard of Gloucester to his side. Both boys had spent their recent years in the North under his control and if the king's obsession with the Woodvilles was making him a distant figure, the same would not be true of the royal brothers. He offered Clarence his elder daughter in marriage, the surest way of keeping a man and his estates under one roof, but Edward heard of the plan and stopped it. Undeterred, Warwick played the foreign statesman, negotiating with Louis of France to back him in his long-standing feud with Burgundy. He assured the French king that Edward would gladly be his ally (reversing the policy of England for the last hundred years) and arranging that Edward's sister Margaret would marry a French nobleman. Richard would marry Louis' second daughter and with it would come the Burgundian lands of Holland, Zeeland and Brabant. Had this supremely ambitious pitch come off, Richard may well have left the North – and England – for good.

Paul Murray Kendall conjectures that Richard was not happy in this dazzling London-based court and that he missed the North, which he already regarded as his natural home. He surmises, as many historians have, that the young Gloucester hated the Woodvilles with their arrogance and greed, but perhaps he paints too unyielding a portrait of Richard as dour, bent on service and duty and not prone to laughter or entertainment. The fact is we have no idea of this aspect of Richard's character, even when he was standing centre stage as king. We know that he enjoyed music, both religious and secular, but the minstrels who played before him were actually employed by his mother and later his wife and son.

In February 1467, Richard and Clarence worked together at York in a commission of oyer and terminer (literally, to hear and decide) on criminal cases in the county. The king's justices oversaw trials, but oyer and terminer was a preliminary weeding out process. At the age of fifteen, this was probably Richard's first excursion into the realms of the law. Four months later, however, in an extraordinary move, the king visited George Neville, his chancellor, at Charing Cross, London and took the great seal from him. Neville was fired. Worse was to follow the next year when Earl Rivers' house in Maidstone was sacked and Warwick was widely believed to have been behind it. He refused to leave Middleham to answer charges and was seething at the marriage engineered by the king of his sister Margaret to Charles, son of the Duke of Burgundy. In June, Edward, Clarence and Richard waved her a fond farewell at Margate.

In October 1468, Richard turned sixteen and reached the age of majority. He was given the estates of Lord Hungerford (executed for treason four years earlier), and presided again in oyer and terminer in the case of Hungerford's son, Thomas, and the Earl of Devon's brother, Henry Courtney, both charged with treason against Edward by conspiring with Margaret of Anjou. Richard passed the sentence of hanging, drawing and quartering, which had been the standard punishment for traitors for centuries, but allowed Thomas's mother to keep the income from nineteen manors. The rest of the Hungerford estate was used to set up a charity and almshouses in Salisbury.

Trouble came from the North in the spring of 1469, led by Robin of Redesdale (probably Sir John Conyers) who, among a mass of local grumbles, demanded the restoration of Henry Percy as Earl of Northumberland. John Neville, who actually held that title now, put down the rebellion outside the gates of York, killing the local leader, Robin of Holderness, in the process. Redesdale ran to Lancashire and continued to agitate from there. Edward, with seventeen-year-old Richard in tow, led an army north, but he took his time about it, visiting the shrine of Our Lady at Walsingham. It was from near there, at Castle Rising in Norfolk, that we have Richard's first letter, the postscript of which is in the Duke of Gloucester's handwriting. He was asking for money, which seems a niggardly thing to do, but, as the letter says, he had to raise troops to put the Redesdale rebellion down and that was an expensive business. The fifteenth century saw the arrival of 'bastard feudalism' in which a cash economy was replacing the older concept of fees in the form of land. In short, soldiers had to be paid.

By the end of June, the king and Richard had reached Bishop's Lynn (now King's Lynn) and spent a night at Croyland Abbey (today Crowland in Lincolnshire), whose 'continuator' would claim to know a great deal about the Machiavellian events of the 1480s. It was at Newark that papers fell into Edward's hands, implicating the Earl of Warwick in the Redesdale uprising. The Woodvilles, they said, along with other avaricious earls, were destroying England. The Woodvilles scattered to wherever they felt safest in their newly acquired estates and Edward sent for Lord Hastings and the Earls of Pembroke and Devon to join him with their retinues. Civil war was back on the table; not, this time, between York and Lancaster, but between York and York.

The events of that summer of 1469 are extraordinary even by fifteenth-century standards. First, Clarence went with Warwick to Calais, where he married Warwick's daughter, Isobel, cousins though they were. On their return, Warwick raised loyal supporters in Kent and marched towards Nottingham, where Edward and Richard were awaiting news. Redesdale's rabble joined the rebels, and the king's supporters, the Earls of Pembroke and Devon, were defeated at Lose-Coat field near Banbury, the rebels throwing away their liveried jacks as they ran, giving the field its name. Pembroke was beheaded.

Edward's army, small though it was, seems to have dispersed and the king let himself be taken prisoner by George Neville, still Archbishop of York though no longer chancellor, and be taken to Warwick Castle and then to Middleham. Earl Rivers, Sir John Woodville and the Earl of Devon were all executed in the days ahead. This was a coup and the country was in chaos, made all the more so by Edward's calculated 'surrender' having won a battle!

Warwick, however, had an insurmountable problem. Removing one king and replacing him with another had a very long precedent in English history. Replacing him with a nobleman who had not been anointed by God's choice was an altogether different proposition. This would not be tried until the Interregnum of the 1650s, when Oliver Cromwell desperately tried to find an alternative to monarchical government; he failed. While most other European countries toppled their kings and emperors over the centuries ahead and proclaimed republics instead, England alone remained wedded to the principle of monarchy, however watered down it has become. In the 1460s, men refused to follow Warwick until they could be assured that the king was alive. Accordingly, Edward was released and turned up at York by 29 September, to witness the execution of Henry Neville of Brancepeth in the city. This may have been Edward's plan all along.

We do not know where Richard was during these weeks, but in all probability he was somewhere in the North. Certainly, by the end of September, he and Hastings had cobbled together yet another army and met Edward at Pontefract. Then they marched south, making for London, which the king entered with his entourage and a huge loyal turnout of the great and good.

The Warwick coup had rattled Edward and he was wary of giving the Woodvilles the prominence he once had. Clarence, too, was unreliable, easily seduced by Warwick's flattery and now married to his daughter. Richard alone, although only seventeen, was steadfastly loyal and Edward made him Constable of England. In this context, he could raise armies and put down revolts, hand out punishments including execution, with or without trial. His first use of this was in putting down a potential rebellion in Wales, which had always had Lancastrian sympathies and would provide, in the years ahead, Richard's nemesis, Henry Tudor.

This was Richard's first real taste of action as a commander rather than as a frightened little boy as at Ludlow and details are sketchy. He retook the powerful castles of Edward I at Carmarthen and Cardigan and forced the rebels to swear an oath of fealty to the king rather than face imprisonment in some miserable oubliette. By Christmas, the whole thing was over and Richard was in London reporting his success to his grateful brother. The Duke of Gloucester was virtually Viceroy of Wales.

Across the Channel, however, trouble was brewing. Warwick, determined to break Edward's power somewhere, allied with his former enemy, Margaret of Anjou, and the king of France to stage a coup and put the hapless Henry VI back on the throne. Their army landed at Plymouth and Dartmouth on 13 September and marched for London. Edward was about to leave the North for the capital when he heard of the sudden defection of John Neville, the Marquess of Montagu.

What happened now is one of the strangest twists in the tale of York versus Lancaster. Edward could not rely on Clarence, it is true, but he could and did trust Richard. He also had a large number of Yorkist lords, spearheaded by Lord Hastings and Earl Rivers and he had been a popular king now for seven years. Even so, the four of them – Edward, Richard, Hastings and Rivers – took ship for Calais, abandoning England to Warwick and Margaret. Calais was a convenient bolthole; both Edward and Warwick had used it in the past. At some point, there was a change of plan and the four ended up in Alkmaar, in what was Burgundian territory.

Warwick can hardly have believed his luck. He entered London unopposed and the 're-adeption' of Henry VI took place. The king was brought out of the Tower, shaved, bathed and given new clothes and prayed publicly at St Paul's. Clarence was with him, so was Thomas Stanley, part of a family who changed allegiance as the wind blew. Edward's queen Elizabeth, pregnant with the boy who would briefly become Edward V, went into sanctuary at Westminster Abbey. The kingmaker had made another king, albeit an existing one.

Oddly, Richard is not recorded as joining Edward for some weeks and it may be that he stayed behind in England to recruit men or at least to observe at first hand what was happening in the capital.

Edward worked on Clarence, using his mother Cecily as chief messenger because it was clear that Warwick had no intention of sharing power with anyone except Henry VI and, at a pinch, Margaret. On Thursday, 14 March, the exiled king landed with a small fleet at Ravenspur on Humberside, the formerly thriving port that was now rapidly falling into the North Sea, and marched to York. He told the mayor and aldermen that he only wanted his earldom back, but this fooled nobody and, gathering men, he marched south. John Neville, Lord Montagu, was waiting for him at Pontefract, but Edward outmanoeuvred him and made for Sandal, his father's castle at Wakefield.

Warwick raised his bear and ragged staff standard at Coventry as Edward marched to Nottingham, men joining him as he went. There was a family meeting at which Clarence again joined his brothers and the Plantagenet Yorkists marched on to London. Yet again, the capital was everybody's target and both leaders, Edward and Warwick, had written to the mayor and aldermen asking for their support. The Archbishop of York, woefully out of his comfort zone in the south, paraded the increasingly mad-looking Henry VI around London's streets again. The mayor took to his bed and the Londoners put up no resistance when Edward's now sizeable army arrived. Edward met Henry in person and took his hand. 'My cousin of York,' Henry said, 'I know that my life will be in no danger in your hands.' He was taken to the Tower, along with the Archbishop of York and the former king never saw freedom again.

On Good Friday, Edward held a council of war, with Richard and Clarence in attendance. Warwick, they heard, was coming south and everyone knew that Margaret of Anjou and her 'hitman', the Bastard of Fauconberg, had not yet joined him. The king's army marched north-west out of the city, taking the road to St Albans across Barnet Heath.

Here, across the modern A1081 near Hornsey, the outriders of both sides clashed and Edward's troops drove Warwick's back, seizing Barnet town for Edward. Richard, given his first major command of the vanguard at the age of eighteen, got there first and sent word to Edward telling him of the situation. The plan was to push forward under cover of darkness, forcing Warwick to give battle in the morning. Richard's men walked as quietly as their weapons and armour would allow, holding their horses' muzzles to keep them quiet, and there were to be no torches. The battleground, now Hadley Common, was a treeless expanse of gorse and heather. At some point, Warwick's artillery opened up, but he had no idea how close Richard was and the cannonballs whizzed harmlessly over the Yorkists' heads. They did not fire back. Men got what sleep they could.

Just as the snow had blighted Towton, so a thick fog shrouded Barnet as dawn broke. It muffled sounds in the battle preparation, but when the fighting was joined, caused all kinds of confusion.

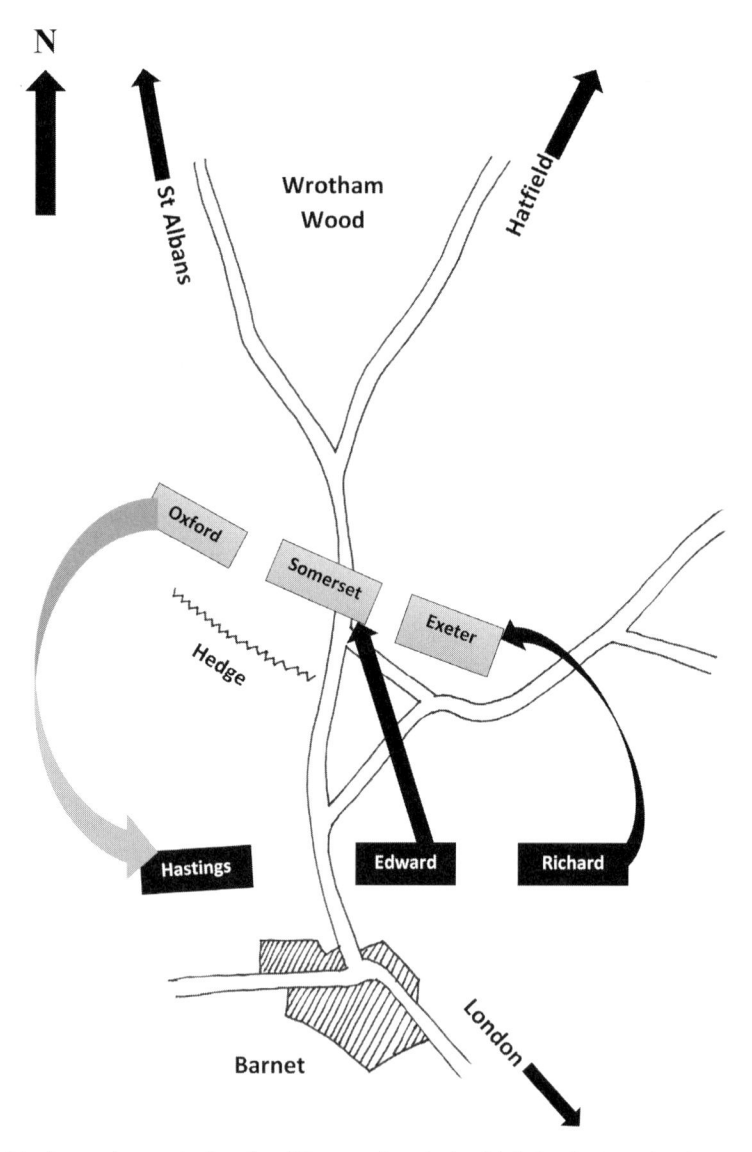

The probable formation at the battle of Barnet, fought in thick fog in March 1471. Because of the very limited visibility, the 'battles' were not drawn up in line, but Richard of Gloucester's right wing would have missed the enemy entirely if he had not swung left.

The Yorkists had divided their army into three 'battles', Edward in the centre against Somerset with or without (the sources differ) a cavalry reserve behind him. Hastings commanded the left wing, facing Oxford and Montagu. Richard led the right, with the village of Monken Hadley behind him and Lord Exeter ahead. The problem was that, in the fog, the armies were not aligned. Hastings was facing the Lancastrian right wing and the centre, while Richard, as he marched ahead down the slope, met nobody. The wings overlapped and by the noise, he knew that the fighting had been joined to his left.

It must have been a bizarre and unnerving experience for Richard. This was his first major battle. Visibility was almost nil and there was no enemy ahead. He ordered his captains to swing left, marching uphill to the plateau top, crashing into Exeter's left flank and forcing him to wheel in line with the road. Richard was in the middle of it all, according to one account swinging a battleaxe, but reinforcements were adding to Exeter's numbers and Richard's wing was brought to a standstill. Those reinforcements were Warwick's reserve, positioned at the fork in the roads to the north that led to St Albans to the left and Hatfield to the right. While a battle royal was going on there, on the far side of the field, the Earl of Oxford was forcing Hastings' flank backwards and reaching Barnet's streets, began plundering already. Some of Hastings' riders fled the field, bringing news to London that Edward and his brothers were dead.

In the centre, the battle line having swung to north-south from east-west, Edward was holding his own against Somerset's centre. Gallopers were sent backwards and forwards. If Richard could just hold on … if Edward could break the stranglehold … if … if … All Medieval battles hung on that moment when somebody's nerve cracked, when exhaustion kicked in, when hope was lost. Then defeat became infectious and panic became the new order of the day.

Oxford's men had pursued Hastings back to Barnet, but Hastings himself had rallied a hard core of supporters and Oxford had to haul his men out of the town and bring them back to the action. In the fog, Oxford's star banner may have been confused with Edward's sun in splendour, though it seems unlikely. Whatever the reason, Somerset's struggling force fired a volley of arrows at Oxford's troops – a rare, but not unique instance of friendly fire. In this war, where men changed allegiance at the drop of a hat, Oxford assumed that he had been betrayed. There were shouts of 'Treason!' and his men broke. He himself rode north to the safety of Scotland.

On what had been Richard's right flank, now at the northern end of the battlefield, the duke himself was wounded. It cannot have been serious and there are no accounts of exactly where or how he was hit. He lost two squires alongside him during the day. Exeter's men began to waver in the centre, the duke himself was down, stripped naked and left for dead – that crucial moment had arrived. With the natural instinct of a born soldier, Richard ordered his trumpeters to sound the advance and they battled forward, driving the enemy down until they reached Edward's centre. Now the rout began, men fleeing north, away from London across the hollow from which Richard's flank had swung west and were hacked down by Edward's reserve of knights in an area known today as Dead Man's Bottom.

Big names had fallen. John Neville, the Marquess of Montagu, was killed and his death was the subject of colourful rumours for months. The chroniclers came out with the usual platitudes – that he had been fighting manfully for his brother Warwick. Others said that his own troops had turned on him and murdered him out of sheer frustration. There was an even sillier story that under his armour he wore the arms of Edward, ready to change sides at a moment's notice.

Warwick himself, fighting on foot as he had been, hurried north beyond the road's fork to Wrotham Wood where the horses were tethered. He was caught here in the Yorkist pursuit and hacked down. Stripped of his expensive armour, he was carried to London along with his brother, their naked bodies displayed for two days at Paul's Cross outside the cathedral. Warwick would make no more kings.

The battle of Barnet had lasted perhaps three hours, beginning as dawn broke. It was all over by 8pm. There were perhaps 3,000 dead, nothing in comparison with Towton, and Edward had fought off Warwick's rivalry once and for all. The king marched for London, Henry VI in tow, to peals of bells and general gratitude. London once again had hedged its bets and, not for the first or last time, come out on top.

Edward presented two battle-torn banners for blessing at St Paul's.

Richard, for his part, licked whatever wound he had and set up regular prayers for his fallen comrades; John Milewater, Christopher Warsly, Thomas Huddleston, John Harper and Thomas Parr had all died fighting for him. They were all from the North.

The more one reads of the details of the Wars of the Roses, the more it resembles a 'Mob movie' script! In what was actually a sordid squabble over power and had nothing to do with principles or chivalry, neither side was prepared to take defeat lying down. The Yorkists, momentarily, had triumphed, but Henry VI still lived and he had a son, Richard's age, who was technically still the Prince of Wales. He and his mother Margaret, with French backing as always, landed at Weymouth on the day after Barnet, with Edward's new wife, Anne Neville, the kingmaker's daughter, in tow.

As usual, disaffected lords rallied to the queen's banner from the counties of the south-west. She may have intended to link up with Jasper Tudor, the Earl of Pembroke, in Wales, and to get there she had to take the city of Gloucester. Edward guessed this and sent gallopers with orders that the city must hold out against the queen. This they did, troops lining the walls and threatening the Lancastrian army with cannon. As the May sunshine grew hotter, Margaret marched north, looking for another crossing of the River Severn at Tewkesbury. They followed the Severn banks, along what is today the M5 motorway, with Edward reaching Chipping Sodbury via Malmesbury and swinging north to Cheltenham, half a day behind them. If Margaret could cross into Wales, it would be the devil's own job to reach her in the mountains, so Edward had to strike fast.

Richard was commanding the vanguard again, in effect the left wing, so whatever the nature of his wound at Barnet, it could not have been serious. The main 'battle' was led by Edward, who kept Clarence with him under a watchful eye; Warwick may have been dead, but men like Clarence could never be given a free

Barnet and Tewkesbury 73

rein. Hastings and the Marquess of Dorset led the rearguard and the reserve. The Yorkist army, which had fought last in thick fog, now had to contend with burning sun. The only stream they crossed was so churned up south of Tewkesbury, by gun carriages and bullock carts, that the water was undrinkable.

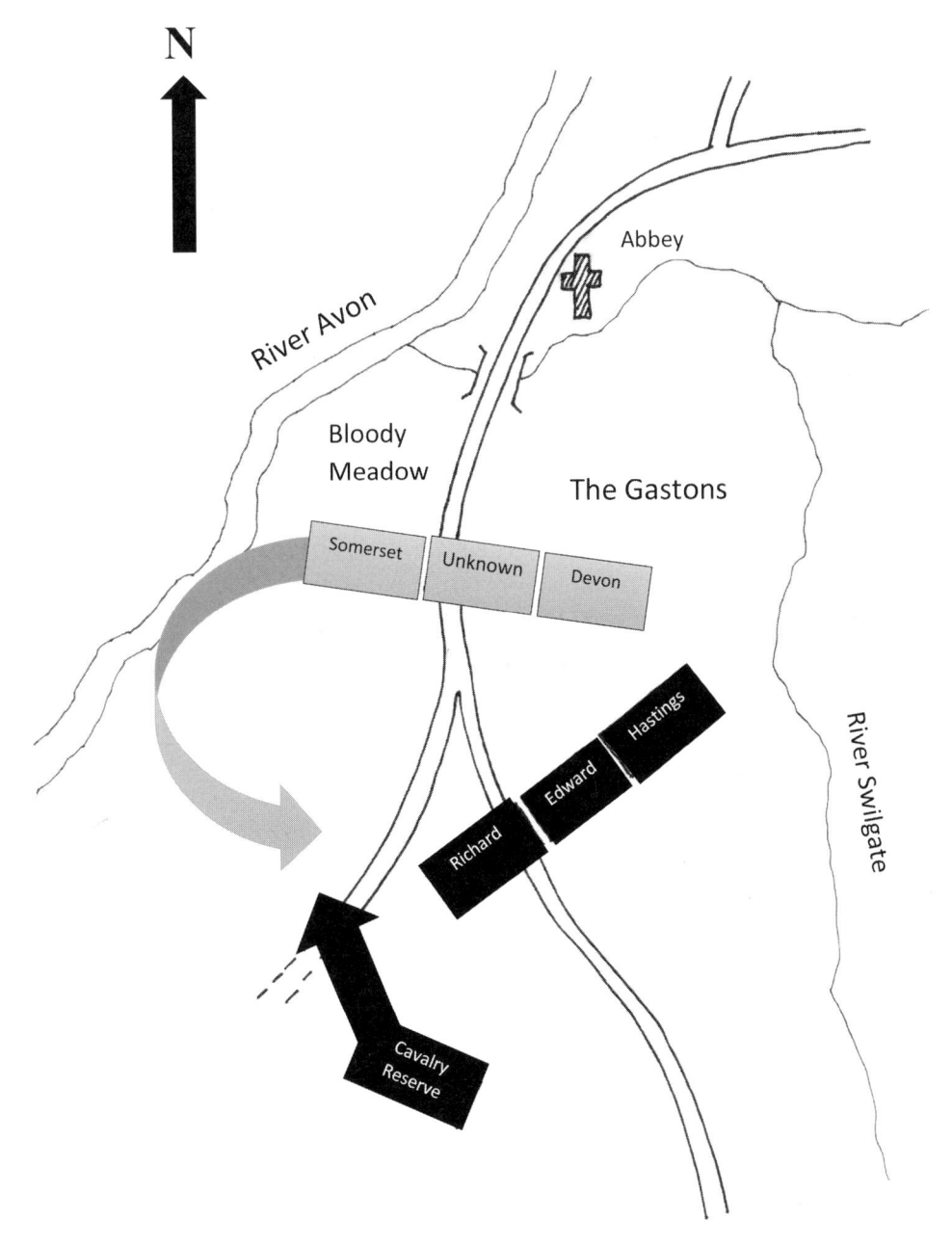

The formations south of Tewkesbury Abbey, May 1471. The Earl of Somerset's attempt to outflank the Yorkists was blocked by the advance of Edward IV's cavalry reserve.

On the early morning of Saturday, 4 May, St Godehard's Day in some parts of Christendom, the Lancastrians, led by Edmund Beaufort, Duke of Somerset, took up their positions in the Gastons, an area of sloping ground south of the abbey, with the town of Tewkesbury behind them. Today, re-enactors of the battle take life very seriously, camping near the battlefield and going through their paces with as much accuracy as they can muster. The town is permanently hung with copies of the banners carried by the various lords who fought that day. The Lancastrians had dug a ditch beyond their lines, probably with sharpened stakes behind to deter cavalry. One Yorkist chronicler referred to the Gastons as 'a right evill place', but today it is simply a gentle slope from the River Severn on the left and the Swilgate to the right. The lower area is frequently flooded, but that was not a problem in May 1471. The large trees that screen the abbey would not have been there then and the whole area would have been more open than today, albeit with hidden lanes and copses. The Lancastrian formation was probably three 'battles' in echelons. One of their commanders, Lord Wenlock, had seen this at Towton ten years earlier. He had fought for Edward then, but now was chancing his arm with Margaret and her Lancastrians.

Somerset's plan, for which he had carefully reconnoitred the ground the evening before, was to march westwards through what is today Tewkesbury Park and the Severn bank before swinging east again to outflank Edward. We have no idea of the numbers involved; sensible suggestions are 7,000 for the Lancastrians, 6,000 for Edward, although the king was probably outnumbered in terms of archers and gunners. Edward sent a cavalry detachment to the west to watch the thick trees of the Park in case of the very manoeuvre Somerset was planning to undertake.

Richard's vanguard opened up with a 'right a-sharp showr' of arrows and cannon fire, which startled the Lancastrians who fired back, although they seem to have been very shaken by the Yorkist attack. Battle was joined in the centre, slowed up by dry drainage ditches which made hand-to-hand fighting difficult. Somerset landed his outflanking manoeuvre from Tewkesbury Park and Edward met him, driving the Lancastrians back. His cavalry reserve, with perfect timing, pitched into Somerset's flank and drove them back towards the Severn, the area that would later be christened Bloody Meadow. Somerset himself retreated to the main battle to find Wenlock pinned down by Richard's vanguard. He was furious. Wenlock had not even moved from behind his ditch and Somerset screamed at him, calling him a traitor and smashing his head with his battleaxe. As Young and Adair comment in their *Hastings to Culloden*, 'History records no more summary dismissal of a divisional commander.'

The rump of the Lancastrians cracked and ran, some into the carnage of Bloody Meadow, others drowning in the deep millpond of the Swilgate, still others hoping to find sanctuary in the abbey itself. If this was the plan, it did not work. They were dragged out, no doubt kicking and screaming while the monks, presumably, made themselves scarce. The story that a priest carrying a sacrament, begging a pardon from Edward, stopped the slaughter, was almost certainly a later fabrication by the writer of the *Chronicle of Tewkesbury Abbey*. A number of the soldiers were summarily executed. This is where the story of the execution of Edward, Prince of Wales, comes from. It morphs from Edward being killed in the rout, by far the most likely interpretation, to a kangaroo court in which King Edward slaps the boy's face and leaves it to Richard, Clarence and Hastings to stab him to death. In Shakespeare's still more tainted version, Richard stabs the prince:

> 'Lascivious Edward, and thou perj'or'd George, [the Prince of Wales snarls]
> And thou, mis-shapen Dick, I tell ye all
> I am your better, traitors that ye are.'

The king strikes first, then Richard, then Clarence. Margaret, standing by, screams, 'O kill me too!' and Richard is ready to oblige – 'Marry, and shall' – but Edward stops him. That gives Richard the chance to nip off to the Tower to attend to the murder of the Prince of Wales's father, Henry VI. So far, so ludicrous. The stories of Edward's end grew in the telling under the Tudors because, of course, it was necessary not only to blacken Richard's reputation but King Edward's too. The Prince of Wales emerges almost as a martyred saint, the notion kept alive by the memorial stone to him in Tewkesbury Abbey today. There was further killing at the church of Dillbrook nearby, indicating that the Yorkists were tired of letting Lancastrians go to fight another day.

On Monday, 6 May, captives from the battle were brought before Richard in his capacity of Constable of England to be tried for treason. The Duke of Norfolk presided with Richard as Earl Marshal, but there is no record of exactly where the court was held. It may have been in the abbot's lodgings next to the abbey or the newly built Crofts Hall, near the market square. Here, they were hanged and buried, but without the quartering of their bodies usually reserved for traitors.

Margaret herself was captured by William Stanley as she tried to go north in a carriage. Contrary to the Shakespeare version, she had to be told of her son's death; she was not there in person. There was a flutter of uprisings in the North, easily put down, and the Bastard of Fauconberg's rather feeble attack on London was beaten back, the earl himself riding for the port of Sandwich as fast as he could.

On Tuesday, 21 May, Richard of Gloucester led his brother's victorious army into the gates of the capital. Like a general's triumph in the brave days of Rome, Margaret appeared in a 'chariot' that was not much better than a cart. That night, someone killed Henry VI in the Tower. According to some historians, the decision to dispatch Henry was made by Edward IV who sent Richard, as Constable of England, with an order to have the killing carried out. Shakespeare has the Duke of Gloucester talking to Henry on the walls of the Tower, which seems oddly in the open when a murder is about to be committed. While Henry rants about Richard's evil, the duke loses his temper – 'I'll hear no more; die, prophet, in thy speech' and the poignard blade goes in. Henry, of course, has time to gasp, begging God to forgive his sins and Richard's, for he is sure there is more blood to come.

'Down, down to Hell,' Richard snarls, 'and say I sent thee thither,' before telling his audience that Clarence is next in his bid to get the throne.

None of this, of course, is true. The only contemporary comment on Henry's death comes from the Croyland continuator who wrote, 'he who perpetrated this has justly earned the title of tyrant'. This, even assuming that the continuator knew something he has not told us, may well refer to Edward. The king's body was taken to St Paul's at night, with an armed guard carrying torches, and placed in an open coffin for all to pay their respects. The word went out that he had died 'of pure displeasure and melancholy', but no one commented on any tell-tale marks on the body that could say otherwise. Henry was embalmed and taken by barge up the Thames to Chertsey Abbey. In 1484, when he was king, Richard had the body brought to Windsor for a royal burial. Was this the work of a guilty man whose conscience was bothering him? Or of a pious one who regarded Chertsey Abbey as an unfitting burial place for a king?

Henry VI's body was dug up again, on 4 November 1910. Astonishingly, adipocere was still present, the desiccated remains of soft tissue which usually disappears after years, still less centuries, in the ground. The remains were examined by Professor MacAlister of Cambridge University who described a man of 5ft 9in in height (an inch or two taller than Richard) and the bones had been dismembered when placed in the rectangular box in which MacAlister saw them. There was a clump of hair attached to the skull, brown in colour and, according to the professor, matted with blood. This would have been perfectly natural if Henry was beheaded, as convention dictated, with an axe.

At the end of his *Richard III*, Shakespeare puts words into the mouth of the victorious Henry Tudor, the future Henry VII:

> 'Now civil wounds are stopp'd, peace lives again;
> That she may long live here, God say amen!'

This was after Bosworth in 1485, but the sentiment could easily have been expressed after Barnet and Tewkesbury, back in 1471.

Chapter 8

Lord of the North

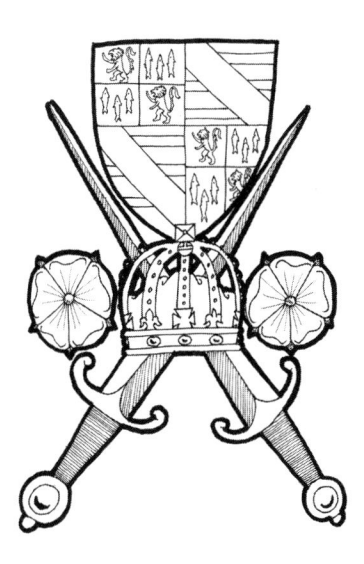

Arms of Henry Percy, Earl of Northumberland. The Percys had controlled the North of England for centuries before the arrival of the Neville family and Richard, Duke of Gloucester.

> 'The North is full of tangled things and texts of aching eyes,
> And dead is all the innocence of anger and surprise.'

So wrote G.K. Chesterton in his poem *Lepanto*, celebrating the Christian naval victory over the Ottoman Turks in 1571. Chesterton was in fact talking about Northern Europe generally, but southern Englishmen in the fifteenth century regarded Northern England with a mixture of fear and hatred. The place was lawless, wild and licentious, a brutal frontierland that abutted warlike Scotland.

Richard's handling of the Scots we shall look at in another chapter, but it was as predictable as night following day that, whenever England was in trouble, the Scots would come south across what had once been the Roman wall built by Hadrian, with or without their king, to cause havoc. They were held partially in check by the Percy family, the hereditary earls of Northumberland, but latterly, their power had been supplanted to a large extent by the Nevilles. After Tewkesbury, the kingmaker was attainted, his lands distributed between the crown itself and the royal brothers, Clarence and Gloucester.

We do not know whether Richard actively petitioned Edward for the Warwick lands in the North, but in view of later events, it seems likely that he did.

He was Constable of England, Lord High Admiral and possessor of handsome, lucrative estates, as well as being Warden of Wales. He was only nineteen years old. In 1471, the Duke of Gloucester could not have expected to inherit a kingdom. His brother the king was thirty years old and a healthy bouncing boy, Edward, created Prince of Wales and Duke of Cornwall, had been born in the year of Tewkesbury. His wife, Elizabeth Woodville, had already produced three daughters and the breeding programme seemed strong. Even if, by some mischance, Edward's immediate family should be wiped out, there was still his brother George, Duke of Clarence, whose wife was Isobel, daughter of the kingmaker. He was only twenty-two and although Isobel had lost a baby already, a girl, perhaps called Anne, in a ship crossing to Calais the previous year, no one doubted that there would be more children. Richard, then, was not the heir or even the spare and he set about carving a mini-kingdom for himself north of the Trent.

It was some time during these months after Tewkesbury that Richard of Gloucester became a father, not once, but twice and the birth of these children gives us an unusual insight into the man who was about to take the North in a charm offensive. The only writer to produce a detailed history of Richard's children is Peter Hammond, former research officer of the Richard III Society, but most telling is the attitude adopted by Charles Ross, one of those unfortunates who went to press before the finding of the king's bones and who therefore had to speculate a great deal about Richard's body and his character.

Richard's first born was John of Gloucester. We cannot be accurate about the boy's birth date, but from later details of his life, it may have been 1474, the year in which Richard married Anne Neville. His mother has been tentatively suggested as Alice Burgh, a gentlewoman at Middleham where Richard made his home in the North. Richard gave her 20 marks a year for life for 'certain special causes and considerations'. Since Alice had received similar (smaller) annuities before, from Edward IV, it may be that the 'consideration' referred to something else entirely and even that the long-serving Alice was an old woman. She is, incidentally, the only female among twenty-two people recorded as receiving fees at Middleham in 1473–4. John was knighted at York Minster in 1483, the year Richard became king, and was captain of Calais two years later. He may be 'the lord bastard' referred to in various documents concerning clothing and land-rent throughout the 1480s. The concept of illegitimacy has swung full circle over the centuries. Today, when wedlock itself is becoming something of a rarity (according to official statistics recently released by the Church of England) being born out of it is neither here nor there. Nor was it in Richard's day. Bastards born to the aristocracy carried a bar sinister (pointing left) on their shields. Royal bastards often took the suffix 'Fitzroy'. But in neither case were they prevented from promotion, wealth and power. It was the Victorians who made illegitimacy taboo and that only among the middle classes.

Richard's second child was Katherine Plantagenet. The first record of her comes from 1484 when William Herbert, Earl of Huntingdon, signed an accord 'to take to wife Dame Katherine Plantagenet, daughter of the King before Michaelmas [September]' of that year. In 1484, there was only one king old enough to have a daughter and that was Richard. Unfortunately, the marriage to Huntingdon (which Richard paid for, as well as settling lands on the happy couple) does not give us her age. As we know, little girls were betrothed to older men and even, for reasons of politics, went through a marriage ceremony with them. Peter Hammond extrapolates a possible birth date of 1470 for Katherine, making her older than John, but this can only be guesswork. The same guesswork has been applied to her death. We know that she was buried in the church of St James Garlickhythe in London, possibly having died of the endemic sweating sickness which struck the capital with force in 1485.

No one suggests that Richard produced any more children by other women after his marriage to Anne. And this may have a bearing on Charles Ross's take on Richard's sense of morality. Kings were expected to have mistresses – Edward IV was notorious for the number of his conquests, fathering four illegitimate children while married to Elizabeth Woodville. Richard did not; or at least, none that we know of.

Ross quotes Richard's letter to his bishops in 1484, 'our principal intent and fervent desire is to see virtue and cleanness of living to be advanced, increased and multiplied' and he promised a crackdown on 'all such persons as set apart virtue and promote the damnable execution of sins and vices'. Ross then points to the bastards John and Katherine, contending that 'Nor was Richard himself blameless in this respect', claiming, in a rather over-the-top Victorian phrase, 'both were probably the product of his bachelor lusts'.

Ross believes that Richard was obsessed with sexual morality, citing his attack on Buckingham's supporters in the 1483 rebellion and the followers of Henry Tudor the next year – 'the malice of the said traitors and punishing their great and damnable vices'. He also cites Richard's forcing the ex-royal mistress (Edward IV's) Jane Shore to do public penance in London's streets. The problem that Ross has ignored is that 'vices' can refer to anything. It was, after all, a vice to betray (as Buckingham and Henry Tudor both did) their anointed king. Likewise, Ross seems to believe that the 'delectable' Mistress Shore has come in for unfair criticism by Richard. Elizabeth Shore, known as Jane, was the mistress, after Edward IV, of Lord Hastings and the Marquis of Dorset. Just because Thomas More had a soft spot for her – 'Proper she was, and fair' – does not mean that Richard did not know a manipulative schemer when he met one. Richard's stand on this was very much in keeping with a general trend in the late fifteenth century, spearheaded inevitably by the Church, to clean up public morals.

We shall look more closely at Richard's morality later, but in the early 1470s, his principal concern was to establish control of the Neville lands and that led to

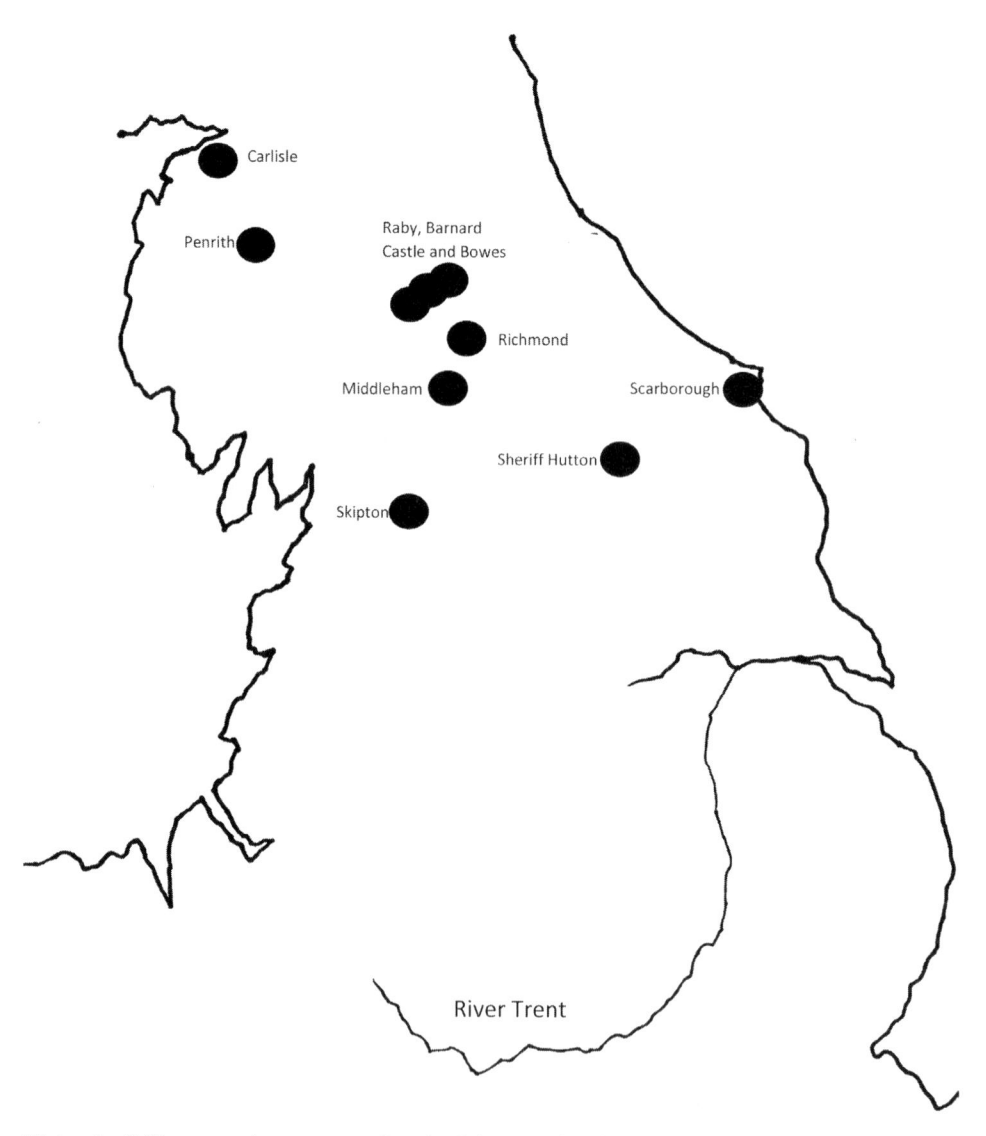

Richard of Gloucester's estates as Lord of the North. The River Trent marks the southern boundary of what was regarded as the North in the fifteenth century. Richard's estates made him the principal landowner in this area.

a head-on confrontation with his brother Clarence. For once, Shakespeare got it right: 'false, fleeting, perjured Clarence' was a liability. Unreliable, greedy, perhaps mentally unstable, he expected more from the king than did Richard, by virtue of being older, ignoring the fact of his treachery against Edward by joining Warwick. In his increasing softness, Edward let him get away with it. He first gave Richard the office of Great Chamberlain and when Clarence complained, took it off him again and gave it to Clarence. The dispute between the king's brothers over the Neville

Conisbrough Castle, perhaps the birthplace of Richard, Duke of York.

Fotheringhay Church from the castle. The current church, containing the tombs of several of the Plantagenet family, is half the length of the original. The rest was destroyed by Henry VIII.

Pulpit built under orders from Edward IV in the 1460s.

The vaulted roof of the chapel inside Ludlow Castle where 7-year-old Richard would have attended service with his family 1459.

Ludford Bridge from Ludlow Castle. Henry VI's Lancastrians would have been camped in the wooded area beyond the bridge.

The keep of Sandal Magna Castle, Richard of York's principal stronghold in the North.

Possible site of the sallyport at Sandal Castle. Did Richard of York lead his rescue party out from here in 1460?

The battlefield of Wakefield from Sandal Castle. The buildings in the distance were not there in 1460 and somewhere on this slope, Richard of York and his son Edmund of Rutland were killed.

Micklegate Bar, one of several entrances to the Medieval city of York. Richard of York's head was impaled on the battlements after his defeat at Wakefield.

The battlefield at Towton, fought in a snowstorm in March 1461. We are facing the Lancastrian position and the battlefield itself has changed little in five and a half centuries.

The River Cock from the Towton battlefield. This was the site of Bloody Meadow, where most of the slaughter took place. The mounds under the trees are burial pits.

Tewkesbury Abbey from the Yorkist position at the bottom of the slope in May 1471.

The Dacres Cross in the centre of Towton battlefield. This was possibly part of the chantry erected by Richard III when he became king. People still leave flowers at the site.

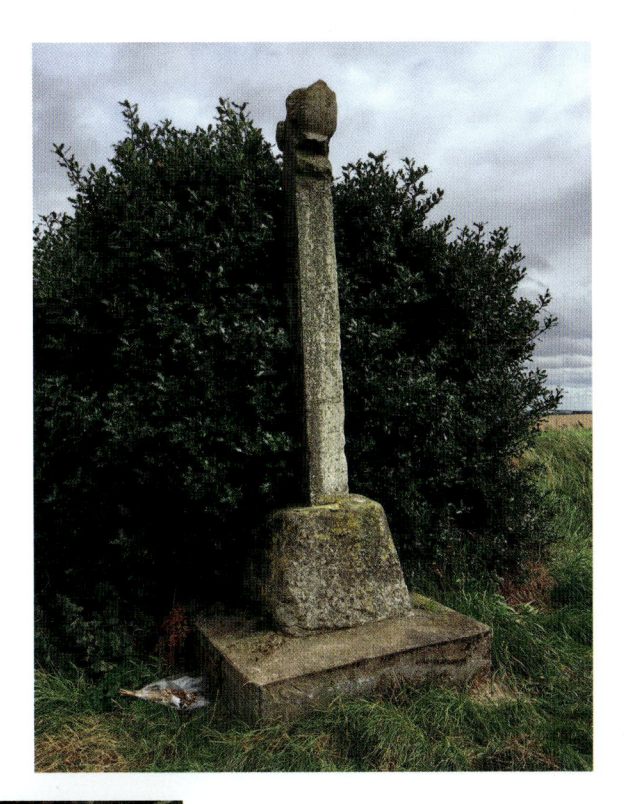

Middleham Castle, Yorkshire, Richard's principal stronghold in the North and family home. His son, Edward of Middleham, was born and died here.

Above: The tomb of Edward of Middleham? This stands in Sheriff Hutton Church and is more likely to be that of a member of the Neville family. All the evidence that would have clinched the child's identity has now gone.

Left: Fifteenth-century stained glass in Sheriff Hutton Church, showing the sun in splendour device of Edward IV.

Above: Sheriff Hutton Castle, a possible meeting place for Richard's Council of the North. Edward of Warwick, the son of George Duke of Clarence, spent his childhood here.

Right: The Neville coat of arms on the font at Staindrop Church. There are several members of the family buried here.

Barnard Castle from the River Tees. Richard planned to set up an ecclesiastical college here.

Above: Bowes Castle on the site of a Roman fort. The austere lines of the keep mean that Bowes was regarded as a fortress, not a family home by Richard.

Right: Rather worn bas relief of Richard's white boar device on the wall of St Mary's Church, Barnard Castle.

Left: Carved head of Richard III from the nave of St Mary's Church, Barnard Castle. (*Tali Trow*)

Below: Scarborough Castle on the clifftops overlooking the town. This was the headquarters of Richard as Admiral of England.

York Minster, the heart of what many regard as the capital of the North. Richard set up an ecclesiastical college here and had his son, Edward of Middleham, invested as Prince of Wales.

The battlefield at Bosworth from Richard's position on Ambion Hill. The hedge to the left was not there in August 1485, but the waterlogged area in the distance was probably the site of the marsh where Richard was killed.

The sun sets on Plantagenet England. Richard's white boar standard still floats over Ambion Hill, Bosworth Field.

inheritance was not pretty and is tortuous in the extreme. Neither of the royal dukes comes out of it with much honour, but Richard at least had *earned* the estates and titles; Clarence had not.

He was already Warden of the West Marches centring on Carlisle. Now, Edward added the East and Middle Marches, which gave Richard precedence over the tricksy Lord Percy, the Earl of Northumberland. He also obtained all Warwick's estates in Yorkshire – Middleham, Sheriff Hutton and Penrith as well as the lordships and castles of Skipton-in-Craven, Scarborough and the title of sheriff of Cumberland for life. By 1478, he had added Richmond to the impressive tally.

Penrith had a Neville castle, standing on the River Eamont, eighteen miles south-east of Carlisle. The church of St Andrew was already there in Richard's day as was the grammar school. Its market and fairs date from the thirteenth century.

Skipton in the district of Craven, close to the River Aire, had been defended by a castle since Norman times. Its squat, round gatehouse towers dated from the early thirteenth century. The church of St John stood in its grounds when Richard became Lord of the North.

Scarborough was the Saxon *Skardeburg* and it had been given its town charter in 1181, returning 'two knights of the shire' to parliament since 1295. Boasting a Cistercian abbey as well as a castle, it held a special place for Richard because of its role as a naval base and his role as Lord Admiral. Henry II had been personally responsible for the construction of the castle's square keep, not merely to keep an eye on the ever-dangerous Scots, but the possibility of invasion by the French. It came under the spotlight in the fourteenth century when it was the property of Edward II's favourite, Piers Gaveston. The town that Richard knew was a busy fishing port, but Richard III House, a seventeenth-century building on the sea front has no real link with the admiral at all.

We know that Richard had been High Admiral of England since 1462 when he was ten. He remained in this post until he assumed the crown in 1483, at which point the title and duties passed to John Howard, Duke of Norfolk. The kingmaker briefly held it in 1470, but his death at Barnet put paid to all his ambitions. A whole book could be written on Richard's navy, but that said, sources are notoriously vague and limited. There was a resurgence of naval power under the Tudors, highlighted by the sinking of Henry VIII's *Mary Rose* in 1545 and the Armada campaign under Elizabeth. Naval battles were rare in the fifteenth century, largely because the sea was nobody's idea of a sensible place to fight. Richard's ships, like those of France, the most likely enemy, were essentially slow, sluggish merchantmen, short and broad-bellied with 'castles' of timber mounted fore and aft. The term 'focsle' (forecastle) lasted for centuries in the Royal Navy. Cannon on board ship were heavy and unreliable, especially in rolling seas and most of the long-distance fighting was accomplished by archers firing from the 'castles'. At close quarters, grappling hooks were thrown to hold an enemy ship steady and hand-to-hand fighting followed as if on dry land.

Richard's navy was probably more about show than anything else – warships streaming with flags and heraldry, especially in numbers, gave the illusion of strength. There was no serious French invasion attempted in this period, although it is noticeable that no attempt was made to stop Henry Tudor's invasion at sea and most of the action of Richard's navy involved scaring off individual pirate ships prowling the Channel.

Richmond Castle stood on the banks of the River Swale, fifty miles north-west of York. Its original owner was Alan Rufus who also held Middleham and formed the focus of the area known as the Honour of Richmond. There was a triangular Great Court and a smaller one, the Cockpit. The outer bailey is now built over by the bustling town. The keep was 100ft high and it became a tourist attraction to the Georgians, later lovingly photographed by Francis Frith. There was a Grey Friars priory in Richard's day, as well as the thirteenth-century church of St Mary. It is rather ironic that one of the Duke of Gloucester's estates should be forever associated with Henry Tudor, who was, of course, the Earl of Richmond.

One Neville property that is barely mentioned in works on Richard is Bowes, originally a Roman fort called Lavatris on the road between Carlisle and York. It stands near the River Tees and Barnard Castle and is a dull, solid-looking building constructed by 'Richard the Engineer' for Alan Rufus who held many of the Norman castles in the area. Ralph Neville, Earl of Westmoreland, added it to his extensive list of estates in 1444 and it became Richard's after Barnet.

One way to keep Clarence's undoubtedly grubby hands off the rest of the Neville lands was to marry the kingmaker's daughter, Anne. Shakespeare has portrayed this girl as frail and weak, a pawn in a man's game. Alongside the feisty women who fought for their men in this story – Cecily Neville, Richard's mother; Margaret of Anjou, wife of Henry VI; Elizabeth Woodville, wife of Edward IV; and Margaret Beaufort, Henry Tudor's mother, it may be that she pales. But the endlessly weeping half-child, portrayed by Claire Bloom in Olivier's film, wooed, according to Shakespeare, by the 'foul toad' who murdered her first husband, bears no relation to reality.

Anne was four years younger than Richard, born in her father's great castle of Warwick over the Avon. Because she died (probably of tuberculosis) at the age of twenty-nine, even the Ricardian Paul Murray Kendall calls her 'frail'. When her father rode out on the Barnet campaign, Anne was effectively a fugitive. She sailed, along with her mother and sister, to Calais and then rode on to Normandy. Here she was told that she would marry Edward, Prince of Wales, as part of the deal that her father had struck with the boy's mother, Margaret of Anjou, and Louis XI of France. Only weeks later would she meet the sixteen-year-old prince in person. She had just turned fourteen.

Far from the 'gentle, mild and virtuous' description of Edward by Shakespeare, he was very probably a psychopath. The Milanese ambassador in France wrote of him at the age of thirteen, 'This boy . . . already talks of nothing else but of cutting off heads or making war' – which is hardly surprising bearing in mind the rambling lunacy of his father and the fact that Edward had, at that point, spent half his life being dragged around battlefields. The couple were married in Amboise, probably on 13 December 1469, but on their return to England, they heard the news of Barnet and Warwick's death. Weeks later, Anne was hiding in an abbey west of the River Severn when news reached her that her husband, too, was dead, killed in the rout at Tewkesbury.

The story of Richard and Anne's relationship reads like a novel and some of the details are unlikely. Kendall, using words like 'doubtless', imagines a scenario in which Clarence, the pantomime villain, has hidden the girl away from Richard's 'prince charming' galloping to the aid of the hapless girl who has suffered too much already. Other historians doubt whether the two of them even knew each other, but they seem to be ignoring the fact that for two years at least, they were at Middleham together.

The story goes that Richard found Anne disguised as a scullery maid in the house of one of Clarence's London friends. He took her to the relative safety of sanctuary in the church of St Martin le Grand. This is the version of the Croyland continuator, who may or may not have been in a position to know the truth, if only we knew who he was. In the end, by February 1472, Richard agreed to relinquish half of Warwick's lands to Clarence, as long as he was allowed to marry Anne. The pair were cousins and papal dispensation was necessary for the marriage to take place. Clarence had needed similar papal authority and for the same reason, for his marriage. In Richard and Anne's case, the pontiff was Paul II (Pietro Barbo) the strikingly handsome Venetian nobleman who toyed with calling himself, when elected to Peter's chair, Formosus (the beautiful) – wiser counsel prevailed. The wedding took place, either in Westminster Abbey or St Stephen's Chapel next door, on 12 July. If they had a honeymoon at all, Richard and Anne spent it at Middleham. There is no doubt that this was a political marriage as virtually every other noble match was in the fifteenth century. Far too many people have believed the Tudor apologists, especially Shakespeare, that Anne was seduced by a murderer and her acquiescence in falling for him makes little sense. There is no evidence one way or another for the couple's actual relationship, but it certainly gave Richard the whip hand in terms of inheritance. What clinched the whole thing, of course, was Clarence's renewed treason against the king, with which Richard of Gloucester had nothing to do.

Some historians have claimed that Richard's stay in the North was some sort of reclusion, that he deliberately turned his back on the court of Edward IV because of the cloying control of the Woodvilles. That was undoubtedly partly true, but Richard could not avoid all southern contact. He had to attend parliament, whenever it met, and the king's Great Council. He also had duties as admiral, which took him to the coast (most royal shipyards were south of the Trent). But there is no doubt that he had come to love the North and, before 1483, made it a mini-kingdom under the king. Where, exactly, was this?

Richard's headquarters, perhaps because of the fond memories he may have had of the place under Warwick's wardship, was Middleham. The couple entertained on a lavish scale. We have eyewitness accounts of the great feasts and public ceremonies as well as the scientific evidence of Richard's diet, particularly in the last years of his life. The daily events, visitors, food consumed and wine drunk is more vague, but people must have been coming and going all the time to Middleham, the great and good who owned the Northern shires – families like Dacre, Greystoke, Fitzhugh and Scrope who all held estates within a few miles of Middleham. An army of servants would have been needed to accommodate, feed and entertain them all and most of these would have come from the villages nearby.

We know more about Richard's eating habits as king, but it is likely that he acquired various tastes earlier. The soup that formed the first course of any meal was 'frumenty', a porridge-like concoction of wheat, milk of almonds, venison and saffron. 'Brewer of Alyman [Germany]' was a dish of rabbit seasoned with cloves, ginger, nutmeg and galingale (the root of an aromatic water plant), sprinkled with raisins. The third course was often blaundsorr, a pottage of rice and capon, forming a savoury blancmange. Really exotic dishes, perhaps served up to impress visiting dignitaries, included pike cooked in three ways – boiled at the head, fried in the middle and roasted at the tail. This was called 'glazed pilgrim', with eels served to resemble the staffs of travellers to shrines all over Europe. Each course was punctuated with jellies, using garish colours.

For his coronation (details of which have survived) Richard had a number of dishes decorated with heraldry, like the jelly called 'te deum laudamus'. The boar was of course a particularly handy choice for serious eating!

The castle had briefly been at the centre of political events in 1469, when the kingmaker was living in Middleham and Edward IV was his prisoner there before Warwick was virtually forced to release him. But the spotlight was never turned off in those years. In June 1473, Richard brought his mother-in-law, the largely disinherited and landless Countess of Warwick, now a widow of course, to Middleham in the care of James Tyrell, one of Gloucester's closest advisers. In the Shakespeare version, Tyrell is a discontented nobleman whom Richard barely knows, who is brought in as a hitman to snuff out the princes in the Tower. In reality, he was a solid confidant of several years' standing to Richard and, perhaps oddly, would survive for some years under the Tudors.

Many of the servants who had worked for Warwick before his fall at Barnet were Middleham men or from close by. Twenty-two of the original thirty-six transferred their allegiance to Richard, probably, but not exclusively, because of their ties to the area. Sir John Conyers of Hornby Castle was one of these, having been steward of Warwick's Richmondshire estate with a (sizeable) fee of £13 6s 8d (more than £285,000 today). Richard increased the fee to £20. Conyers was probably on Richard's Council of the North (see below) and became a knight of the body on Richard's coronation in 1483. James Metcalfe, of Nappa, five miles from Middleham, went into Richard's service from Warwick's in 1471 and at the coronation became Chancellor of the Duchy of Lancaster, another of Richard's titles. His brother Miles served Richard in the Council of the North as a lawyer and became, thanks to Gloucester, recorder of the city of York.

We know that, at Middleham, Richard and Anne enjoyed mummers' plays, the pantomime antics loved by all classes and which were a welcome relief from the sermonizing miracle or mystery plays, religious motifs performed, for example, at York. We also know that Richard obtained royal permission from Edward for Middleham to hold not one but two fairs a year, making village and castle a serious focal point in Yorkshire.

It is at Middleham that Richard's only legitimate son was born, but the date is debatable. Earlier books on Richard usually claim 1474, the year of Richard and Anne's wedding, but today 1476 is considered more likely. The south-western tower of the keep is traditionally called the Prince's Tower, but we cannot be certain exactly where the boy was born. The D-shaped tower is described in a survey of 1538 as 'the round tower', but it was next to the 'Nursee', so it is probably the actual birthplace. Even though the tower was rebuilt in the 1870s, it clearly had latrines (garderobes) and fireplaces. Because traditions changed so little in the Middle Ages, the rituals concerning Anne's pregnancy and Edward's birth and early infancy would not have changed appreciably since Cecily Neville gave birth to Richard a quarter of a century earlier or even since Cecily's own birth in the year of Agincourt.

A set of ordinances, or rules, for births and baptisms has survived from the Percy family, traditional rulers of the North before the Nevilles and Richard arrived. They date from 1500, but describe customs that would have been in operation for years before that. Anne would have chosen her own bedchamber, perhaps in one of the new rooms with windows that Richard had had enlarged – the septfoil window in the Prince's tower is unique to the castle. There would be thick curtains to cut out light and a portable altar for Mass to be said, especially if things went wrong during the delivery. Next to the birthing chamber would have been a larger room – perhaps the 'Nursee' – where family members, invited guests and Richard himself would have waited for news.

Edward was born in the spring and a month before that, Anne would have attended a private service in the castle chapel with the steward, clergy and Richard's liveried supporters in attendance. During the High Mass, Anne joined the company, knelt before the altar and kissed the *pax*, an ivory disc representing the presence of Christ. She took communion, tasting the bread and drinking the wine. Anne had been fasting for up to two weeks by this point and was given a cup of spiced wine to fortify her before she was escorted to her chamber and the men left.

When Edward was born, the priests sang a *Te Deum* and there was rejoicing all round. There is a tendency with Edward (who died aged eight), Anne (who died aged twenty-nine) and Richard (killed at thirty-three) to assume that the whole family was sickly, but there is no evidence for this. It may be that the boy's infancy followed perfectly normal lines; certainly, since his role in history is so limited, there is none of the Tudor nonsense of abnormal gestation and monster births. Edward of Middleham would have been baptized according to a long-established ritual, but this could not be carried out in a private chapel, so it may have been in the church of Sheriff Hutton, another of Richard's estates.

Here, the priest splashed water from the font in four directions to the points of the compass. Then he breathed three times on the water still in the receptacle and dipped wax from a candle into it. Chrism oil was added and he took the naked Edward, placed his right hand on the boy's forehead and asked his godparents (we do not know who they were) questions in Latin. They replied in the same tongue.

> 'Abrenuncius sathane? (Do you renounce Satan?)
> 'Et omnibus operibus einis? (And all his works?)
> 'Et omnibus pompis einis? (And all his pomp?)'

– to which the godparents, speaking for little Edward, replied that indeed he did. The priest made the sign of the cross, baptized the boy in the Name of the Father, the Son and the Holy Ghost and dunked him in the holy water. If Edward was not crying already, he almost certainly was by now! The priest warned that it was the godparents' duty to keep the child from harm by fire and water until he was seven. They were to teach him the Paternoster (the Lord's Prayer), Ave Maria and the Apostles' Creed.

The godparents would have brought presents for the boy and it is just possible that one of these was found by metal detectorists in 1985 in the East park near the castle. Today known as the Middleham jewel, it is a late fifteenth-century 68g lozenge pendant made of gold. It has a ten carat blue sapphire in one corner and carved into its gold surfaces are a nativity scene and the effigies of thirteen saints. It would originally have had pearls around its rim. The back panel slides open to reveal a hollow interior with three discs (and a fourth, broken one) of silk embroidered with cloth of gold, which may be from a reliquary. An inscription in Latin on the outside is a charm to ward off epilepsy or for protection during childbirth. The jewel was bought by the Yorkshire Museum, York, for £2.5 million. Two other archaeological finds have come to light from Richard and Anne's time at Middleham. One is a gilded copper livery badge of the white boar which would have been sewn to the doublets (usually quartered in the murrain and blue of the house of York) and the other is a circular copper alloy plaque, possibly from a casket lid, three inches in diameter, that has the entwined initials 'R' and 'A' and a French motto, *A Vo Plaisir* (for your pleasure).

Middleham also sheds light on Richard's religious leanings. All members of the aristocracy were supposed to support the Church, usually by way of setting up chantries and other donations. After the king, the Church was the richest landowner in England and later generations would accuse the landowning classes of buying their places in Heaven. In Richard's case, however, all the evidence points to a man who genuinely was a believer and not merely paying lip-service to a tradition.

His *Book of Hours*, which still survives, carries several extra prayers, handwritten perhaps by Richard himself or if not, certainly including special prayers that meant a lot to him. Some relate to Christendom defending itself against Islam, at a time when the Ottoman Turks were becoming the scourge of Europe. Others refer to saints who had a long affinity with the North, especially Ninian, Katherine, Cuthbert, Anthony, Barbara and George. George was perhaps to be expected; the Praetorian martyr killed by the Emperor Diocletian was a warrior saint and patron of England – his red cross standard was carried by both sides in the battles of the Roses. Barbara was another martyr, a Greek of the third century who had become by Richard's time, the patroness of armourers and artillerymen. Katherine was, after the Virgin Mary, the most popular saint of the Middle Ages, a fourth-century martyr who had, according to tradition, died strapped to a wheel. St Catherine's College in Cambridge was established in her honour the year before Richard and Anne's marriage.

Anthony was a Franciscan monk from Padua who died, probably of ergotism, in the thirteenth century. Bearing in mind the discovery of the Middleham jewel, he was the patron saint of lost things. He was also associated with the boar, the only animal that kept the saint company during twenty-four years of living in the wilderness.

The most Northern saints were Ninian and Cuthbert. Ninian was an eighth-century missionary working with the pagan Picts who had come to dominate what was, by Richard's day, Scotland and the Marches around Carlisle. Cuthbert was altogether more local. His tomb and wall painting can still be seen in Durham cathedral and, as Lord of the North, Richard would have had many dealings with William Dudley, the bishop of the richest See in England after Canterbury and York. This was the land of the Prince Bishops, a powerful theocracy which most Medieval kings left alone to govern itself. Cuthbert's plain white altar cloth was carried in battle against the Scots in all campaigns up to the Reformation; it is likely that this applies to Richard's in 1482.

In July 1478, Richard ensured that all these saints, as well as Christopher, Joseph and Julian, were venerated in two religious colleges, one at Middleham, the other at Barnard Castle. The Barnard Castle college seems never to have operated, perhaps because Richard opted for the grander setting of York instead, but at Middleham, six priests were employed to pray for Richard and his family.

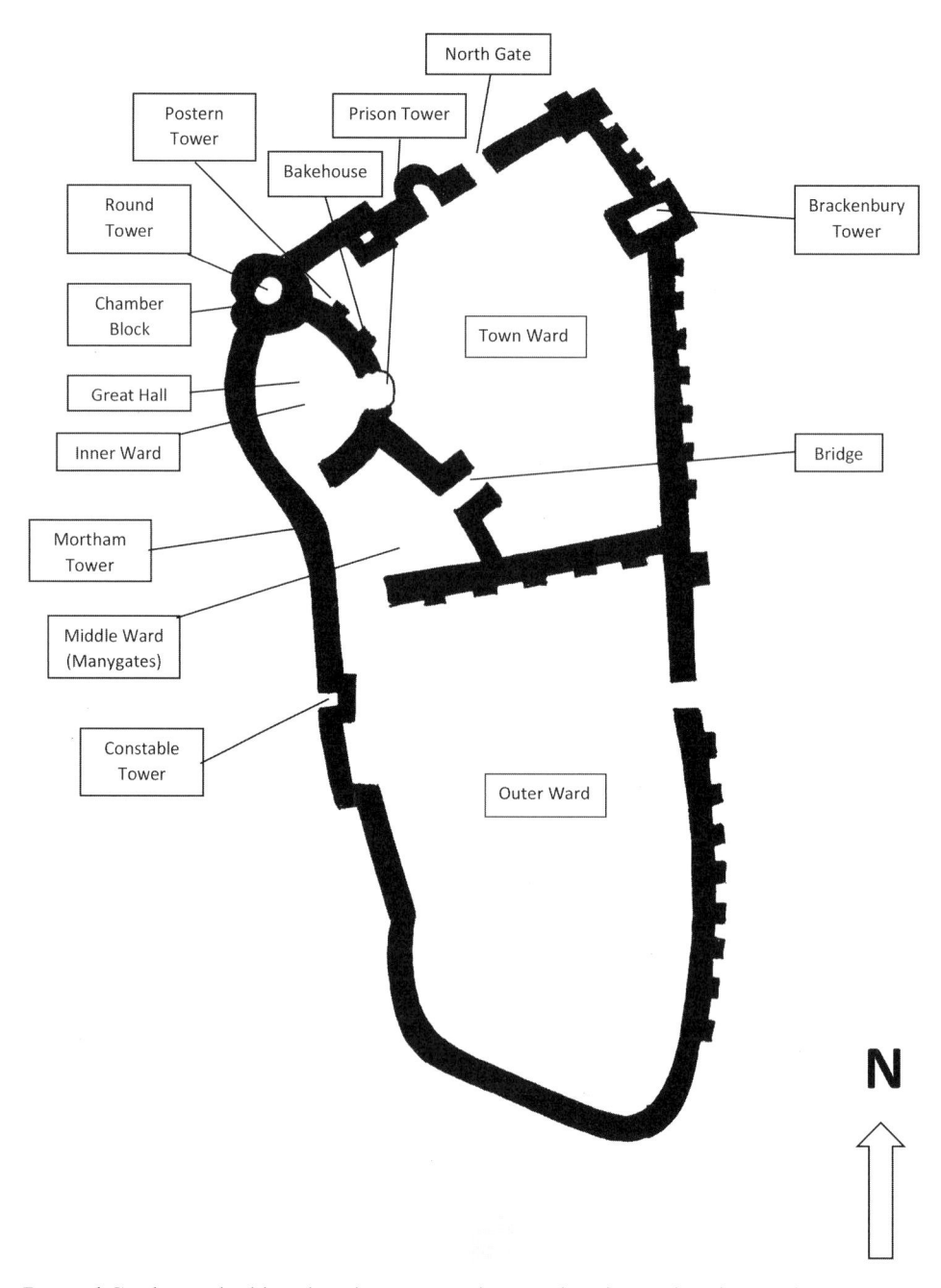

Barnard Castle overlooking the River Tees and protecting the road to the North.

'Know ye,' the Middleham documents proclaimed, 'that where it hath pleased Almighty God … to enable, enhance and exalt me His most simple creature, nakedly born into this wretched world, destitute of possessions, goods and inheritaments, to the great estate, honour and dignity that he hath called me now unto, to be named, knowed and reported and called Richard Duke of Gloucester.' The instructions for the services and saying of prayers were detailed and the feast days of George and Ninian were to be particularly celebrated, along with St Cuthbert's Day in Lent and St Anthony's in January. The priests could not visit inns nor sleep away from Middleham college without the dean's permission. They were to be fined for slander and charged with a fourpenny fine for drawing a knife. It seems bizarre to us that priests should carry knives at all, but these were dangerous times and violence at all levels a way of life.

There were other Northern links too. St Wilfrid of Ripon was included in the Middleham prayers; so too was William of York. St Alkelda (who may actually be totally fictitious) was the patroness of the parish church in Middleham. And Richard's piety included generous gifts to various institutions. In 1472 and 1473, he repaired the parish church at Coverham near Middleham (which also had an abbey of its own) and extended the church at Barnard Castle. Gargoyle heads of Richard and Edward IV can still be found in the nave there, as can a bas relief of the white boar above a window on an outside wall at the east end, perhaps originally one of a pair. Unusually for an heraldic animal, it faces right. The shipmen of Hull, the most important trading port in the North, received a bell from the duke, to be hung in the Trinity Guild chapel.

Richard's personal fiefdom spread all over the North. Sheriff Hutton, where he had often stayed as a boy, was said by some to have been a meeting place of Richard's Council of the North as early as 1478, but there is no evidence for that. In 1480, the duke was there when news came of Scottish raids further north. Aldermen from York were constant visitors here, asking Richard's advice on all sorts of issues which, as a feudal lord, it was his duty to sort out. As at Barnard Castle, Richard extended and developed the comfort of the place, perhaps looking forward to a time of peace despite the constant rumblings from over the border.

Barnard Castle stood on the River Tees with the town behind it. It was the birthplace of three members of the Balliol family who became kings of Scotland in the fourteenth century. The castle itself was under siege in the sixteenth century, and attracted artists such as J.M.W. Turner in the romantic period of the early nineteenth. Richard's involvement in the castle, as elsewhere, was to convert a grim fortress into a family home suitable for a duke of royal blood. The Brackenbury Tower, which was built in the thirteenth century, takes its name from Richard's faithful supporter who was Constable of the Tower of London in 1483. Another steward of the castle was Miles Forest, who, according to Thomas More, was one of the murderers of the princes in the Tower.

Inevitably, York held a special place for him. One document, dictated by Richard, talks of the 'great zeal and tender affection that we bear in our heart unto our faithful and true subjects the mayor, sheriffs and citizens of the city'. The Minster was the focus of Richard's royal progress in 1483 (see Chapter 12) when Edward of Middleham was invested as Prince of Wales. The documentation in the Minster library still contains, on vellum and written in a priestly hand, the plans for the religious college he intended to set up, on a far greater scale than that at Middleham. There were to be 100 priests, worshipping 'God, our Lady, Saint George and Saint Ninian'. Six altars were to be erected in a separate building that was probably never begun before Bosworth ended all such plans. Soon after his coronation, Richard gave the Minster a huge crucifix on six bases, studded with rubies and sapphires. No doubt, it was melted down by Henry VIII and disappeared into the Tudor royal purse in the 1530s.

The city was the second largest in the country after London, with perhaps 13,000 inhabitants. The military base of the VI Legion, Eboracum was also the second See in the country after Canterbury. Its walls and barbicans still stood firm in Richard's day and most of the walkways are still there now. The castle itself was decaying simply because York was seen as a religious centre and because there were plenty of castles in the surrounding countryside. The religious buildings of the city apart from the Minster, newly finished in 1472, included St Mary's Abbey, St Leonard's Hospital, Holy Trinity Priory and the friaries of four Orders. Civic buildings proliferated too, with a Guildhall and the halls of both the Merchant Taylors and the Merchant Venturers who traded as far east as the Baltic. Even the bridge over the Ouse had a conical chamber and a chapel.

The city dignitaries were headed by the mayor and included aldermen and twenty-four councillors, all intensely proud of the charter of liberties granted to the city and church by former monarchs. Wool merchants dominated among the great and good, but as ever the craftsmen and artisans working in gold, silver, copper, timber and textiles provided a flourishing 'shopping centre' along what is today called the Shambles (originally a meat market). True to the insular tradition of the North, 'Easterlings' (Hanse merchants from Bruges and further east) were mistrusted, as were the Scots, whose constant violence spelt loss of profits to city money men.

York loved Richard. He usually stayed in the buildings of the Austin Friars in Lendal and was given fine presents by them in exchange for his patronage. Fish from the Ouse and the sea, barrels of wine and 'demain' (dominus) bread of higher quality than usual were packed onto the backs of the duke's packhorses to take back to Middleham or Sheriff Hutton on his return journey.

In late spring, Richard and Anne attended the pageant of the festival of Corpus Christi. The city guilds performed mystery plays, Biblical allegories of up to fifty scenes staged by an astonishing 500 performers. At the break of day, heavy wagons carrying sets, costumes and players set out from Toft Green, rumbling through the narrow, cobbled streets to perform at various holy sites or outside the houses of merchants rich enough to pay. The goldsmiths' guild re-enacted the coming of the Magi with their exotic gifts. The vintners retold the miracle of the water into wine at the marriage feast at Cana. The shipwrights and fishmongers told the tale of

Noah and his Ark as well as the feeding of the five thousand. It goes without saying that everyone in the city, whether performers or audience, believed every word of the stories they were telling, whether from the Old or New Testaments.

In 1477, Richard and Anne became members of the Guild of Corpus Christi (Cecily Neville, Richard's mother, had joined twenty-one years earlier). They walked in solemn procession from the Holy Trinity Priory to the Minster, the priests in their robes and carrying crosses, past houses hung with tapestries and over pavements covered with spring flowers.

In return for the largesse given to the ducal couple, Richard worked hard and did not miss minor details. He wrote to Hastings and to Thomas Stanley to back him in removing a greedy clerk from the city Council in 1476. A year later, he was defending the users of the Ouse from the illegal creation of fishgarths, weirs and nets designed to catch fish in a chaotic and uncontrolled way. Large numbers of letters have survived from various interested parties asking for Richard's help, all of them addressed to 'Right high and mighty prince … our full tender and especial good lord'.

At Sandal, his father's castle overlooking Wakefield, Richard improved all defensive and domestic aspects and we know that the Council of the North met here from time to time. Anne, too, became crucially involved in Northern affairs, joining the sisterhood at Durham's cathedral priory in 1476, perhaps soon after the birth of Edward. When Richard became king, he presented the cathedral with his coronation robes of blue velvet, decorated with the golden leopards of England.

Men who were not part of the Neville connection became the duke's trusted retainers. Thomas Gower from Sheriff Hutton and Stittenham fought for Richard in Scotland and was made a knight of the body. Thomas Markenfeld, who held estates of the same name near Ripon joined his service, as did the old soldier Thomas Eveningham. Both these men received an income of £200 a year from Richard, far more than people of their relatively lowly rank could have expected. It is still tradition for historians to see the Tudors as the royal family who deliberately elevated humble men to key positions, bypassing the old aristocracy on the grounds that they were too volatile and fickle to trust. In Richard's choice of men like Markenfeld, Eveningham and even more the 'unholy' trio of Richard Ratcliffe, William Catesby and Francis Lovell, the evidence proves that the Plantagenets got there first and that Henry VII was merely building on an existing tradition.

Richard also controlled Cumberland and Westmoreland, in effect taking on the Neville ascendancy over the Percys. John Huddleston of Millom was a trustee of Gloucester's Middleham lands and was granted more territory further south. His brother Richard became a knight of the body and took over the Marquess of Dorset's northern estates when he fell from grace in the coup of 1483. The Musgrave family all served Richard, as did the Redmaynes of Leven Hall and Harewood. Sir William Redmayne was a knight of the shire (MP) for Westmoreland in 1478.

Where Richard was at his dazzling political best was in soothing relations between the older and newer branches of Anne's Neville family and in working with, but as superior to, the Earl of Northumberland and the Stanley family, lords of Derby. He selected members of parliament for the area through the 1470s and early 1480s, as well as offering his advice on the appointment of justices of the Bench. This involved power-sharing and often walking a tricky tightrope, but Richard did it well. None of this would have been possible had he been the sour-faced, dour and humourless personality as portrayed by his enemies, still less the Machiavellian schemer from the pen of Shakespeare.

As we have seen, the highest order of chivalry was the Garter, and men held the coveted blue garter for life. Seven vacancies occurred during Richard's reign and he filled six of them with Northerners – John Tunstall, John Conyers, Thomas Burgh, Richard Ratcliffe and Lord Stanley. The sixth was Francis, Viscount Lovell, who served Richard so loyally that he was considered, like the duke himself, an honorary Northerner.

Richard was at Middleham in May 1484 and already king when he met the Bohemian knight Nicolas von Poppelau. This royal watcher, centuries ahead of his time, got himself invited to so many royal European courts that he can only have been a spy, reporting back on what he saw to his boss, the Holy Roman Emperor, Frederick III. Von Poppelau gave an eloquent address, in Latin, to Richard and his court in the great hall. The two men were clearly impressed with each other and the king shook the Bohemian's hand and dined with him twice during his nine-day stay. When von Poppelau spoke of the Ottoman threat from the East, Richard told him enthusiastically that if his kingdom lay on the frontiers of Turkey, he would be delighted to take them on, 'with my own people and without the help of other princes'. In that context, the king may have been thinking of Vlad Dracula, the Impaler, who had defended his kingdom of Wallachia in precisely that way fifteen years earlier. This tiny, unlooked-for glimpse of Richard at home in the North, surrounded by his friends and intimate family, may, just briefly, show us glimpses of the real man. His son had died just weeks before.

Richard's lasting legacy, although it was almost destroyed by Henry VII, was the Council of the North. It comprised all the Northern counties (Yorkshire, Durham, Cumberland, Westmoreland and Northumberland) and survived as a vital powerhouse until well into the seventeenth century. The Duke of Northumberland was appointed Warden of the Marches once Richard was king, but a separate council under Richard's nominated heir, John de la Pole, Earl of Lincoln, met at York and Sandal to run the rest of the area. The men who sat on the Council, deliberating with Richard, or in his absence, with the Earl of Lincoln, were almost exclusively Northerners.

Chapter 9

Scotland

The arms of the kings of Scotland. The lion rampant (on its hind legs) was probably the most common symbol in Medieval heraldry. It represented courage and nobility. The thistle became the flower of Scotland, as opposed to the rose of England.

'The trouble with Scotland,' says the actor Patrick McGoohan in Mel Gibson's *Braveheart* (1995) 'is that it is full of Scots.' McGoohan was playing Edward I, the *Malleus Scotorum* (Hammer of the Scots) who had already subdued Wales and was one of the great warrior kings of the Medieval period.

With the death at sea of Queen Margaret, the 'Maid of Norway' in 1290, it was effectively Edward I who chose her successor. He was John Balliol and demands a footnote in this book because he and at least three of his children were born at Barnard Castle long before it passed into Richard's hands. There was a resurgence of Scots' independence under Robert le Brus (the Bruce), crowned king of Scotland at Scone Abbey in Perthshire in March 1306.

By the time Richard of Gloucester was Lord of the North, the Scottish crown had passed into the control of the Stewart family. The name came from the title – steward – which their ancestors had held as High Stewards of Scotland since the late thirteenth century. James III was a few months younger than Richard, born either at St Andrew's Castle, Fyfe, or at the far more formidable fortress of Stirling. He was crowned, an eight-year-old, on 10 August 1460 at Kelso Abbey, Roxburghshire, continuing a tradition which haunted England too, of a boy-king expected to control a wild, ambitious and greedy aristocracy.

The southern Scots had, for generations, taken any sign of weakness in the English government as an excuse for raiding the Northern shires, sometimes as part of the 'auld alliance' with France. This is why the Percy earls of Northumberland were so important in keeping these border raiders in check. It is also why the Neville ascendancy, which threatened that, had to be constrained by the English king and why Edward IV was so keen to give Richard his head in the North.

In the late 1470s, tension began to build among the Scots, while the French king, the slippery Louis XI, was anxious to destroy England's ally, Burgundy. To ensure that Edward did not send troops to Burgundy's aid, James III broke his treaty with England and sent men south to the spectacular coastal castle of Bamburgh, twenty miles inside English territory.

It is difficult to know what was happening to Edward IV as his reign progressed. The hero of Richard's boyhood, victor of Towton, Barnet and Tewkesbury, the popular warlord was growing middle-aged and fat before everyone's eyes. In 1475, he led a massive army, the vanguard, as ever, commanded by Richard, into France to support the Burgundians. Then, the opposing kings seemed to backtrack from an all-out renewal of the Hundred Years War and signed a peace treaty on the bridge at Picquigny, effectively buying the English off. This may have been clever realpolitik (Henry VII would do exactly the same at Etaples when he became king), but it left a bitter taste in the mouths of the rank-and-file soldiery who expected booty for their weeks of sore feet and dysentery. Richard of Gloucester expected military action and glory – clearly Barnet and Tewkesbury had given him a taste for warfare and he refused to be present when the documents of peace were signed. Only later did he grudgingly accept presents of horses and silver plate from Louis at his court in Amiens.

Perhaps Edward now took his role as king more seriously, playing the dove to Richard's hawk. The brothers, along with the ever-shifty Clarence, reburied their father and elder brother Edmund in the Plantagenet vaults at Fotheringhay the following year, in which ceremony Richard, as the youngest, was chief mourner. A life-sized effigy of Richard of York had been carried all the way from Pontefract, wearing the dark blue robes of a king, edged with ermine. The journey took a week and all who witnessed it along the roads from the North to the Midlands were in no doubt at all that Richard should have been king all along and that Edward, his eldest surviving son, fully deserved his place on the throne. The tombs on display today at Fotheringhay church are Elizabethan replacements. The originals, which would have been canopied with alabaster figures like those at Staindrop, had become decayed by the 1560s and Elizabeth visited them in 1573. Then, the collegiate church had no roof and the extension built by Edward had been torn down. When Cecily's tomb was opened prior to being moved, there was a silver ribbon around her neck, a pardon from the Pope himself. Small pieces of brass from these original tombs are still visible today.

The next year, they all attended the investiture of Edward's eldest son, also Edward, as Prince of Wales and in January 1478, the wedding of his little brother Richard, Duke of York, to five-year-old Anne Mowbray, daughter of the Duke of Norfolk. Richard knelt in front of the four-year-old prince, his nephew, and paid him homage for the Norfolk lands he held. The little boy thanked him, no doubt with formal words he had been taught.

That year of 1478 was an ominous one for the house of York. Edward had negotiated a peace with James of Scotland, but Richard, as Lord of the North, was not interested. In his role of admiral, he ignored any charges of piracy against Scottish ships, such as *Le Salvator* in 1474, and continued to be as difficult as he could in working with the Scots. Edward's chaplain, Alexander Lee, was sent north by the king to apologize to James and to remind Gloucester of his duties to keep the Scots sweet. It may be that Richard's creation of a Northern affinity outside Edward's influence is a symptom of a cooling of relations between the brothers, but by 1478, the real problem was the third brother.

Clarence had been forgiven by Edward for his earlier treasonous efforts with Warwick to make himself king, but the facts themselves could not be forgotten. Clarence's wife, Isobel, Anne's sister and Richard's sister-in-law, died suddenly at Warwick Castle in December 1476. She was buried in the abbey at Tewkesbury where her father's old allies, the Lancastrians, had been defeated five years earlier. Rumours swirled about poison and, whether true or not, speak volumes of the reputation and growing instability of Clarence himself. Clarence had Ankarette Twynyho, a former servant of Isobel's, executed for murdering her mistress. When Edward effectively scotched attempts by his younger brother to marry again, this time Mary, heiress to Burgundy, Clarence flounced off to Warwick Castle and stayed there. By 1477 then, effectively both the king's brothers were absent from court, Clarence in a fit of pique, Richard in disgust at Edward's increasing pandering to the Woodvilles.

There had been a bizarre incident two years earlier in which three astronomers, including one of Clarence's household, were convicted of 'imagining and compassing' the king's death by prophesying that he would have a short life (which, of course, as it turned out, was to be true). Two of them were executed and Clarence was implicated – guilt by association.

Clarence got wind of this and burst into the meeting of the King's Council at Westminster in Edward's absence and demanded that all allegations against him be dropped. The following day, the king arrived from Windsor and had Clarence placed under guard in the Tower. In the Shakespearean version, Richard drip-feeds the already ailing Edward with prophecies implicating someone with the letter 'G' associated with his name as a potential traitor to the crown. The 'G' is of course Gloucester, but Edward believes it is *George* Clarence.

The duke languished in prison for six months, even offering trial by combat to prove his innocence. It was not accepted and the Council found Clarence guilty of treason. His mother Cecily did her best to soften Edward's heart, but he was determined that Clarence should die. Historians such as Charles Ross believe that Richard was indeed involved in Clarence's end in order to obtain his brother's Neville estates. Obtain them he did, as the only brother the king had left, but there is not a shred of evidence linking Richard with Clarence's death. No one at the time mentioned it and the Italian visitor Dominic Mancini recorded that the London rumour was that the Woodvilles were behind it, which is entirely in keeping with their animosity to all Plantagenets except Edward. There is no doubt that Richard behaved badly in amassing estates all over the country, although most of the complaints about this and demands for recompense came to the attention of the Tudors, when Richard was no longer there to defend himself.

The murder by Malmsey story refuses to go away, but I cannot believe it actually happened. 'That notorious butt of malmsey wine' Charles Ross calls it. Chris Skidmore posits that it happened 'possibly at [Clarence's] own request [?]'. The only contemporary accounts of Malmsey come from the York Civic Records and York is over 200 miles away from the scene of the crime. Richard was not involved, however much he benefited later. Indeed, there are rumours that the execution of Clarence drove a further nail into Richard's relations with Edward and meant that his stay in the North was likely to continue. The fact that two days later, Richard announced his religious colleges at Middleham and Barnard Castle is proof, suggest some historians today, of Richard's guilt. Equally, there is such a thing as coincidence and Richard did nothing, if he were involved, to make things right with Clarence's immediate family.

On the day that Clarence died, 18 February 1478, Richard was appointed Great Chamberlain of England, a title that the greedy, petulant Clarence had taken from him six years earlier. Richard was now, after the king, the greatest landowner in England, a warrior and a supporter of Edward through and through, at least as far as policy and the world went. And Edward needed his loyal brother in Scotland.

On 12 May 1480, Richard was made Lieutenant General of the North, a new title which would not re-emerge until Oliver Cromwell's rule of the Major Generals in the 1650s. Edward and his council decided to invade Scotland in reprisal for the attack on Bamburgh and the king would lead the army himself. Richard stood down as Lieutenant General, only to be reinstated two years later as Edward decided not to command the army after all. It may be that the king's health was already deteriorating. He ate and drank far too much and his increasing weight meant that he could not exercise in the way that he had. It may be that an arduous campaign was beyond him.

During 1481 and 1482, intermittent clashes occurred along the Scots border, including a half-hearted siege of Berwick, always a source of rivalry between the two countries. Margaret of Anjou, who had been sheltered along with Henry VI by the Scots, had bartered it away in 1460.

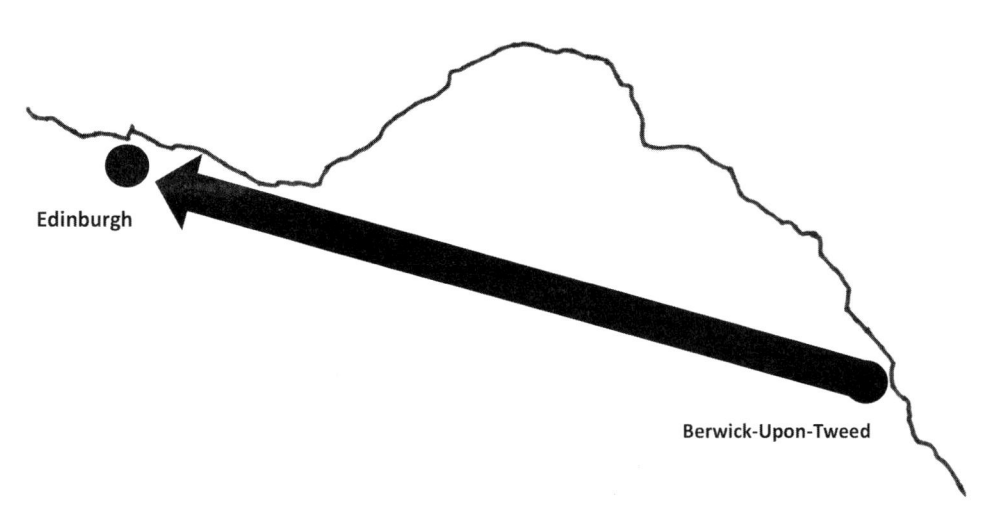

Richard of Gloucester's campaigns in Scotland, 1482. He was criticized at the time for not destroying either town.

When Richard took up command again, it was to aid a pretender to the Scottish throne, Alexander, Duke of Albany, James III's brother. He was two years younger than the Scots king (and Richard) and his various titles and estates had been taken away from him in a family dispute in 1479. The Stewarts of this period were every bit as quarrelsome and dysfunctional as the Plantagenets. A treaty was signed at Fotheringhay on 3 June 1482 and Richard got his army together by the middle of July. With the obvious exception of the retainers of the Marquess of Dorset and Edward Woodville, virtually all Richard's troops were Northern. Northumberland and Stanley were his seconds-in-command and Richard dubbed five knights – Scrope, Lumley, Greystoke, Lovell and Fitzhugh. By the end of the month, he had made forty-nine knights and baronets, all but four of them from the North. If Richard had not been the loyal brother he was; had he been Clarence, for instance, he could have made life very difficult indeed for Edward.

Richard had seen the Scots' threat coming for some time. He paid out of his own purse for the renewal of the fortifications at Carlisle, including new artillery and gun-emplacements. Carlisle had been Luguvallum under the Romans, an important base of the VI Legion. The Vikings had destroyed it in the ninth century, but William Rufus rebuilt and fortified it, complete with castle and walls 200 years later. The Augustinian church became a cathedral in 1133 and the city was always at risk from Scottish incursions. Richard had garrisoned the town, waiting for word from Edward, but the king was playing a waiting game. Perhaps he did not want to face the fact that he could no longer lead such a campaign (which may even explain the events at Picquigny seven years earlier) and did not want to give either too much power or glory to Richard. By February 1482, the Lord of the North was frantically buying food supplies for the Carlisle garrison. He had already, if only to keep up morale, led raids into Scottish territory, knighting men in the field for their courage.

This kind of guerrilla warfare was typical of the later Middle Ages and it ground down morale. Out and out victories or defeats like Towton or Tewkesbury got results and turned the tide of war: nibbling at the borders did not. The next month, Edward owed Richard 2,000 marks for his services as Warden of the West March, but sent bows and arrows from the Tower in lieu of cash. How much of this was Edward's own policy and how much of it was the machinations of the Woodvilles is impossible to say. In the same period, the king continued to pay small fortunes for banquets and sumptuous clothes, even importing expensive armour from France for a campaign he never intended to lead.

It is possible that Richard was wounded in clashes with the Scots or at least, he was suffering from the ill effects of campaign that far north in the long winter months. Edward's personal physician, William Hobbes, was sent to Richard with six other doctors, and John Clerk, the royal apothecary, brought 'divers medicines' for Gloucester's use. It is a fact, of course, that more men died from disease in any Medieval campaign than ever fell in the field.

With the Fotheringhay treaty now in the bag, Richard and Albany at last marched to York. They were there by 18 June, in the city that loved Richard and relied on him. We know the state of military finances in that month – Richard had £15,000, enough to keep his 20,000 men in the field for a month. Of those 20,000, there were 1,800 German, Swiss and Burgundian troops, possibly the first time that the brightly uniformed *Landsknecht* infantry had appeared on a British battlefield.

By the third week in July, Richard had reached Berwick, defended by only 600 men. The formidable earthworks and stone wall defences visible today were not there then – they are Elizabethan – so the old Medieval walls would have been vulnerable to Richard's cannon. The town surrendered leaving the garrison of the castle over the Tweed to hold out for as long as it could. It was now that news reached Richard that James III had been overthrown at Lauder by his own generals and dragged to Edinburgh for a showdown. Leaving a skeleton force to threaten Berwick Castle, Richard led a forced march of thirty miles and found the capital's gates open to him.

Edinburgh had been a fortress since pre-Roman times, one of the principal settlements of the Celtic Gododdyn tribe, when it was Din Eidin. Its massive castle, built on an outcrop of formidable natural rock, would have taxed any Medieval army and, as at Berwick, the town surrendered; the castle did not. Inside, the captors of James III, the Earls of Buchan and Atholl, as well as the king himself, refused to negotiate with Richard. The English army was now miles from the border with Gloucester's friendly Northerners, and Albany, far from pressing his claims to the throne, now merely wanted his lands and titles back.

Negotiations dragged on for days, with Richard doing his best to make some capital out of his lightning campaign. He had taken two towns inside a week without a shot being fired and knew how Scottish mindsets worked. He carefully wangled his way around the matter of the proposed marriage between his niece Cecily and James III's son, who would become James IV. By 11 August, Richard had raised the siege, retaining a nucleus of troops and had marched back to Berwick. The Croyland continuator, among others, criticized him for not destroying Edinburgh, but it says a good deal for Richard's magnanimity in an age of notorious European cut-throats, that he let the city live.

Back in Berwick, Richard found Thomas Stanley, commanding the skeleton army there, nervously complaining that he had been left undefended by Gloucester. As always with the Stanleys, if there was something to whinge about, they would find it. There was some fighting, but the castle surrendered on 24 August and the Scots' war was over.

Berwick was in English hands again after twenty years and would now remain so for ever. There were street parties and bells were rung all over the country – even as far away as Calais – but the whole thing was a bitter disappointment, especially to Richard. Edward's policy had been one of vacillation; Albany had proved a weak and fickle ally. Richard's fault lay, perhaps, in that he had waited to see what Edward's orders were and no orders came. He was too loyal and too subordinate to a man who was clearly, by the summer of 1482, losing his grip.

The king, and parliament, officially thanked Richard for his restraint in Edinburgh and even Pope Sixtus IV was impressed by it. Then came the summer of 1483.

Chapter 10

Pontefract

Arms of Anthony Woodville, Earl Rivers. The Woodville family, linked to the Plantagenets through marriage, were seen as upstarts trying to carve a name for themselves at the expense of 'the old guard'.

In March 1483, Edward IV stayed at his castle in Windsor where plans were afoot to rebuild the chapel of St George which would become the much-embellished headquarters of the knights of the Garter. He was back in London by the 25th, complaining of exhaustion and chest pains. These got worse over the next five days and he took to his bed. There were a number of theories, but no one, least of all the king's doctors, had any real idea of the problem. The Croyland continuator wrote that Edward 'was neither worn out with old age nor yet seized with any known kind of malady'.

Today we might consider a coronary thrombosis as the most likely cause. He had been fishing on the Thames and had caught a cold, which, given Edward's obesity, might have developed into pneumonia. It could also have been diabetes and/or pleurisy, which would explain the chest pains. He died in the early hours of Wednesday, 9 April. He was not yet forty-one. The sudden death of a relatively young king sent London into a panic. The king's son, now unexpectedly Edward V, was at Ludlow. His only remaining brother, Richard of Gloucester, was at Middleham. The ship of state suddenly had no one at the helm. 'We [know] not', John Gigir wrote to the Bishop of Winchester, 'who shall be our Lord nor who shall have the rule about us.'

Used as we are to a constitutional monarch who is largely a figurehead, we find this sense of bewilderment a little peculiar. But the experience of everybody in the previous thirty years – an entire generation then – was that a young or weak king spelt chaos and disaster for the nation. Somebody must act to stop the rot. And the Woodvilles moved first.

We do not have to buy into the conclusion drawn by R.E. Collins and Annette Carson that Edward was poisoned, probably with arsenic which in fifteenth-century terms leaves no trace and was probably administered by the queen, to accept nevertheless that the Woodvilles were a grasping bunch of upstarts who, having tasted power, could not bear to relinquish it. With Edward gone, the late king's will should have been consulted. During his brief illness (perhaps ten days long) the king had done his best to reconcile the elements of his family and closest advisors, but the breach was too great. Although the actual will has not survived, all contemporary accounts contend that Edward left the welfare of his sons – and hence, the kingdom – to his brother Richard of Gloucester. That meant either a regency or a protectorship until the elder boy was of age to rule by himself. That in turn meant that Richard would be pulling government strings for another four years. And the Woodvilles could not stomach that.

Edward had been brought up in the castle at Ludlow that Richard must have had mixed memories of as a child, by his mother's brother Anthony, 2nd Earl Rivers. The man was a scholar and a champion jouster, but his military experience was limited. The late king had taken the captaincy of Calais from him and given it to William, Lord Hastings, but he still held the role of Deputy Constable of the Tower of London and, above all, he had the new king. If Shakespeare's version can be believed, young Edward was a cocky child, as precocious as any Plantagenet and he would have been a mummy's boy through and through. He would barely have known his uncle Gloucester.

Rumours reached London that Edward and Rivers were coming from Ludlow with an army. The Council, well remembering the threat of Margaret of Anjou's Northern Lancastrians back in 1469, baulked at this, complaining that control of the king should not be purely in Woodville hands and Hastings insisted that the retinue from Ludlow should be no more than 2,000 men.

Edward Woodville, Dorset's uncle, was given command of the fleet on the grounds that the French, having heard of Edward IV's death, were upping their presence in the Channel. As High Admiral of England, these decisions were Richard's and Dorset had no right to give his uncle the commander's job at all. In addition to that, Woodville took a carrack moored in Southampton Water containing £10,250 in gold coins (almost £8.5 million today). Edward IV's Treasurer, the Earl of Essex, had died five days before the king, so the country's finances were momentarily out of whack. As Deputy Constable of the Tower, Dorset helped himself to massive amounts of coin from the fortress, which was at once the royal mint and the 'Fort Knox' of its day.

Throughout the Middle Ages, the royal treasure, including the Crown jewels used on state occasions, travelled everywhere with the monarch. Not until Elizabeth's reign would London become the permanent headquarters of the monarchy and the treasure remained in the Jewel House of the Tower from then on.

Control of the fleet, the royal funds and the new king could only mean one thing – the Woodvilles were attempting to overthrow Edward IV's will and establish themselves as the power in the land. This was plain old-fashioned treason, although with the king in tow – and presumably happy to go along with it – this was a difficult case to put. The only solution for Richard was to grab the boy himself and his little brother and see him crowned in the way that Edward IV intended, with Richard as 'Protector and Defender of the Realm and Church in England and Principal Councillor of the King'.

Richard wrote letters of condolence to the queen and the council in London and held a memorial service in York Minster. Everyone was dressed in black and everyone swore an oath of fealty to the new king. Richard was the first to do so. At this juncture, with the whole country holding its breath, Harry Stafford, Duke of Buckingham, came from nowhere to be Richard's right hand man. He had started writing to Richard after Edward IV's death, perhaps because he was a pushy lord who had not climbed as high as he would have liked, despite being married to a Woodville (the queen's sister Catherine) and being descended from Thomas of Gloucester, the youngest son of Edward III. It was this that probably rankled with him – the Cliffords, the Percys, the Nevilles, all of whom had married Plantagenets; not to mention Richard of York's sons themselves – all outranked him in terms of power. The fact that he adopted the arms of Thomas of Lancaster, without the usual heraldic symbol of differencing, speaks volumes for the man's ambition; on the battlefield, he would have worn on his tabard the same cognizance as Richard of Gloucester – the leopards and lilies.

Richard left York about 23 April, St George's Day, with 300 men. Various historians refer to Richard's spy network, which kept him informed on developments in the south, but no one provides details of what was, and remains, the black art of espionage. The first *acknowledged* royal spymaster was Francis Walsingham in the reign of Elizabeth I, but there must have been intelligencers, men listening at keyholes and watching roads long before that. Buckingham offered Richard 1,000 men to match the young king's entourage coming from Ludlow, but Richard asked for only 300 and that seems to have been agreed.

There is some confusion as to where the parties met. Shakespeare follows the Croyland continuator in plumping for Stony Stratford near the modern Milton Keynes. Dominic Mancini has Northampton, fourteen miles further north. Stony Stratford was an estate (Grafton Regis) belonging to the king's mother, so that seems the more likely. Despite Edward's entourage outnumbering Richard's four to one, the Protector arrested Rivers, Grey and Vaughan who led the party on the grounds that they had been laying an armed ambush for him. Grey was Sir Richard Grey, Rivers' half-brother, who had also enjoyed the custody of Edward at Ludlow. Thomas Vaughan, also a knight, was Edward's chamberlain at the castle.

We cannot know after all these years whether this ambush was real or more a very real possibility in Richard's mind. Why, on the other hand, would Rivers bring so many men with him? In defending his position as Lord Protector of the boy king, Richard had every right to arrest the trio, however much the Croyland continuator wrings his hands over the action. Edward IV's will had been very clear – Richard was to have control of the boy and the council in London concurred. To be on the safe side, Rivers was sent under guard from Richard Ratcliffe to Sheriff Hutton. Grey went to Pontefract and Vaughan to Middleham. There they could wait until Richard decided what to do with them and Richard, Buckingham and Edward continued on their way to London. An odd piece of parchment survives from these days, perhaps written at St Albans en route to the capital on 3 May. It contains the signatures of these three. First, in a not-very-accomplished hand, comes 'R. Edwardes quintes'. Then 'Richard Gloucester' and his motto *'Loyaulte me lie'* and finally 'Harre Buckingham' and his motto *'Souvente me souvene'* (remember me often). Richard sent Rivers' troops home to Ludlow, but kept their wagons of weapons, just in case.

At this point, with the new king and his Protector arriving in triumph in London, we need to examine the sources that exist for the story. So far in Richard's life, we have a smattering of political and church records, as well as buildings that speak for themselves. But in the last two years of his life, every event is open to scrutiny in a way that does not exist for earlier kings.

There had been renaissances before, cultural explosions of art, literature, architecture and science that changed the thinking world, but the fifteenth century saw the birth of the greatest of them, emanating from Italy. A glance at Shakespeare's playlist of a century later proves the point; Italy was everywhere. There are his two gentlemen from Verona, his Jew of Venice, his Moor (Othello) from the same city. His shrew is tamed in Northern Italy. Even his supposedly English heroes and heroines have oddly Italian names. All this, as well as the arrival of the printing press, gives us a formal, European gloss wholly missing from earlier chronicles.

Foremost among the Italian commentators was Dominic Mancini, living briefly in London during the 1480s and about fifty years old. He was a spy working for Angelo Cato, the Archbishop of Vienne, councillor to the French king, Louis XI. It is most unlikely that he spoke English, but got by with the Latin in which he wrote his *De Occupatione Regni Anglie Per Ricardum Tertium Libellus* (The taking of the throne of England by Richard the Third), which was not rediscovered until the 1930s. He probably came to London at the end of 1482 and left soon after Richard's coronation in July of the following year. He was not an insider, almost certainly never met Richard – and probably never even saw him – and his whole anti-Richard bias seems to have come from the Woodvilles or their supporters. Because he is a contemporary, historians have been forced to consider his work, but all he really is is a Woodville hack anxious to blacken the new king's reputation. Other Italians followed, particularly Polydore Vergil, writing in 1512–13, but since he was a professional historian employed directly by Henry VII, we can add him to the typical list of Tudor propagandists and we are at liberty to doubt everything he says.

There were two English chroniclers who were eyewitnesses of the extraordinary events of these years, although both of them have obvious bias issues. The first is John Rous, the chantry priest and chaplain of St Mary Magdalene at Guy's Cliffe, Warwick, who wrote two versions of the *History of the Earls of Warwick* (now more usually called the *Rous Roll*) between 1477 and 1485. He had probably seen Richard and may even have met him during one of Gloucester's stays at Warwick Castle (his from 1478) and certainly knew Anne, who had been born at the castle.

The earlier version, beautifully written with elaborate heraldic drawings of all concerned, praises Richard:

> 'The most mighty prince ... by the grace of God king of England ... all avarice set aside ... punishing offenders of his laws, especially extortionists and oppressors of the common people ... by which discreet guiding he gives great thanks to God and [has] the love of all his subjects, rich and poor and great praise from people of other lands.'

Rous's second version has expunged all that. Now (when he was safely dead) Richard was a monster, born with teeth and shoulder-length hair. Even the portraits have changed. Edward of Lancaster, Anne's first husband killed at Tewkesbury, now stands in this version between her and Richard. Whereas Mancini was in London, at the heart of events in 1483, there is no record that Rous ever left Warwickshire.

The final chronicler is the most difficult to fathom of all. *Ingulph's Chronicle of the Abbey of Croyland* was written by different, anonymous monks, one continuing where another left off. Much of the detail of these turbulent months seems to have been written after Richard's death, but the second continuator was an outsider, not of the abbey itself, and somebody very well informed of the internal workings of the Council in the last months of Edward IV's reign and the 'usurpation' that followed. The jury is out as to who this man was. Most historians plump for John Russell, Bishop of Lincoln, who had easy access to Croyland as well as a role on the Council in London. Or it may have been Dr Henry Sharp, an official in the royal Court of Chancery. Whoever wrote *Croyland*, the author is increasingly pro-Woodville and anti-Richard and of course, unlike Mancini, there is a moralising 'goody-two-shoes' tone which we might expect from a senior churchman.

To sum up on these commentators, we can discount Rous entirely, both his smarmy praise of Richard during his lifetime and the puerile rubbish after his death.

Mancini was a foreigner who only reported what he heard – and rumours are not facts. Croyland was informed but partisan. Nowhere in these chronicles do we have the voice of Richard himself.

Once Elizabeth Woodville, now queen-dowager, heard of events at Stony Stratford, she took her youngest son, Richard of York, and his sisters to the safety of sanctuary at Westminster Abbey. If Richard Gloucester was to have Edward, he would not have his brother too. There was unrest in the capital, Dorset doing some broadsword-rattling before realizing Richard's popularity in the city and joining his sister in sanctuary. When Richard and Buckingham arrived, they brought with them the carts of weapons, marked with the Woodville arms. Mancini claimed that these were stashed outside London for a renewal of war against the Scots, which is preposterous. The man had no idea how far away the Scottish border was or that Richard had ample weapons and men in the North to cope with that problem. The young king was placed in the Bishop of London's palace at St Paul's and all the city dignitaries swore him allegiance, as Richard's Northerners had already done at York.

The coronation, originally planned by the Woodvilles for 3 May (indecently soon, we might think, after Edward IV's death) was now put back until 22 June. Parliament ratified Richard's role as Protector and the king was moved to the Tower, to keep him safe and to prepare him for the arduous six-hour ceremony of the coronation in Westminster Abbey.

On 5 June, Anne arrived from Middleham, leaving little Edward behind. The boy was only seven, the age of his father when he had been shocked by the blast of trumpets at Ludford, but the journey was 200 miles long and would have taken an exhausting eight or nine days. Five days later, all Hell broke loose and Richard's first thought was to write to his Northerners for help. To the Corporation of York, he wrote:

> 'We heartily pray you to come to London in all the diligence … possible … with as many as you can make defensively arrayed there to aid and assist us against the Queen, her bloody adherents and affinity, which have intended and daily doth intend to murder and utterly destroy us and our cousin the Duke of Buckingham and the royal blood of this realm.'

What had happened? Extraordinarily, Hasting had changed sides. The man had always been a loyal supporter and friend of Edward IV, commanding the rear at Tewkesbury and carousing and revelling with the king at his various progresses in time of peace. They shared at least one mistress, Jane Shore, but there was always something self-serving about Hastings. We know that he was on the take from both the king of France and the Duke of Burgundy, sworn enemies. It may well be that the sudden appearance of the Duke of Buckingham as Richard's right-hand man had annoyed him, in that he saw himself in that role. But the *real* reason for Hastings' sudden disaffection was the bombshell dropped by Robert Stillington, Bishop of Bath and Wells, to Richard and the Council on Monday, 9 June,

Stillington was an immediate witness to the reality of what had happened. He had been a loyal servant of Edward IV, his keeper of the Privy Seal and Chancellor. He was also a doctor of canon law and understood both the legal issues and the precepts of the Church through and through. Above all, he had officiated, while still an ordinary priest, at the hole-in-corner wedding of Edward and Elizabeth Woodville in 1464. He also knew why the wedding had been hole-in-corner, held in a private chapel rather than a church and with none of the dignity befitting a king and queen. This was because Edward was already married to Lady Eleanor Butler, daughter of the Earl of Salisbury. The confusing term bandied about in those weeks of the summer of 1483 is *precontract*, but all that means is that it was a marriage undergone and consummated before the later one.

When Stillington announced this to the Council, the impact was clear and immediate. All of Edward's children with Elizabeth Woodville were automatically declared illegitimate. They could still hold titles and estates and marry within the nobility, but they could not take the throne. Opponents of Richard, then and now, find Stillington's revelations too pat and the timing too neat. There was talk that there were various attempts to smear Edward IV still further, by implying that he was not Richard of York's son (looking nothing like his father), but the result of a fling between Cecily and an archer named Blaybourne or Blaueborne. Stillington did not claim this; neither did Richard. In fact, when the bombshell hit, Richard was actually living with his mother at Baynard's Castle. There is no record of any enmity between them and 'Proud Cis' was altogether too loyal and virtuous a lady to make the Blaybourne fling at all likely. The only surviving letter from Richard to his mother is one of complete duty and affection.

Hastings grasped the fallout from all this at once. He had expected to serve Edward V as he had his father (giving the boy time, presumably, to work up to the drinking and wenching bit!), but with Edward and his little brother eliminated, the crown must go, legally, to Richard. And there is nothing to suggest that Richard and Hastings were ever close. The transfer of loyalties of William Catesby, the East Anglian lawyer, from Hastings to Richard does not prove friendship; merely that Catesby knew which way the wind was blowing. As a footnote, historian Peter A. Hancock paints Catesby as all kinds of villain, simply because he was out to feather his own nest; it was the fifteenth-century way.

Matters came to a head, ironically for Hastings, on Friday, 13 June. Richard called a mini-Council meeting at the Tower, with Hastings, John Morton, Bishop of Ely, Buckingham, John Howard, Duke of Norfolk, Archbishop Rotherham of York and Thomas Stanley in attendance. Shakespeare's version, from fiction supplied by Morton and passed to his student Thomas More, is such good drama that many people have swallowed it wholesale. As historian Annette Carson sums it up:

> 'The reader is invited to consider whether the entire scene ... with the Bishop of Ely innocently sending for strawberries and the protector suddenly transformed into a raving despot, might not have been one of Morton's favourite after-dinner anecdotes.'

At first, Richard is all sweetness and light – they have met to discuss the king's coronation. Then he leaves the room and suddenly returns, screaming that the queen and Mistress Shore have conspired against him by using witchcraft, leaving him with a withered arm and fearing for his life. Oh, and by the way, Hastings is in on it too!

So far, so farcical. Only Thomas More has the witchcraft angle; it is not in any of the other chroniclers' accounts. Why does More have it? Because he was a drama queen himself, prepared to believe any of the vitriolic nonsense that Morton spouted about Richard and because he was writing (in the 1530s) when witchcraft was looming as a serious issue for the first time in England. 'I will not to dinner till I see thy head off!' Richard screams, even though dinner in the fifteenth century was eaten three hours before this meeting took place. Troops were called and the two bishops and Hastings were placed under guard. Whereas the churchmen were released later (in the case of the malicious Morton, a serious mistake by Richard) Hastings was taken outside to Tower Green. A makeshift block was erected using a plank of wood and the headsman sliced off his head with his axe. The removal of Hastings is cited by anti-Ricardians as an example of the protector's duplicity and lust for power. Now he had decided to rule himself, bypassing Edward V entirely. But Stillington's bombshell had made that a given anyway. By removing Hastings – an avowed opponent of the Woodvilles – Richard was actually narrowing his support. The only sense this makes is that Hastings, for the reasons outlined above, had buried the hatchet with the queen's kindred and had, in effect, joined the enemy. It may be that Gloucester acted too precipitately. It may be that he regretted it later.

Richard saw to it that Hastings was given a fitting burial in St George's Chapel, Windsor, near the tomb of Edward IV, still a work in progress at this time, and a chantry chapel was set up for him. His innovative and lavish brick-built castle at Kirby Muxloe in Leicestershire, however, has remained unfinished to this day, as the workmen were told to down tools and go away.

On Monday, 16 June, after considerable persuasion from Richard, the queen allowed Richard of York to leave the abbey and go to join his brother at the Tower. She herself and her daughters elected to stay put. This act itself poses all sorts of questions. To the anti-Ricardians, convinced that Richard was making a grab for the throne since the death of his brother, this is proof of the protector's intent. He now had both boys in his clutches and could do what he liked with them. While this is true, the fact that Elizabeth and her daughters remained in sanctuary is inexplicable. Why let the boy go if she despised and mistrusted Richard as much as Morton and the Tudor apologists contend? On the other hand, why not accept Richard's offer for the whole family to come out of sanctuary? It implies either that Elizabeth was perfectly happy to trust the protector or she was appallingly negligent in respect of her son. The fact that the protector had stationed troops around the abbey (as he had around the Tower) proved nothing. The Council had sanctioned it, London was alive with rumours and the flimsy evidence that we have indicates one or more plots to 'rescue' the boys during those days. Perhaps the conciliatory words of Thomas Bourchier, Archbishop of Canterbury, who had acted as go-between, had won the queen over, but it still does not explain her deliberate splitting of her children.

The other child to be protected by the protector was Edward, Earl of Warwick, Clarence's son, then aged about eight. He was moved to Sandal Castle, Wakefield, in the summer of 1483 and lived there in comfort and as befitted his high-born rank. For twelve years after the accession of Henry Tudor, Warwick was held prisoner in a cell and then promptly executed.

With the pronouncement made by Stillington being made public, first in a sermon preached by Dr Ralph Shaw at St Paul's Cross outside the cathedral (the rough equivalent of a press conference today), then by the Duke of Buckingham to the mayor and aldermen of the city at the Guildhall the next day, matters moved on quickly. Edward V's coronation and the parliament to follow it had already been delayed and was now postponed. Nevertheless, enough lords and gentry had already arrived in the capital to constitute the three estates who comprised parliament (the lords spiritual and temporal and the commons) and they officially petitioned Richard at Baynard's Castle to accept the crown. Shakespeare has Richard, flanked with priests, being horrified at the offer and refusing at first, while Buckingham whips up the crowd's support. This is pure invention by Dominic Mancini, Thomas More et al, who all conveniently ignore the fact that the three estates had spent several hours debating the Stillington issue in full.

While Richard was poised to accept the crown in the south, fate was closing in on Edward V's former advisors in the North. Anti-Ricardians have painted Richard Ratcliffe as the villain in this story because he organized Gloucester's Northern Council to attend the trial of Rivers, Grey and Vaughan at Pontefract. Too many writers have taken William Collingborne's later polemic, pinned up in London – 'The rat, the cat and Lovell our dog rule all England under a hog' – as serious, unbiased political commentary. In fact, Collingborne was a Tudor spy attempting to undermine Richard's rule in the capital and they duly hanged him for it. Richard Ratcliffe – the 'rat' – was certainly a loyal servant of Richard Gloucester, but the implication that the trio were some sort of Machiavellian cabal is pure propaganda. *Somebody* had to call the Northern Lords to Pontefract and that was Ratcliffe's function.

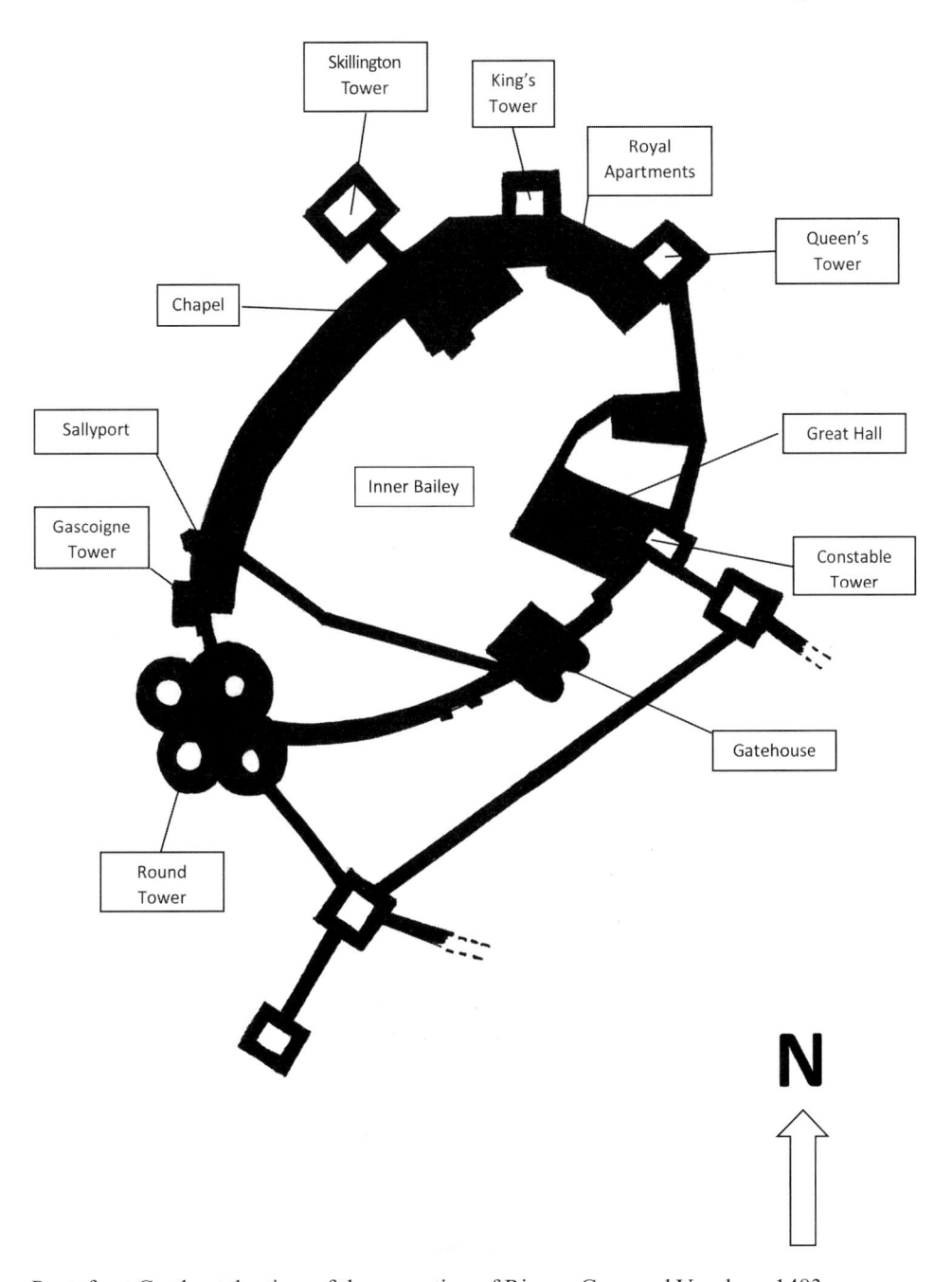

Pontefract Castle at the time of the execution of Rivers, Grey and Vaughan, 1483.

The castle itself was built by Ilbert de Lacy on a rocky outcrop above All Saints church. It was a royal castle for much of its existence, reverting to the crown under Henry I, John and Edward II. Much of the building, however, the donjon and outer curtain walls, was the work of the de Lacys and John of Gaunt, who spent a fortune on it in the fourteenth century. Today's ruin gives only a hint of the power and splendour which it once possessed. Almost unique was the Skillington Tower, an example of *torre albarrana*, a free-standing tower joined to the curtain wall by a bridge. This style of castle-building is not usually found outside Spain and it may be that Edward, the Black Prince's campaign at Najera in 1367 led to its construction at Pontefract.

The place also had a reputation for murder and grisly death even before Rivers, Grey and Vaughan ended their days there. 'Pomfret, Pomfret!' wails Rivers in the Shakespeare version:

> 'O thou bloody prison, fatal and ominous to noble peers! Within the guilty closure of thy walls Richard the second was hacked to death, And, for more slander to thy dismal seat We give thee up our guiltless blood to drink.'

As we have seen, Richard II was probably poisoned, not hacked to death, but nobody ever accused Shakespeare of avoiding a dramatic exit. If Richard II died in the castle's cellars which doubled as dungeons, Thomas of Lancaster had preceded him. Defeated at Boroughbridge on 16 March 1322, Lancaster was executed on the orders of Edward II, perhaps in the great hall, perhaps outside the castle gates. His body was taken into the town that had grown up around the castle and buried at the priory, a Cluniac house that had been established in Pontefract in 1090 and of which no trace survives today.

Here, at the shrine of St John the Evangelist, various miracles were attributed to Lancaster's spiritual intervention until Edward II heard of this and impounded all the offerings made by pilgrims. More pertinently to recent events, Richard of York and his son, Edmund of Rutland, had been buried there after Wakefield, the removal of their bodies to Fotheringhay having taken place only seven years earlier.

Now it was the turn of Rivers, Grey and Vaughan. Because no details are known of the trial (there was no Mancini or Croyland to snipe at what was happening) it is often assumed that this was a kangaroo court with only the most cursory nod in the direction of justice. The judge was the Percy Earl of Northumberland and the trial – of three men who had colluded in what amounted to a coup d'état and the kidnapping of a king – was almost certainly held in the great hall. Trials of this type happened routinely in the late fifteenth century. They did not follow proceedings as we now know them and we should not try to apply twenty-first-century notions of justice and democratic fairness to them.

Judged guilty by Northumberland and his peers, the three were executed with an axe (exactly where is unknown) on 25 June. Two days earlier, Rivers wrote his will:

> 'I, Anthony Woodville, in the castle of [Pomfret] bequeath all my lands … my heart to be buried (if I die south of Trent) …'

As we have seen, the River Trent marked the legal and cultural boundary between North and South. It was usual for men to will various parts of their body (the heart was believed to be the home of the soul) to different burial places. Rivers' horse, banners and clothes were sold and the money given to the poor. He was buried, as were the others, away from the dead heroes of Wakefield, in St John's Priory, the bodies left naked in the hall there so there could be no doubt about their deaths. The deep, scholarly Rivers was found to be wearing a hair shirt under his clothes when he died – the sign of a penitent intent on suffering – and this was hung on the altar of Our Lady of Doncaster, a Carmelite friary in the town. He was forty-one. Grey was twenty-three and Thomas Vaughan, a very old man for his times, was seventy-three. The axe took them all.

But if some people believe that what happened at Pontefract was pure political murder, what about the two murders that were supposedly carried out 200 miles further south, in the Tower?

Chapter 11

The Black Deeps

The arms of Edward V. The boy was only king for eleven weeks and was never actually crowned. Even so, he had his own herald, a pursuivant called Ich Dien (the Black Prince's motto meaning 'I serve'). The bend sinister (bar across the shield) was the badge of bastardy in that Parliament and Richard of Gloucester decided that Edward was in fact illegitimate.

The troops that Richard had sent for arrived under the command of Henry Percy, Earl of Northumberland and were kept somewhere to the north of London in case there were to be other attempts to 'rescue' the royal princes. Richard reviewed them at Moorfields, the undrained fenland later known as Finsbury. Dominic Mancini, presumably well used to seeing French and Italian soldiers, was impressed by them:

> 'There is hardly any without a helmet and more without bows and arrows … [these are] thicker than those used by other nations, just as their bodies are stronger than other people's, for they seem to have hands and arms of iron.'

The petition presented to Richard, almost certainly at Baynard's Castle, became *Titulus Regius*, an Act of Parliament setting out Richard's right of inheritance because of the bastardy of Edward IV's children. It was this document that Henry Tudor tried to airbrush out of history on his accession by having all copies of it destroyed. One escaped, however, and we still have it today.

On Sunday, 6 July 1483, Richard and Anne walked barefoot, as was the custom, to the doors of Westminster Abbey, for centuries the crowning-place of kings. No expense had been spared. Like his brother Edward, Richard understood the need to impress with all the pomp and splendour available. Londoners would never forget the scene; neither would the Northerners who had come south, probably never having seen the capital before. Foreign dignitaries were there too, keen to report back to the courts of Europe exactly what happened that day. The Archbishop of Canterbury and his supporting bishops led the procession. Northumberland carried the blunted Sword of Mercy; Lord Stanley had the Constable's Mace; John de la Pole, Duke of Suffolk, held the sceptre and his son, also John, Earl of Lincoln, had the orb. The crown itself, the golden circlet allegedly worn by Edward the Confessor at his coronation in 1042, was carried by John Howard, newly created Duke of Norfolk and Marshal of England. His son Thomas, Earl of Surrey, carried the sword of state. Alongside Richard walked the Earl of Kent and Francis, Viscount Lovell, carrying the swords of justice. As the senior duke, Buckingham held the king's velvet and ermine train and the lesser nobility walked behind him. Anne's entourage came next, suitably followed by other aristocracy.

At the altar, Richard and Anne were stripped to their underwear above their waists. In Anne's case, there must have been a modicum of chasteness about this; it was hardly dignified for a soon-to-be queen of England to bare her breasts in public. And no one commented on the supposed deformity in Richard's spine or shoulders, which surely would have been remarked on by *somebody* that day, had it been an issue. They were dressed in cloth-of-gold, the costliest fabric available and crowns were placed on their heads. They took communion from the Archbishop and a *Te Deum* was sung. Then the whole party crossed the square to Parliament Hall for the lavish coronation banquet. One redoubtable woman who was there, in body if not spirit, was Margaret Beaufort, the mother of Henry Tudor. She helped carry Anne's train.

The feast details have survived. There were three courses of fifteen, sixteen and seventeen dishes each, but because it took so long to eat, it was dark before the third course, and wafers and hippocras (spiced wine) were consumed instead. The actual food of the course was probably eaten by the army of cooks, waiters and scullions who had prepared it all. Only those at Richard's top table would have access to all the goodies; the 'commons' (knights of the shire) had only one course of three dishes. The game birds on offer included heron, egret, crane, bittern, rail and partridge. There were also rabbit and suckling pig, beef, mutton and venison, served with salt and/or a variety of sauces. Tarts, eaten between the meat dishes, included custards (in reality, quiches) and 'flampaynes' (pork pies).

The fish dishes included carp and bream cooked in foil, a thin pastry. The really exotic birds, like peacocks, were carefully skinned before roasting and their feathers replaced for the table. The same went for pheasants. An astonishing 63 gallons of wine were drunk, as well as 116 of hippocras. Vegetables hardly feature and were associated with the peasantry. The previous year, however, we have entries from the household books of Howard of Norfolk that mention herbs used for salads.

The whole would have been decorated with flowers (it was high summer), ornaments of sugar, a relatively new import, and marchpane (marzipan). Most guests would have left their tables very full and probably quite merry!

Things had gone so swimmingly for Richard that with hindsight (which the Tudors used in spades) it looked as though taking the throne was the culmination of his cunning plan all along. Snatch the princes, trash the reputation of the Woodvilles (not difficult), silence any would-be opposition (Hastings), declare Edward IV's offspring illegitimate (Stillington), and put pressure on parliament to offer Gloucester the crown. There were, of course, other interpretations of all these events which we have looked at already. Edward IV's will had given clear custody of the princes to Richard, not the queen and certainly not her grasping family. It was they who had tried to overturn this by bringing Edward V south for a quick coronation and perhaps planning to ambush Richard at the same time. Hastings would possibly have opposed Richard on grounds of morality anyway, but since he had thrown in his lot with the Woodvilles over his petulant objection to Buckingham's rise to the top, he had tipped his hand and plotted, in effect, against the wishes of his old friend, Edward IV. It was not Richard who declared the princes illegitimate, but Robert Stillington, Bishop of Bath and Wells, who had officiated at the bigamous marriage of Edward and Elizabeth in the first place. Parliament had accepted this, not, as Mancini and Croyland would have us believe, through fear, but because it was the legal and right thing to do. The pressure that Richard is supposed to have exerted was presumably through the presence of his Northern army, but, contrary to Mancini's impression above, most Londoners found the Northerners, with their shabby armour and peculiar accents, something of a joke.

But there remained the problem of the princes in the night-time. I have approached this issue, for most people all they know of Richard III, from the point of view of a crime writer, not an historian, which I believe has been the wrong vantage point for years. It would be tempting to paraphrase American television's *Dragnet* crime series of the 1950s, where detective Joe Friday (Jack Webb) was always asking witnesses for 'just the facts, Ma'am'. The problem in the summer of 1483 is that we do not know what the facts are. The usual witnesses in this case were partisan to say the least. As historian Michael K. Jones points out, 'the insupportable drawback remains the absence of a contemporary, or near-contemporary, narrative which told the story from Richard III's point of view'. This may once have existed, but Henry Tudor's victory at Bosworth saw to it (as the removal of *Titulus Regius* nearly did) that everything pro-Richard was lost. London, we are told, was a hub of Yorkist support, perhaps reflected in the three estates' support for Richard, but all we have is Mancini and Croyland, who are clearly in the opposite camp, casting doubt and aspersions on everything the protector/king does. Even so, they *are* all we have, so we will try to piece together what might have happened.

The *Great Chronicle of London*, mercifully beyond the clutches of Mancini, Croyland or the Tudors, tells us that Edward V and Richard of York were 'well treated within the king's lodging'. Tradition (rather than fact) suggests that this was the Garden Tower, now called the Bloody Tower because victims of the Tudors were usually housed here prior to their executions. The Garden Tower stands on the inner curtain wall and is the nearest to the river entrance called Traitors' Gate. Historian Annette Carson suggests that the Lanthorn Tower further east would have been more appropriate. It had recently been refurbished and there was a garden, as a play area, for the princes' use. Wherever they were housed, the boys had their own servants and all their creature comforts, as well as their own doctor, John Argentein.

It is important to establish the status of the boys at this time. They were no longer in contention for the throne of England, so Edward V could never, legally, be crowned (not that that stopped Henry Tudor after Bosworth). Even so, they were the sons of a former king and the nephews of a current one, so they should be treated with all the tenderness and respect that that entailed. Edward was three months short of his thirteenth birthday; Richard of York was a month short of his tenth birthday and because of the dynastic marriage arrangements of the time, was already married to Anne Mowbray, daughter of the Duke of Norfolk. She had died two years earlier at Greenwich Palace (Placentia) and was buried in Westminster Abbey. Both boys had numerous titles which, had they survived in the outside world, they may have been able to keep.

After the coup that eliminated Hastings, the *Great Chronicle* tells us that the boys were 'holden more straight', in other words, kept in tighter security. Although little is made of it, there is evidence that there was at least one attempt to get the boys out by adherents of the Woodvilles. When Richard was travelling the country in his royal progress (see Chapter 12) he wrote to his Chancellor, John Russell, from Minster Lovell:

> 'And whereas we understand that certain persons of such as of late had taken upon them the fact of an enterprise, as we doubt not ye have heard, be attached and in ward.'

The 'enterprise', which the historian John Stowe claimed years later was part of a Woodville-inspired coup to break the boys out of the Tower, is a cryptic phrase on Richard's part. Aware of his opposition, he was loath to be too obvious in a royal letter that he had to send by mounted messenger and which could fall into enemy hands. Even so, he is warning Russell to be on his guard. This letter is dated 29 July and implies that Richard believed the princes were still very much alive then. The move of the boys to the Tower, therefore, was for their protection. 'The children of king Edward were seen shooting [archery] and playing in the garden of the Tower [at] sundry times.'

It is not clear who saw this. The Tower of London was an armoury, an arsenal, a barracks, the royal mint and it housed hundreds of people on a daily basis. Contrary to the ominous rumblings of Shakespeare – 'I do not like the Tower, of any place' and 'rude, ragged nurse, old sullen playfellow for tender princes, use my babies well. So foolish sorrow bids your stones farewell' – the whole place would have been alive with comings and goings; not an ideal crime scene. Presumably the children were seen playing by servants and visitors as July and August wore on and the weather was good.

Mancini now takes over to tell us that the princes were 'withdrawn into the inner apartments of the Tower proper', the keep called the White Tower where it is most unlikely the Italian had ever been. This was the oldest and strongest part of the castle, the base of its walls 20ft thick in places, but it did not yet have a sinister reputation; that, again, was the legacy of the Tudors.

We know that the boys' servants were changed, again for security reasons. A warrant for 18 July authorised wage payments to fourteen servants of 'Edward Bastard late called king Edward the Vth'. A second possible rising, which may or may not have been focused on the princes, took place in July or early August, led by John Welles, half-brother of Margaret Beaufort whose Northamptonshire estates were confiscated and who ran to the safety of Brittany and Henry Tudor's court-in-exile.

Among the many people Mancini talked to was John Argentein, Edward V's doctor. 'Day by day', Mancini wrote, '[the boys] began to be seen more rarely behind the bars and windows, till at length they ceased to appear altogether.' Argentein 'reported that the young king, like a victim prepared for sacrifice, sought remission of his sins by daily confession and penance, because he believed that death was facing him …'

'We can rest assured,' Annette Carson says, 'that information derived from Argentein was rock solid.' Actually, we cannot. Allowing for any misunderstanding between the doctor and Mancini (unlikely, because both men spoke Latin and probably Italian) we have no way of assessing Argentein's memory, or honesty. His evidence is suspect, because he is playing into the hands of those who believe that the boys were murdered. Why should Edward have seen himself as a sacrifice? Why did he believe he was facing death? Admittedly, he had been through a lot in a very few weeks. His father had died (but his father was as remote to him as the king's own father had been). He had been taken away from the people who had brought him up, deprived of his title and a coronation and now he was effectively in gaol, with his own servants replaced. He cannot have been happy, but that is no reason to assume that he was going to die.

The last mention of the princes alive comes from Croyland. While Richard and Anne were celebrating the investiture of Edward of Middleham as Prince of Wales in York, the chronicler wrote, 'In the meantime … the two sons of King Edward remained in the Tower of London with a specifically appointed guard.' This takes us to, at the earliest, 8 September, so we know that the boys were alive until the early part of that month.

By the end of September, rumours were flying in London that the princes were dead. Mancini himself had already left England when he wrote, 'whether … he [Edward V] has been taken by death and by what manner of death, so far I have not at all discovered.' Because of the foreign-reporting angle, such rumours swirled around the courts of Europe, especially France, where every bit of anti-English gossip was lapped up and believed. What is extraordinary is that so many modern historians put such emphasis on these 'facts' whereas all they are are malicious muck-raking and speculation, which we see in the world press's 'fake news' today.

When Henry VII came to the throne, he made enquiries about the fate of the princes. This became a matter of urgency when Perkin Warbeck turned up in Cork, Ireland, claiming to be Richard, Duke of York, the younger of the princes. Gleefully seizing the opportunity to make mischief, the very courts that had openly claimed that both boys were dead and killed by their uncle Richard, now backed Warbeck. The French, the Scots and especially the new Holy Roman Emperor, Maximilian, claimed to be convinced that the boy was genuine. He was not. His small, ragged army, defeated at Exeter by the king, Warbeck allegedly confessed his imposture and was hanged as a common criminal at Tyburn in November 1499.

The turn of the new century seemed to be a time of confessions, although in the case of the next one, it never actually happened. James Tyrell, far from being the disgruntled 'hit man' of Shakespeare's play, was, as we have seen, a loyal supporter and confidant of the king. At Richard's coronation, he had ridden the king's horse of estate, its trappings emblazoned with the arms of England, in his role as Richard's Master of the Horse. He was to take Buckingham to his trial and execution at Salisbury after his failed rebellion in October 1483. In January 1485, as the on-off rebellion by Henry Tudor began to build momentum again, Tyrell was given command of the garrison at the castle of Guisnes, near Calais, having already been given responsibility for South Wales.

Very belatedly, Tyrell was tried for treason by Henry VII in 1502 (having kept his head down after Bosworth by staying in Guisnes) and made a confession that, by the way, he had killed the princes. Unfortunately for those who like neat solutions to murder stories, this information comes from one source only, the former under-sheriff of London and sometime saint, Thomas More. Because he too died a martyr's death in the reign of Henry VIII for refusing to accept Henry's anti-Rome line over his 'great matter', his search for a son and heir, More has been kindly treated by most historians. They cite his impeccable honesty and when that does not convince, his literary style. What More actually was, was a novelist before the novel was even invented.

'Sir James Tyrell,' he wrote, nearly thirty-five years after the event:

> 'devised that [the princes] should be murdered in their bed, to the execution whereof he appointed Miles Forest, one of the four that kept them, a fellow fleshed in murder before time. To him he joined one John Dighton, his own horsekeeper, a big, broad, square, strong knave. Then, all the other [servants] being removed from them, this Miles Forest and John Dighton about midnight (the sely [innocent] children lying in their beds) came into the chamber and suddenly lapped them up among the clothes so bewrapped them and entangled them, keeping down by force the featherbed and pillows hard into their mouths, that, within a while, smored [smothered] and stifled, their breath failing, they gave up to their God their innocent souls unto the joys of Heaven, leaving to the tormentors their bodies dead in the bed.'

This, said More, was 'very truth' and 'well known'. Except that it was not. No copy of Tyrell's confession has come to light. Neither did Henry VII make any capital out of it, which surely he would have done had it actually happened. All More was doing was elaborating, for whatever purpose he had in mind, on the raft of rumours whirling about since 1483. Miles Forest was a Constable of Barnard Castle in Richard's North and, no doubt, More had read the name somewhere or Bishop Morton dug it out as 'evidence'. The *Great Chronicle of London* speculated that the boys (like their uncle Clarence, allegedly) were drowned in a wine butt. Other ideas involved poison. Tyrell may have been involved, but it could have been any of Richard's servants. Croyland, writing in 1486, was extremely vague – 'the princes, by some unknown manner of destruction, met their fate.' Only the malevolent John Rous, now turned against Richard, echoed the gossip of the European courts – 'within about three months [of the Stony Stratford meeting] he killed him [Edward V] together with his brother.'

Fast forward to 1674. In a very different world from that of the Plantagenets, the Stuarts now ruled in the over-the-top figure of Charles II. The Civil War (always more ideological and religious than the Wars of the Roses) had come and gone and Oliver Cromwell's Interregnum, the 'experiment in government', had failed. Restoration London was full of bawdy plays, ladies' plunging necklines, the last great outbreak of the plague and a rumbling war with Britain's great maritime rival, the Dutch. In 1666, in a catastrophe attributed to both God's wrath and the Devil's mischief, much of London burned in the Great Fire. But the Tower was untouched.

And there, during routine refurbishment of the 600-year-old building, workmen at the Tower found the remains of two young humans. The story of the princes' disappearance and supposed murder had, of course, become embedded in English history, even if the details were vague. It was decided, with no forensic evidence at all, that these were probably Edward V and Richard of York and the bones were placed in an urn inside a suitably embellished Rococo tomb in 'Innocents' Corner' in Westminster Abbey.

The tomb was opened in 1933, with the permission of Church authorities clearly more enlightened then than today and two experts, Keeper of Monuments Dr Laurence Tanner and anatomist Professor William Wright, examined the bones. This was the same decade in which an amateur 'dig' of the grave of Vlad Dracula at Snagov church, Romania, produced very disappointing results and only a few years after the discovery in England of 'Piltdown Man', a hoax still accepted as archaeological fact when Tanner and Wright were at work. Neither man was an archaeologist, and Tanner's credentials in particular seem only tangentially relevant to the problem in hand.

The 1678 tomb (the bones had been kept by the Keeper of the Royal Mint for the four years since the discovery) contained, as such finds often do, a mixture of animal bones. The bodies were said to have been found at the foot of a staircase (a particularly busy station, one might think, of daily Tower life in the 1480s). The conclusion that Tanner and Wright came to was that the bones were those of children, one between twelve and thirteen and the other between nine and eleven. The older child suffered from osteomyelitis, which resulted in a painful condition of the jaw and may perhaps account for Dr Argentein's depressed and pitiful Edward V. The 1930s was long before DNA or carbon dating, so there was no hope of pinning down the identities of the bodies or when they died. Neither could the experts determine sex. Now, of course, these problems could be overcome. With the extraordinary find of Richard III's bones in the Leicester car park and the tracing of his descendants via DNA, a re-opening of the abbey tomb would give us hard evidence of who these bodies are, when they met their end and even, perhaps, how. What it will not tell us, of course, is who, if they were murdered, actually killed them.

Charles Ross speculates, using expert analysis of the Tanner/Wright report, that these probably *are* the bones of the princes. This is wishful thinking. Rather like Thomas More, Ross is today held up as the pinnacle of historical rectitude. Actually, he is anti-Ricardian and snidely calls the *Daily Mail* 'a fount of historical authority' because it wrote a good review of Josephine Tey's brilliant *Daughter of Time*. And while he is on the subject, Ross mentions 'a number of others, nearly all women writers, for whom the rehabilitation of the reputation of a long-dead king holds a strange and unexplained fascination'. Could it be that those 'women' are interested in the truth? The only sensible pronouncement on the bones, as even Ross admits, comes from Dr Juliet Rogers of the University of Bristol who wrote 'the only certain evidence here available is that they are pre-1674'.

So what are we left with? The serial killer John George Haigh, committing murder in 1940s London, took the legal term *corpus delicti* to mean the physical existence of a body, without which he believed no crime could be proven. He was proved wrong and they hanged him at Wandsworth in 1949. We do not need the bodies of the princes to prove murder, but so little else exists that we are forced to speculate on what might have been.

The great orator and lawyer Marcus Tullius Cicero was fond of posing the question in criminal trials – *qui bono?* (who benefits?). On a superficial basis, the answer in the case of the princes is Richard of Gloucester. Putting forward the tired old trio of the police – means, opportunity and motive – Richard had two, not necessarily all three. No one has suggested that Richard killed the boys himself; he had a watertight alibi in York at the time. But as king, he had people for things like that. And even if it was not Tyrell, Forest and Dighton, *somebody* could have been pressed into carrying out the killing, assuming the money was right. So, via his minions, Richard had the opportunity – the boys imprisoned in the Tower beyond the reach of possible rescuers. He had the means – loyal servants who would do his bidding. And then, it falls apart. Because Richard had no motive. The princes were already declared illegitimate in the early summer of 1483 and this had been ratified by parliament. They could not rule. So to claim, as anti-Ricardians do, that Richard could only take the throne if Edward and Richard of York were dead, simply is not true. So, we can answer Cicero's question more accurately – who benefits? Not Richard.

The established legend, from Thomas More up to modern historians who should know better, is that the boys were killed, probably by suffocation, at some point between late July and early September. This would have been done in the night while the Tower's inhabitants slept and guards patrolling the battlements might well have been paid to turn a blind eye. The Constable of the Tower was Robert Brackenbury, portrayed rather oddly as a man of scruple by Shakespeare, but who was, in reality, one of Richard's Northerners, with estates at Selaby near Raby, the king's mother's home. Brackenbury too was prepared to look the other way out of loyalty to Richard. Then, one of two things happened to dispose of the bodies. They were either buried at the foot of the staircase, involving the noise and commotion of digging in a relatively public place; or they were carried to a barge waiting beyond the water-gate and taken downstream to a point in the Thames estuary called the Black Deeps. There, suitably weighted, they were rolled into the water.

But if Richard were indeed guilty of this, why did he do nothing as a follow-up? Along with the curious problem of the princes in the night-time, we have the curious problem of the king in the daytime. On his return from the royal progress, he made no pronouncements at all about them. If, as More would suggest years later, the boys were smothered, why not show their bodies in St Paul's or the Abbey, to prove that they had died of natural causes? No one in 1483 was aware of petechiae, the tiny blood spots that stain the eyeballs in the case of suffocation or strangulation. A city like London was always suffering from epidemic diseases; two years later, the 'sweating sickness' would kill thousands around the country. Why not claim the boys had fallen prey to something similar?

Why did Richard not simply say that the princes had died of an illness and affect all the grief of a heartbroken uncle? Alternatively, why did he not point a finger at someone else, guilty of the boys' deaths in his absence? And if the boy's mother, Elizabeth Woodville, had any notion of foul play, she never even hinted at it, eventually coming out of sanctuary herself and bringing her illegitimate daughters with her.

Over the years, a number of people have been put in the frame for the princes' murder. If not Richard III, how about the Duke of Buckingham? He was a slippery customer, inordinately ambitious *and* he had access to the Tower, staying in London while the new king was away on his progress. He too was a descendant of Edward III and the princes stood in his way to the throne. It is the same non-argument that is directed at Richard. Then, there is Henry Tudor. Even if the man could scrape an army together, invade and overthrow Richard (which almost everybody in 1483 believed was highly unlikely) he still had the princes to contend with. It was as much in his interest as Richard's to remove them. And although he was not present in London at the time, a number of Tudor followers were – his mother, the tricksy, dominant Margaret Beaufort, his stepfather Thomas Stanley – either of these could afford hit-men and, unlike Richard, were not related to the boys in question. This is intriguing, but it ignores the fact that Henry VII, by his later actions, clearly had no idea what had happened to the princes – hence his neuroses every time a royal pretender turned up.

We have even sillier ideas, however. The princes did not die in 1483 or for many years to come. They were spirited away, perhaps to Richard's Northern castles, where there are unexplained warrants for rich children's clothes to be sent, for example, to Sheriff Hutton. Or they were sent, as Richard himself had been, to a European court, with a changed identity. The silliest of all, however, is that Richard of York at least survived into the reign of Henry VIII and ended up as Dr John Clements, appearing rather furtively in a doorway in Hans Holbein's famous painting of Thomas More and his family in Chelsea. Why More should write such arrant nonsense about the boys' murders by Forest and Dighton when he knew he had the younger son in his household makes no sense at all. It could be, just conceivably, that even as late as this, the Tudors would not tolerate rivals to the throne and that Clement/York's life was at risk if word of his real identity got out.

We are left with a huge question mark. Subsequent generations etched, drew or painted harrowing scenes, best personified, perhaps, by Millais' version, of two impossibly beautiful boys, their angelic golden hair contrasting with their sombre black clothes (neither of which is accurate for the fifteenth century). They are clearly afraid and no doubt Millais believed they were afraid of wicked uncles.

'"Thus, thus", quoth Forest, "girdling one another with their innocent alabaster arms; their lips were four red roses on a stalk, which in their summer beauty kissed each other. A book of prayers on their pillow lay, which once", quoth Forest, "almost changed my mind." But O! the devil? …' the brilliant line that so terrified me in that cinema all those years ago, the actor Michael Gough's creepy voice surging in my ears. This is, of course, the Shakespeare version and he has Richard musing later on how his cunning plans are prospering – 'The sons of Edward sleep in Abraham's bosom …'

And that is all we can be sure of. They certainly do now.

Chapter 12

Royal Progress

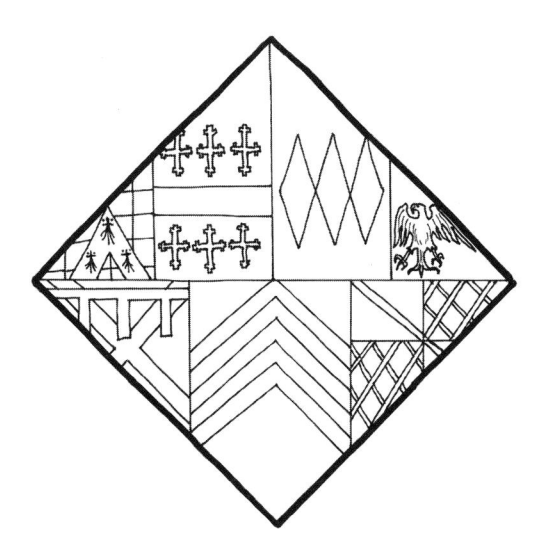

Arms of Anne Neville, Queen of England. As for Margaret of Anjou's coat of arms, I have omitted the leopards and lilies which was the royal device.

Medieval kings had a distant relationship with most of their subjects. Outside the inner circle of Richard III's Plantagenet family, the new king would have met his council regularly, the lords temporal who were the great estate owners and, as we have seen so far, used their personal retinues as private armies to wage war on each other. He would know all the bishops, the new ones being appointed by him and in Richard's case because of how seriously he took his religion. Unlike today, when the Church of England is supposed to stand outside factional politics, the fifteenth-century Church was political from top to bottom. This explains why the bishops of Durham were called prince-bishops and why they were keen to hold on to their territory against relative newcomers like the Percys and the Nevilles.

The rest of the population were the *labori*, those who work, from the inns of court-educated lawyers via the seriously wealthy merchants to the craftsmen, the labourers and the peasants. Bastard feudalism, with its links to an increasingly cash economy and the population loss caused by the plague over a century before Richard's time, had conspired to change the dynamic of English society, but it was still intensely hierarchical, with a 'them' and 'us' element based on wealth which would morph into the modern class structure over time.

The vast majority of people never saw the king, except, very badly depicted, on coins of the realm; the groats and angels of Richard's day carried a 'likeness' that could have been anybody. For this reason, it was important to appear in public from time to time, either at the coronation or a re-crowning ceremony or travelling around the countryside taking in as many populated centres as possible. Villages and hamlets that lay on the route must have been astounded at the sight of Richard's party, bright with heraldry, hung with bells and streamers, lords and ladies on their palfreys; tambours, drums and fifes sounding the approach. There were five bishops to hold divine services at the appropriate times and Edward, Earl of Warwick, Clarence's son rode with them. Edward of Middleham, Richard's own boy, joined the party later. There was no sign of the princes, who remained in the Tower. Security was in the form of mounted knights and perhaps a contingent of footsoldiers. These were dangerous times.

The fourteenth-century Gough map of Britain, while woefully inaccurate for Scotland and Wales, shows the road network radiating out from London as it still does. Rivers are given greater prominence because, where possible, travellers went by boat, even around the coast from port to port. The roads of the royal progress were sometimes cobbled in places near towns, but across the countryside mere tracks. Setting off at the end of July meant that the surfaces were usually firm, but only three months later, Buckingham's October rebellion was literally washed away with rain. John Leland, travelling the same roads sixty years later, comments on the countryside and the distances between towns, but says almost nothing about the road surfaces. They meandered around fields and forests, often taking travellers miles out of their way.

Richard himself set out from Placentia where he had been for six days, travelling by barge, gilded and heraldic, upriver to Windsor. Edward IV's tomb was still being built here, in a special chantry next to the also unfinished St George's Chapel. William Hastings had recently joined the illustrious dead who had once been living knights of the Garter. Buckingham stayed behind to watch the capital while Queen Anne and John Howard, the newly created Duke of Norfolk, joined Richard at Windsor Castle. The lords who were not with the entourage were sent home to their estates after the coronation by Richard, who urged them to govern well and fairly in his name, to be 'against robbery and oppression' and to 'keep the highways free of crime'. At Windsor, Richard dismissed his military escort, which was a calculated move to show his trust of the people, and moved on to Reading.

The town on the junction of the Thames and Kennet had a number of prominent churches as well as the abbey, and Richard, as a new king, had a great deal of business to carry on at the same time as showing his face. Howard went back to London, presumably by boat, and Anne stayed at Windsor for the next four weeks. It is possible that she was already unwell, at least intermittently, during this time, although the jolting slog of travel by carriage or litter, even in good weather,

Royal Progress 125

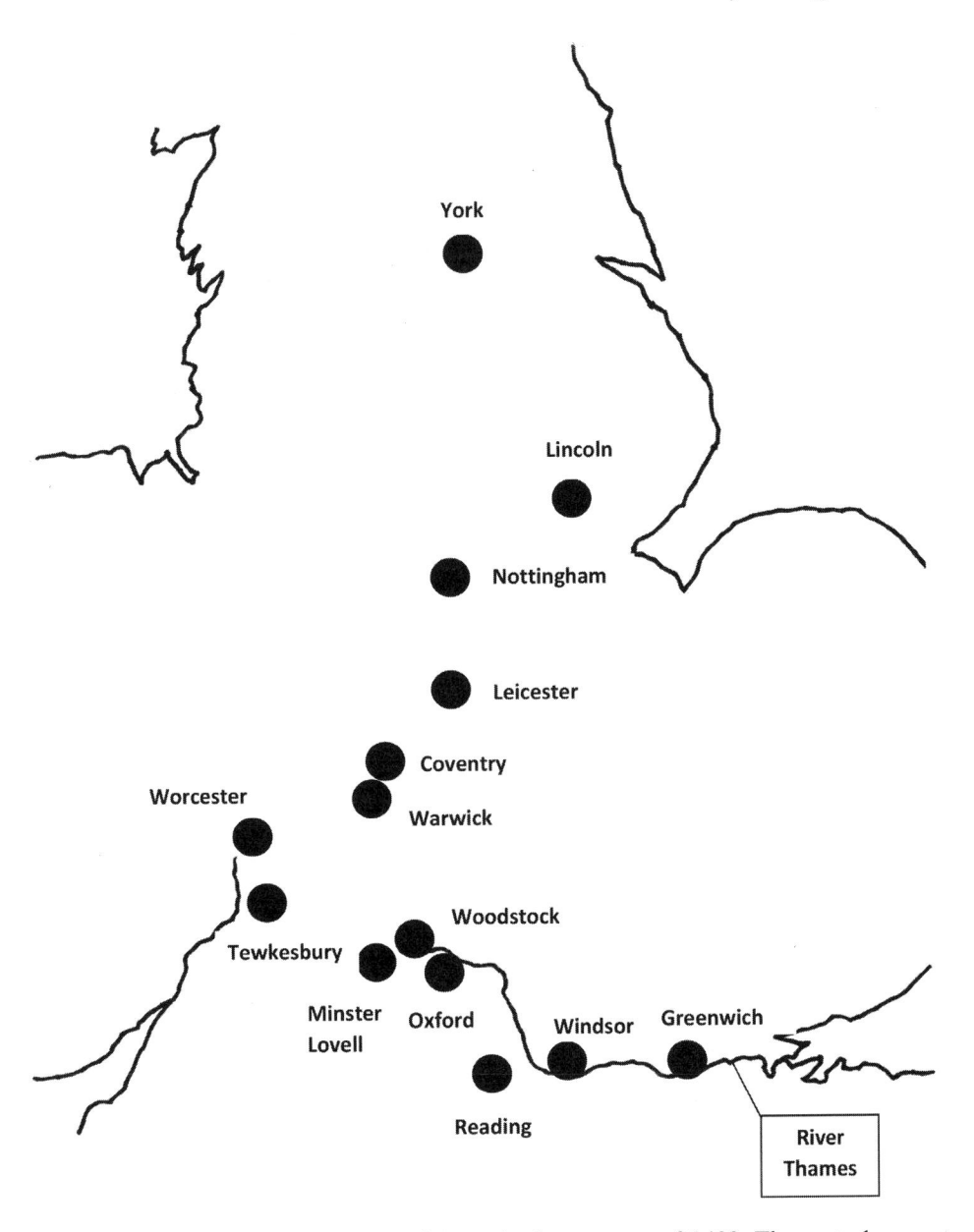

The Royal Progress of Richard III and Anne in the summer of 1483. The party began at Placentia, the royal palace at Greenwich and travelled by river to Windsor. Its most northerly point was York and it ended at Lincoln when Richard heard of the rebellion of the Duke of Buckingham. He presumably intended to return to London via a more easterly route.

was exhausting for anyone. On 23 July, Richard wrote an agreement protecting the widow and children of Hastings. He was not to be attainted for treason, which meant that his family kept their titles and lands. Hastings' brother, Ralph, who may have been implicated in the events of June, was pardoned on 2 August.

The next day, the king reached Oxford. The town had been an important one under the Saxons, and the Normans had built a castle there to keep the population in check. The charter dated from 1155, but it was its role as one of the country's two university towns that gave Oxford its fame. The first colleges were set up by refugee academics from Paris in the reign of Henry I and by Richard's time, at least some of the hostility between 'town' and 'gown' was a thing of the past. William Wayneflete, Bishop of Winchester, arrived in Oxford two days before Richard. He had founded Magdalen College and this was to host the king – 'to receive honourably the most illustrious Lord King Richard the Third'. There was a procession to Magdalen's gates, the university men in their academic robes, and Richard was met by the chancellor, Bishop Lionel Woodville, the dowager queen's brother. The man had followed his sister into sanctuary in May when his name was removed from the commissions of the peace of Wiltshire. By 20 July, however, all was restored and there were real signs of a rapprochement between the king and the Woodvilles.

Always eager to learn and take part in scholarly debates, Richard attended two discourses in Magdalen's great hall. The speakers were Dr John Taylor, Professor of Sacred Theology, and Master William Grocin, a new breed of university lecturer who shared the humanist principles of men like Erasmus, Colet and Thomas More (who would come to spearhead English philosophy under the Tudors). The king was impressed, granting venison and wine to Magdalen and gifts to the speakers. The college accounts end with the words *Vivat rex in eternum* (may the king live forever).

After dinner, Richard rode on to Woodstock, with its church of St Mary Magdalene and its palace associated with Edward, the Black Prince. He was not there long before returning to Oxford for more scholarship and discussion.

From the university town, the king's party travelled through the Cotswolds to Gloucester, of which he had been duke for twenty-two years. The walled town on the Severn had an abbey established there in the seventh century and the Benedictine monastery of 1022 would become a cathedral in 1541. Edward II, the king murdered at Berkley Castle in the county, was buried there in a canopied shrine. William the Conqueror had held his council there and the Domesday Book of 1086 was conceived in the town. Richard gave Gloucester a charter of liberties and received a letter from Oxford University at his next stop, Minster Lovell. This was the home of Francis Lovell, Richard's confidant and the university asked, against the background of goodwill in the reception they had given the king, for Bishop Morton of Ely to be released from the Tower, where he had been since 13 June and his arrest along with Hastings.

By early August, the king reached Tewkesbury where he had commanded Edward IV's vanguard twelve years earlier. He visited the tomb of his brother Clarence, who had fought there too, wrestling with who knows what inner demons and paid his respects to the grave of Edward, Prince of Wales, who Shakespeare would claim, over a century later, had been put there by Richard himself. The king cleared Clarence's considerable debts and on 4 August gave £310 to the abbot.

There was nothing of note at Worcester, Richard's next stop on his progress. The church of Christ and St Mary the Virgin had been built in the eleventh century and had a tower 196ft tall. The crypt was built by Bishop Wulfstan in 1094 and there was still a castle there in Richard's day. The only other king to be as maligned as Richard, John, was buried before the high altar. It is not known whether Richard paid his respects, but, bearing in mind his religious sensibilities, he probably did.

On Friday, 8 August, Richard reached his colossal fortress at Warwick on the Avon. There had been a fortress there since 915 when Ethelfleda of the Mercians had established a royal settlement. The church of St Mary held the tombs of the queen's forebears, the Beauchamp and Neville earls of Warwick, their cross crosslets and bears and ragged staffs much in evidence. The castle had undergone major rebuilding under these earls in the fourteenth century, including a great hall and towers overlooking the river. The Water-Gate was built then, linking the now royal apartments and the motte, and the east front that faced the town was equipped with a flanking tower at each end. The barbican that defended the main gates was particularly impressive, a long, narrow passage protected by two drawbridges and 'murder-holes' through which arrows, boiling oil or hot sand could be dropped on would-be attackers. Guy's Tower and Caesar's Tower, at each end of the new structures were still under construction at the time of Richard's visit and no doubt he was impressed with the workmanship of this latest technological design. Caesar's Tower would rise eventually to 133ft and is tri-lobed, like a clover leaf.

No doubt Richard was acutely aware that this had been the kingmaker's castle, the man who had been his tutor, his friend and finally his enemy. Had things turned out differently, Warwick would have been his father-in-law. Anne joined him here from Windsor, back in her childhood home again. John Rous, the monk from the chantry at Guy's Cliffe, half a mile away, presented the king and queen with two heraldic rolls, one in Latin, the other English, showing Richard (the only surviving contemporary likeness), Anne, Edward of Middleham and the Earl of Warwick in elegant armour and costumes, with crowns on their heads. Rous referred to the new king as:

> 'The most mighty prince Richard by the grace of God King of England and France and Lord of Ireland by very matrimony without any discontinuance or any defiling in law by heir male lineally, descending from King Harry the Second, all avarice set aside, ruled his subjects in his realm full commendably, punishing offenders of his laws, especially extortioners and oppressors of his commons, and cherishing those that were virtuous, but the which discreet guiding he got great thank of God and love of all his subjects rich and poor and great laud [praise] of the people of all other lands about him.'

Rous would be telling a very different story once he knew that Richard was dead. Anne came in for the same over-the-top commendation – 'in presence she was seemly amiable and beauteous … and right virtuous and according to the interpretation of her name Anne full gracious'. It was at Warwick that foreign diplomats first arrived to pay their masters' respects to the royal pair. First among them was Gaufridius de Sasiola, ambassador from the court of Isabella of Castile, who was anxious to arrange a wedding between her daughter and Edward of Middleham. Since both countries detested the pushy arrogance of France, such an alliance made perfect sense; Henry VII would make it a reality a few years later. Accordingly, Richard wrote to his Council in London to make the necessary arrangements and complete the paperwork with his Great Seal.

Over the next few days, as the progress continued to Coventry and Leicester, the king was busy firing off directives to extend a peace with the Scots king, James III (who he had already trounced, of course), and to stop the creeping Irish practice of debasing the currency by minting silver coins of inferior alloy. He sent his herald, Blanc Sanglier (white boar) to Louis XI of France, asking the Frenchman to stop his pirates raiding in the Channel. He knew he was whistling in the wind, which is why he already had sent a small fleet to sort the French out once and for all. The 'spider king' died in the middle of this correspondence. No one cried in England.

The town where little Richard had once gone with his mother, Cecily, to face the 'Parliament of Devils' was a thriving commercial centre, specializing in cloth and ribbons. Coventry's Benedictine monastery was founded by Leofric, Earl of Mercia in 1043 and in Richard's time the city still had its walls, with twelve gates. The church of St Michael, one of the famous three spires of the town, rose to an astonishing 196ft and the new guildhall was one of the most impressive half-timbered buildings of its type in the country. But Richard did not stay there long, moving on to Leicester Castle by 18 August.

The town on the River Soar has particular relevance to Richard today because it became his burial place in late August 1485 and was the centre of some controversy over the reburial in 2013. It was a prosperous place in the 1480s, the wealth of its guilds focused on the wool trade. In the folklore of Richard III, dissected by historian John Ashdown-Hill, there are a number of places in Leicester linked in legend to Richard, but none of them stand up to scrutiny.

Nottingham was another royal castle, like Warwick, that was undergoing a facelift in the summer of 1483, new apartments begun by Edward IV in keeping with the ostentatious show and comfort that was expected of all European rulers at the time. Here, on 24 August, Richard announced the creation of little Edward, still only seven, as Prince of Wales and Earl of Chester. Oddly, there was no inclusion of Duke of Cornwall which was already traditional for heirs to the throne. Clearly Edward had joined his father at Nottingham, because the king presided over the lad having a sword slung from his waist, a garland on his head, a ring on his finger and a staff of office placed in his hand. Richard wrote to his Council and bishops to explain that he had done this 'in the great anxieties which press upon us', to show that the House of York was alive and well and looking to the future.

John Kendall, the king's secretary, wrote ahead to the City of York to make sure that everything was ready, with speeches, pageants, the streets decorated with 'arras work' (tapestries) and a full turnout of the judges, the corporation and the people. Interestingly, in terms of North versus South, Kendall wrote 'for there come many southern lords and men of worship … which will mark greatly your receiving of their graces'.

On the 29th, the royal party entered York under the Micklegate Bar, where twenty-three years earlier, Richard's father's head could be seen rotting on a pole, picked at by rooks and ravens. It was the feast of the Decollation of St John the Baptist, and John Newton, the mayor, made a speech to the royal family. He then presented Richard with a gold cup brimming with 100 marks and another to Anne. A large chunk of this had been donated by York's recorder (senior judge) Miles Metcalfe, a close friend of Richard's from his days in the North. Anybody who was anybody was in the royal party that made its way to the Minster – the earls of Lincoln, Surrey, Northumberland; Lord Stanley and his son George; Lords Lisle and Greystoke and the usual clutch of bishops. The royal couple were sprinkled with holy water and incense by the dean and canons in their blue robes and they heard Mass.

From the Archbishop's palace, where the royals stayed for the next few days, it had to be business as usual. The Archbishop himself, Thomas Rotherham, had been arrested by Richard in the Hastings coup, but he had soon been released and now, presumably, put on a fawning front in the context of the king's presence in his own house. Most importantly, there was the investiture of Edward, which amounted to another coronation for Richard, this time in his beloved North. Banners, gowns and other clothes were sent by Peter Curtys, Keeper of the Great Wardrobe in London, with heraldic emblems sewn to them of St Cuthbert, St George and St Edward, as well as Richard's white boar. There were 13,000 cloth badges of the boar (where are they now?), which were distributed among the people of the city. The hostile Croyland continuator snidely commented that all this was just a form of bribery. The king and queen attended a performance of the Creed play, a mystery event held by the Guild of Corpus Christi in the city.

On Monday, 8 September, Edward was officially made Prince of Wales at a Mass and ceremony in the Minster presided over by the Bishop of Durham. Afterwards, the royal trio sat in state for four hours, receiving visitors and congratulations. Others received accolades too – Richard knighted his illegitimate son John of Gloucester, Clarence's boy Edward and even de Sasiola, the Spanish envoy. While Croyland assumed that the king was made of money, Richard in fact was having to borrow to pay for all this largesse, something that kings had always done and would continue to do in the future. Both John Rous of Warwick and Thomas Langton, the newly consecrated Bishop of St David's in Pembrokeshire were highly impressed by the king's generosity and his evident concern for the poor wherever he went. Ten days later, Richard officially thanked York for its hospitality and wiped over half the taxes due from the city. This was praise indeed.

Before he left Anne with Edward at Middleham, the king set up Edward of Warwick at Sheriff Hutton under the care of his cousin John, Earl of Lincoln. This, along with Sandal, would become a meeting place for the Council of the North which Richard established in the weeks ahead. The progress ended officially at Lincoln, having passed through Pontefract, so recently the departure point of Rivers, Grey and Vaughan, and Gainsborough, on 10 September.

It was at Lincoln that Richard received news of the body blow of Buckingham's rebellion. As Shakespeare's Richard asks rhetorically in Act IV Scene II, 'Hath he so long held out with me untried, And stops he now for breath?'

If Hastings' turning against Richard is difficult to understand, Buckingham's rebellion is incomprehensible. That Richard went on his progress to gather support makes sense, but it kept him away from the capital, always a hotbed of intrigue and malice. This was the time when the princes disappeared from public view and rumours of their murder flew through every alehouse in the city. There were anti-Richard camps everywhere, not least the scheming Margaret Beaufort and her untried son, Henry Tudor, Earl of Richmond. He was overseas, either in Brittany or at the French court, smarming around the French king and a trickle of discontented lords who, not likely to rise any higher under Richard with his established family and his fondness for Northerners, continued to join him.

The only possible explanation for Buckingham's actions in October 1483 is that he wanted to be the king of England. His claim was weak, via Thomas of Gloucester, the youngest son of Edward III, but it was far stronger than Henry Tudor's, who had illegitimacy on both his father's and his mother's side. Buckingham saw himself as another kingmaker and may, in that context, have been responsible for the murders of the princes in the Tower. He deliberately took charge of the imprisoned John Morton, Bishop of Ely, who could plot for England, and whisked him away to his estates at Brecon on the Welsh marches. What we have is an unholy alliance of Morton, Margaret and Richmond, who realized that Buckingham was an important figure to add to the mix. Buckingham does not appear to have been any too bright; perhaps he thought he could outweigh Tudor by reason of his claim to the throne alone.

Messengers thundered through the night across southern England. Ships set sail from Deptford and a handful of Kent ports. Buckingham was raising an army on the Welsh borders and hoped to link up with others from Cornwall to Kent, to seize London and march on the king. To Richard, Buckingham, who had been given so much in terms of land and power, became 'the most untrue creature living' as he wrote to his Chancellor on 12 October. Yet, all his life, Richard had faced treachery and betrayal – they were the yardsticks and the everyday experiences of the Wars of the Roses; he knew how to react.

He sent messengers from Lincoln commanding faithful lords to join him at Leicester with their retinues. Buckingham was declared a rebel on 15 October. Richard was isolated in the Midlands and the raising of troops took time. One man who stayed with him, and had been with him throughout the progress, was Thomas Stanley, whose wife, Margaret Beaufort, was now also a rebel against the king. The ever-duplicitous Stanley may have thought it best to keep a close eye on Richard, ready to jump whichever way suited him best. There was a great deal of confusion as sporadic rebellions broke out across the southern counties. Nothing happened in the loyal North.

John Howard, Duke of Norfolk, had been in London restoring Richard's town house, Crosby Place near Bishopsgate, in August. Now he swept into action, bringing his army from East Anglia and defending London against a Kentish uprising. He stopped it in its tracks.

Now at Leicester, Richard issued a second proclamation targeting the West Country and the southern Midlands as the heart of rebellion and promised a full pardon to all those rebels who went home now. He named the leaders – Buckingham, of course; Lord Dorset; William Norris; John Cheyney; George Brown; not forgetting the Bishop of Ely. They were, in the standard polemic of the day 'traitors, adulterers and bawds'. Richard had no time to pussyfoot around.

On 24 October, the king marched to Coventry, appointing Ralph Assheton as Vice Constable to replace Buckingham who was Constable among his many other titles. His plan was to drive a wedge between Buckingham's Welsh levies and the Englishmen in the south, destroying first one, then the other. It was a tactic that Napoleon Bonaparte would use again and again in the centuries ahead. But local resistance and appalling weather were conspiring to upset the rebels. The Vaughans of Brecon attacked Buckingham's castle at Brecknock and Humphrey Stafford destroyed bridges which alone could carry Buckingham's troops over rivers swollen and dangerous with weeks of rain. John Morton took the earliest opportunity to abandon the duke and make for Henry Tudor in Brittany. Buckingham himself, his forces deserting by the hour, put on peasant's sacking and tried to hide.

In the Shakespeare version, the news of Buckingham's rebellion and its collapse comes helter-skelter, one messenger after another and even in reality, the whole fiasco lasted less than two weeks. The lords and gentlemen of the south, men like Cheyney, Richard Woodville, William Berkley and William Stonor, lost their collective nerve and ran to the ports and Brittany. Richard reached Salisbury on 28 October without an arrow having been fired.

A servant, Ralph Bannester, had handed Buckingham in to the sheriff of Shropshire and he was tried by Assheton in Salisbury. Nobody said that Buckingham had much dignity and he now turned king's evidence, in effect blowing the whistle on just about everybody. He ranted and raved, ill with fever and Richard refused to see him, despite his impassioned requests.

On Sunday, 2 November, a scaffold was set up in the city's marketplace, the tallest spire in the country looming over the day's business. As the bells called the faithful to prayer, the executioner took off the traitor's head with his axe.

But one traitor still rode at anchor off Poole harbour in Dorset and Richard rode south to confront him. On hearing the news, the traitor turned tail and sailed back to Brittany. He was Henry Tudor, Earl of Richmond and, against all the odds, he would have a second chance.

Chapter 13

Bosworth

Arms of Henry Tudor, Earl of Richmond. Although he had his own Richmond coat of arms, Henry made a great deal of his Welsh connections, displaying the oldest of all British heraldic badges, the red dragon.

The events that filled the remaining eighteen months of Richard's reign have been discussed at length by all his biographers, his detractors reading all of them as examples of the king's increasing paranoia and desperation. Looking back, as we can, from the safety of the centuries, Richard's only parliament, which sat in January and February 1484, introduced a number of laws that lasted for years because the Tudors continued them and built on them throughout their reigns. Much of what Richard did was wise: removing the power of magnates to raise private armies and extort ordinary people was a moral and long overdue example.

Historian Chris Skidmore sees this – and other Acts in Richard's parliament – as the king pandering to various sections of society to buy their support. But this ignores the fact that the very men he would need most to face another Buckingham, the great landowners, were the very group he was forcing into line. With all the pettiness and spite of centuries, many of these men ran to Henry Tudor, first in Brittany, then in France. They fought for the pretender at Bosworth – but very few of them would ever see their old power restored as they had hoped.

England had been here before, in the reign of that other unpopular king, John. In the absence of his brother, Richard the Lionheart, on crusade and other wars, the barons had accumulated lands, wealth, armies and power which John attempted to take back. He did it badly, even though right was on his side, and was forced to agree to Magna Carta, one of the most over-rated and misunderstood documents in history. It was not a charter of liberty for the common man (which is how the eighteenth-century American colonial rebels read it) but a list of sixty-three gripes by a self-interested clique intent on keeping the power they had illegally obtained. Even though John effectively tore up Magna Carta and the Pope, Innocent III, condemned it, the power of the aristocracy remained unbroken until the fifteenth century and contributed in no small measure to the Wars of the Roses. It was a kind of gang warfare, with rival families, Mafia-style, using their heavies to gain control.

As for Richard's new laws protecting English merchant interests from foreign competition, especially by the Italians, Skidmore calls this xenophobia. This is to put an altogether twenty-first century, European Union gloss on things. *Every* ruler protected his national interests where possible. In fact, when Vlad Dracula, ruling Wallachia in the 1460s, found that German merchants were swindling his own people (as the Italians were in London), he did not denounce them in parliament, he had them impaled in their hundreds.

What made Richard enemies during those months was his appointment of Northerners to key positions. Because of the nature of land-holding, it is possible to read too much into this; for instance, Edmund Hastings was made sheriff of Yorkshire, but he was not a Northerner born and bred. Likewise, Richard Ratcliffe became sheriff of Westmoreland for life (as it turned out, less than eighteen months), but he was not a Northerner either. Robert Brackenbury, however, from Selaby near Raby, was Constable of the Tower and Vice-Admiral of the Fleet. With Richard's creation of the Council of the North in 1484 (see Epilogue) it must have looked to southern lords in particular as if the writing was on the wall and they saw themselves as a vanishing species.

Through a mixture of sword-rattling and diplomacy, Richard came to a permanent peace treaty with Scotland which was, in Paul Murray Kendall's words 'ineluctably sliding towards Flodden Field and John Knox'. Flodden was a military disaster for the Scots in 1513 where their king, James IV, was killed. John Knox was the Presbyterian zealot whose fire and brimstone sermons did a great deal of harm to Anglo-Scottish relations. His bigotry is best exposed in his infamous 'monstrous regiment of women' tract, written in Geneva in 1558.

Richard came to an accord with the Duke of Brittany and used whatever spy network he possessed to keep an eye on Henry Tudor, who was busy ingratiating himself with the French court. Thanks to the complicity of Archbishop Rotherham of York, who betrayed the king's leniency to him by contacting Morton of Ely in exile, the French court continued to believe that Richard intended to make war again. There is no evidence that he did and, in fact, by 1485, could probably not afford to.

In the middle of April 1484, devastating news reached Richard and Anne, then at Nottingham, that their boy, Edward, had died at Middleham in their absence. Even the Croyland continuator, no fan of the king, wrote, 'You might have seen his father and mother in a state bordering on madness, by reason of their grief.' Because he was only eight, Edward is little more than a shadow in the story of Richard III. We glimpse him briefly at York during his investiture as Prince of Wales and, just as quickly, he disappears again. Because of that, several historians have supposed that the child was sickly (which may, of course, have been true of Richard too) and this explains his being carefully nurtured at Middleham for most of his life. Croyland talks of 'a short illness' and the consensus today is that it was tuberculosis. It was not protocol for a king and queen to attend the funerals even of their children (neither Henry VII nor his queen, Elizabeth of York, went to the burial of their eldest son, Arthur, for instance), but Richard and Anne seem to have dispensed with this, Richard going to Middleham for two days early in May. Nottingham, where the royal couple first heard the news, was known by Richard afterwards as his 'castle of care', the term coined in the epic poem *The Vision of Piers Plowman* by William Langland.

Oddly, we do not know where Edward was buried. The marble tomb, with heraldry and a child's effigy, in Sheriff Hutton church is believed today to be that of one of the Neville family and surely, a Prince of Wales, allowing for Richard's Northern affinities, would be buried in York Minster. Yet there is no record of the burial there, nor anywhere else. There are vague references in royal accounts of expenses referring to John Davney (Edward's treasurer at Middleham) 'for diverse provisions ... by his uncle for the expense of our dear son whom God pardon'. This carries a date of 22 July.

Sheriff Hutton church can be forgiven, perhaps, for insisting that this is indeed Edward's tomb. There is a great deal of Ricardian information in the church today, but the effigy is not helpful. It is clearly of a young boy, perhaps ten years old, in the civilian clothes of the period. Weathering of the alabaster means that the headgear *may* be a crown, but could equally be a hat. Above all, the animal usually shown at the feet of the deceased (as in the Rous Roll) is missing. Was it Richard's boar or the Nevilles' bear?

From all accounts, Anne never quite got over the death of Edward of Middleham. Her sister Isobel died young (poisoned, it was rumoured, by her husband Clarence) and it may be that her intermittent attendance with Richard on the royal progress was evidence of her own frailty. By Christmas 1484, the queen was ill and although she put a brave face on it, dressing sumptuously with Elizabeth of York, now free of sanctuary, all was far from happy in Richard's household. By the end of January 1485, she had been given weeks to live by her doctors and Richard was forbidden access to her bed in case her condition was catching. She died at Westminster on 16 March.

In the Shakespearean version of course, Richard has quietly had her murdered (Edward of Middleham does not appear in the play) and proceeds to court his niece,

Elizabeth of York. Gossips at Christmas 1484 noted how favoured in the festivities Elizabeth was and drew the wrong conclusions. So strong did the rumours become that Richard was forced to deliver a public proclamation that he had no intention of marrying Elizabeth. Not only would this have entailed another dispensation from the Pope (his second) but it would have countered the belief (now enshrined in an Act of Parliament) that Elizabeth was illegitimate and so unfit to be queen.

This denial by Richard is an extraordinary thing to do. No doubt he hoped that the king's word, given with the blessing of the Church, would be enough to scotch the rumours. In fact, by the summer of 1485, his ambassadors were in active negotiations with the courts of Spain and of Portugal to find a suitable princess for the king to marry. In either case, the might of those European countries (Spain especially) and the promise of a New World on the brink of exploration by their navigators would have been a huge coup in terms of England's empire.

In the event, none of this would come to fruition because the discontented lords, Lancastrians, Woodvilles, southerners and mercenaries, backed by French money, were sailing for Milford Haven, the 'white-livered runagate', Henry Tudor, at their head.

The basic problem for anyone expecting an invasion of England is where precisely the invaders would land. Coming from France as Henry was, anywhere along the south or east coast would be likely and the Duke of Norfolk, Robert Brackenbury and Francis Lovell were given orders to cover as many ports as possible. Historian Michael K. Jones has Richard unaccountably at his mother's tiny and run-down castle at Berkhamsted in Hertfordshire. 'Proud Cis', who would outlive all her sons, was becoming a religious recluse by this time, perhaps worn out by all the politics. All other accounts have Richard at Windsor on Ascension Day, Kenilworth in Warwickshire at Whitsun and Nottingham after that. Here, he waited for news.

In the event, Henry Tudor, with a tiny fleet, probably of cogs (merchant ships with fore and aft castles mounted with a handful of guns), sailed around the Lizard and landed in Mill Bay, near the hamlet of Milford Haven in Pembrokeshire. He was unopposed, but then again very few flocked to his banner, even though it was *y ddraig goch*, the red dragon. From that day, 7 August, Henry posed as a Welshman descended from the mythical kings of Wales, including Arthur. As propaganda went, it was puerile and nobody was buying it.

The invaders made their way cautiously north, perhaps hoping to meet up with Thomas, Lord Stanley, who was back in his Lancashire castle of Lathom, supposedly ready to support the king. At Mallwyd, however, Henry turned east. Wales had not risen for him as he had hoped (although numbers increased as he entered England) and his army commander, the redoubtable John de Vere, Earl of Oxford, probably counselled hitting Richard before the king was ready. He had faced the man before, though not directly, in the fog at Barnet and there may have been more than a hint of personal vendetta in this campaign.

Bosworth 137

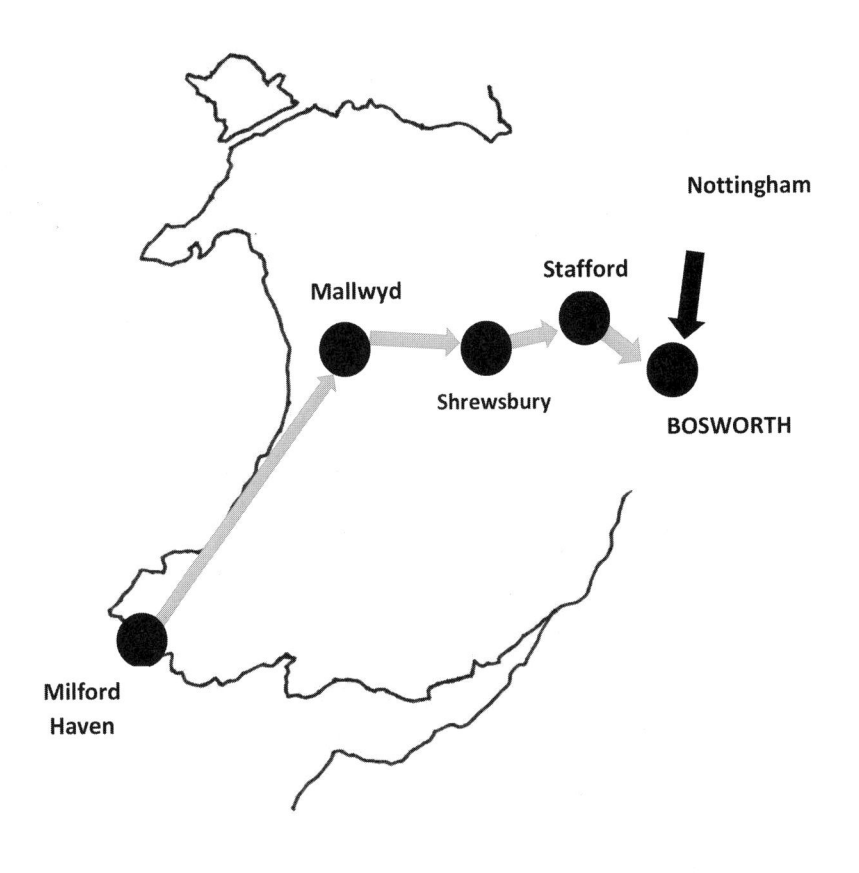

The routes of Richard and Henry in the Bosworth campaign, August 1485. Henry landed near Milford Haven, hoping to attract Welsh support, which never quite materialised. The only leading nobleman to join his standard was the Earl of Oxford.

Shrewsbury opened its gates to Henry, but that was to avoid damage to the town and loss of life. There were no flowery speeches or pageants and very few new recruits joined Tudor's troops. There is considerable evidence to show that Henry himself got lost in the country of the Welsh marches, to the extent that some of his men assumed that he had lost his nerve and fled. On the same day that Shrewsbury surrendered, Richard celebrated the Assumption of the Virgin Mary. Unbeknownst to him, William Stanley, Thomas's equally slippery brother, met Henry Tudor a day or so later at a camp near Stafford. Thomas Stanley marched out of Lathom and reached Lichfield on 17 August. The Stanleys kept their retinues separate from both the king and Tudor, but Richard had sensibly kept George, Lord Strange, Thomas Stanley's son, as a prisoner with him on the march, rather as Edward IV had hauled the hapless Henry VI all over the place.

On the evening of the 20th, Tudor reached Atherstone and may have set up his headquarters in Merevale, a Cistercian abbey nearby. Legend has it that the would-be usurper stayed at the Three Tuns Inn, but this tradition, like others found all over the country in this period, is probably the crafty story-telling of later pub landlords anxious to cash in on national events. That day, Richard left Nottingham with his large army and got to Leicester by nightfall. Norfolk and Brackenbury arrived later and the Earl of Northumberland, who had had farthest to come, the next day.

On 21 August, the king led his men out across Bow Bridge over the River Soar. Contrary to legend, he did not strike his armoured foot on the stonework, nor was there an old crone to hand to prophesy that his head would strike it when his corpse was brought back over the same bridge a day later. It is rattling good story telling, but it is not history.

All battlefields of the Middle Ages are shrouded in legend, mystery and confusion. Considering that it changed the dynasty that ruled the country forever, Bosworth is one of the worst chronicled. There are two ballads – *Bosworth Field* and *Lady Bessy* – which I think should be discounted because they are poetry written by men who were not there. Similarly, the war poetry of the Trenches (1914–18), while it is moving and dramatic, tells us very little except the mindset of a particular poet. Robert Fabyan covered the battle briefly in the *Great Chronicle of London*; Polydore Vergil, Henry VII's historian, dutifully gave the Tudor version; the Croyland continuator is as simpering as ever. Two European sources are intriguing, but cannot be trusted entirely; Jean Molinet was writing for the Burgundian court before 1490 and the French chronicler Philippe de Commines in the same period. Both seem quite well informed, but the oddity written by the Spanish writer Diego de Valera, based on an eyewitness account of Juan de Salazar who fought for Richard, is difficult to assess.

As Michael K. Jones points out, no one can grasp all aspects of a battle. Individuals only see what is immediately around them. Generals loitering at the rear cannot see what is happening at the front and generals in the front line – like Richard himself – were at grave risk. Armchair strategists today are criticized for simplifying things, with war games style manoeuvres and arrows on maps to mark troop directions. In reality, however, how else can it be done? It is the historian's job to make sense of the past, including complex battlefields.

Today's excellent visitor centre and its car park stand on Ambion Hill, traditionally said to be Richard's position at the start of the battle. The centre is one of the best in the country and provides details, visual interpretations and accurate copies

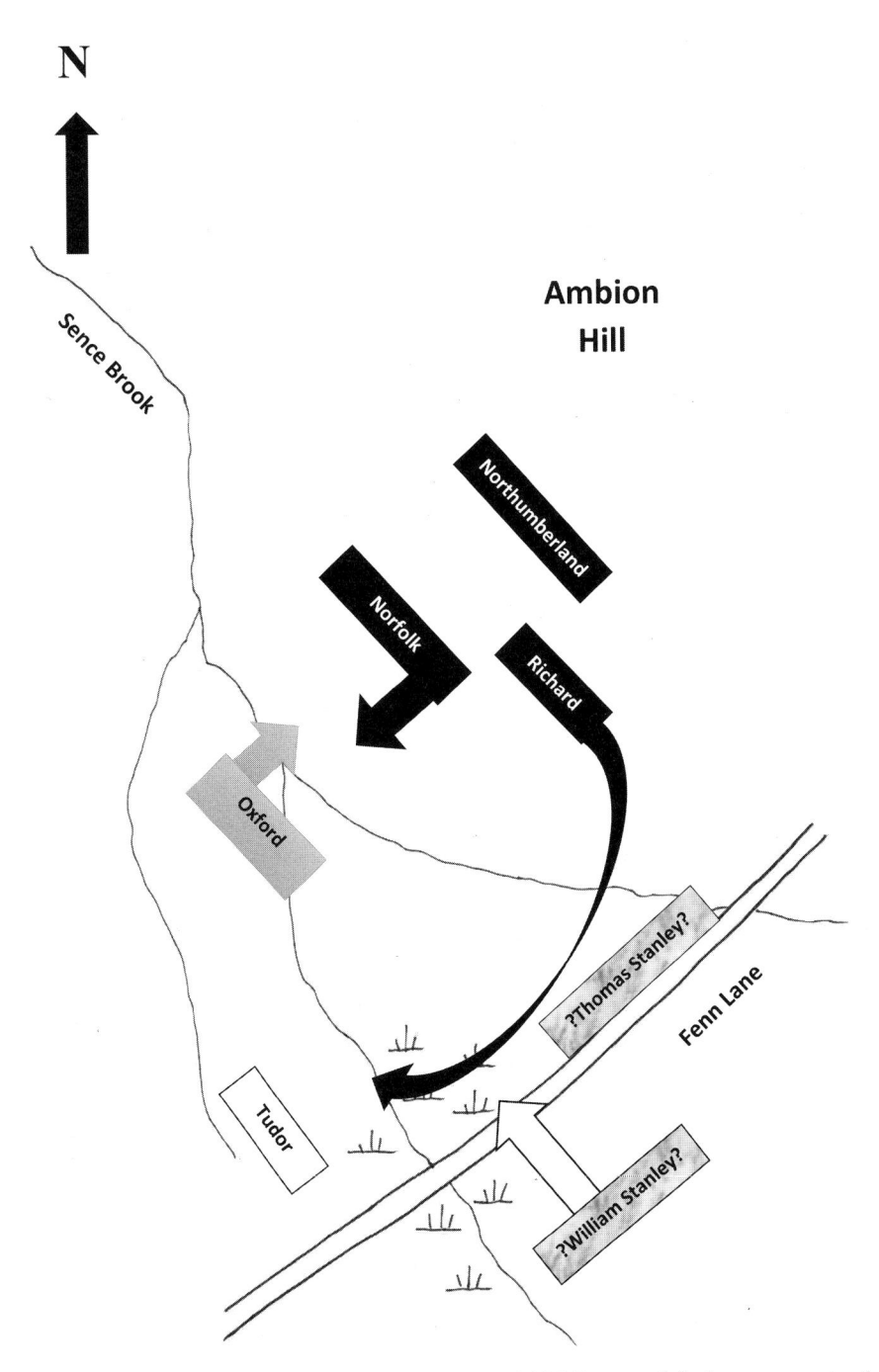

The last battle of the Plantagenets, Bosworth, August 1485. Bosworth is the most contentious battle of the Wars of the Roses, some historians believing that the fighting took place over a mile to the west of the diagram. I have stuck to the earlier belief that Ambion Hill was Richard's vantage point. The position of the Stanley brothers, must be conjectural in that no contemporary commentator specifies exactly where they were.

of artefacts almost wholly missing from other battle sites of the Roses. Richard had never had complete command of an army in battle before, but he had led a campaign in Scotland and had led the vanguard at both Barnet and Tewkesbury. Despite Michael K. Jones' objections, as a tactician of experience, the king would have sought high ground, both to give his attack its own downhill momentum and to give him a clear view of the battlefield. The height of Ambion Hill is deceptive. Driving up to the top, one is not aware of the steepness of the climb, but the view from the summit, where a modern sundial now stands with the banners of Richard and Henry floating in the wind, makes it clear that the king could easily see Tudor's position to the rear of his army.

Based largely on the compensation paid by Henry Tudor (in a very unusual example of largesse by the first Tudor, well known for counting the pennies), Jones suggests that the fighting took place just off the Roman road of Watling Street with Henry Tudor leaving Merevale at dawn on the 22nd, wheeling north-east past the village of Witherley and facing Richard who had taken up his position beyond the Sence Brook. It was for those villages – Merevale, Atherstone, Witherley and Mancetter that the new king forked out his compensation. Equally, of course, this compensation could have been made for depredations made by Henry's men on the night before the battle; how much damage can men do to open countryside, without hedges, during a two-hour engagement? If Jones is right, this gave Richard a relatively weak position, having to negotiate a stream to confront his enemy and does not help explain why the majority of the dead were buried at Derby Spring and Fenny Drayton, over a mile to the rear of Henry Tudor's position. There were also mass grave pits in the churchyard at Dadlington, but no detailed excavations have been carried out.

I cling to the older idea that Ambion Hill was Richard's starting point and the fighting took place at the bottom of this. The battlefield today of course, has modern roads, the hedges of enclosed fields and even a railway line destroying the topography that Richard and Henry would have known. Intriguingly, when I visited the field in December 2019, recent floods had blocked various roads and the area of the 1485 marsh is still waterlogged today.

The king's demon-haunted night, the lack of priests and the sacrament before battle began, no time for breakfast – all this was part of the blackening of Richard's reputation that Henry Tudor and his followers had begun months earlier. One account has Richard dashing to the church at Sutton Cheney to hear Mass. Why, when he had chaplains galore with his own army on Ambion Hill? Michael K. Jones rightly makes a great deal of Richard's solemn and unhurried preparation, parading holy crosses and the wearing of the crown of England.

Henry Tudor had never fought a battle in his life. Other than skirmishes at Pembroke Castle when he was a boy, he had never even seen one. He hung back with a cavalry bodyguard while the Earl of Oxford, commanding a single 'battle' advanced to the left of a marsh (still boggy in late August) up the hill towards Richard. Facing him was the royal vanguard commanded by the Duke of Norfolk, who may have received (but probably did not) the propaganda note earlier in the morning – 'Jack of Norfolk, be not too bold, for Dickon, thy master, is bought and sold'. Richard probably stayed behind with his cavalry, the knights of the body that Paul Murray Kendall calls his 'fellowship of steel' and behind him the rearguard of Northumberland, watching which way the Stanleys would jump.

Exactly where the brothers were is still a vexed question. Some authorities contend that they were between the armies of Richard and Henry, but this is unlikely, because they would have been caught up in the fighting and would have had to commit themselves earlier than they did.

Oxford had cavalry on his wings, led by Gilbert Talbot and John Savage. At least half the infantry was made up of Frenchmen and German mercenaries, fighting solely for pay with no interest in political causes or retribution. Other than the Stanleys, who clearly had their own agenda, Oxford was the only great nobleman to go over to Henry – as an avowed Lancastrian, this was to be expected.

Archers and handgunners opened the action as usual. Various commentators have explained Richard's defeat by implying that he was out of touch with modern tactics and that Tudor's mercenaries ran rings around him. This is nonsense. We know from financial accounts that Richard had spent heavily on serpentines (guns) in the weeks before Bosworth and his artillery would easily have outnumbered Tudor's ramshackle units. The fact was, however, that Oxford's men were doing well, pushing Norfolk's vanguard back up the hill while Gilbert and Savage smashed the wavering Yorkist line with their horsemen.

The battle had been raging for perhaps an hour when Richard came to his fatal decision to charge. Shakespeare says he rode White Surrey that day and although no contemporaries mention the horse's name, it has become synonymous with the king and Bosworth. It may be that the animal was actually White Syrie (Syria), an early imported Arab nearly two centuries before such stock was officially introduced to create the English thoroughbred. De Valera says that Richard put on his coat of arms – either a tabard of the lilies and leopards over his Gothic armour or a shield with the same device and signalled his fellowship to advance. He trotted forward, his standard bearer, Perceval Thirlwell, with the white boar at his elbow. Behind them rode Robert Brackenbury, James Harrington, Marmaduke Constable, Thomas Burgh, Ralph Assheton, William Catesby, Thomas Pilkington, John Sapcote and the Stafford brothers – the men of his Northern Council, the lords of the dales and moors.

White Surrey rose to the canter and the gallop. Richard had seen, in the hazy morning sun, the red dragon of Henry Tudor. The man was isolated and a target. Kill him and the venture was all over; the day was won. Some modern commentators have poured scorn on Richard's last charge – it was delivered by a man with a death wish, whose family was gone; a man heavy with the guilt of the murder of his nephews. Others have pointed to the old chestnut of a reckless cavalry charge delivered in the face of artillery and modern technology. But the artillery had already done its stuff earlier in the battle. The gunners, along with the archers, were now in the melee, hacking with swords and daggers. And, most importantly of all, the gamble *nearly* paid off. William Brandon was Henry Tudor's standard bearer and Richard drove his lance into the man's chest, killing him and sending the red dragon flying. John Cheney, a giant of a man and a champion jouster, tried to block the king, but Richard was faster and smashed him out of the saddle with his war-hammer. For Richard to have reached these men meant that he was within *feet* of Henry himself. The invader's followers were impressed in the telling and re-telling of the story; that Henry did not run at this critical moment. That, I believe, was because he was shell-shocked. A wall of steel was coming at him at upwards of twenty miles an hour, led by a man who had just dismissed in seconds two of his bodyguards. Henry Tudor was rooted to the spot with fear.

Now was the time for the Stanleys to strike. Wherever they had been positioned, they now closed in on Richard whose attack had been slowed by the marsh. Michael K. Jones conjectures that it was Henry Tudor's German *landsknechte* pikemen who saved his life and stopped the king, who would never have seen their deadly 18ft long pikes in action before. But of course, he had – Richard had had 1,500 Burgundian and German troops with him in Scotland; he must at least have seen them training, going through their paces. Had the Stanleys opted for Richard, of course, had the Duke of Northumberland not hung back on the hillside doing nothing until he retreated, the king would have won Bosworth and Henry Tudor would have been a very little footnote in history.

White Surrey went down and Richard with him. Even his detractors – and in the years ahead, there were many – were impressed with his death, 'fighting manfully in the thickest press of his enemies'. A number of men claimed to have killed him and with his loss, the fight went out of the Yorkists who limped away if they could, to fight another day.

We now know what all chroniclers and historians before 2012 could only guess at – how did Richard III actually die? From the evidence of the bones found in the famous Leicester car park, six of Richard's wounds were to the head. This tallies with similar bodies discovered at Towton, one of which is on display in the Bosworth centre. Wounds to the jaw imply that his helmet was hacked off. A puncture wound, either from a dagger or a poleaxe point brought him to his knees. Finally, the blade of a halberd sliced off the back of his skull, suggesting that, not unlike the Olivier film that frightened me all those years ago, the king was surrounded. Then someone finished him off with a sword thrust through the head.

The crown was picked up in the debris of battle, although no one at the time mentioned a thorn bush and it was placed in a rough ceremony by exhausted and shell-shocked men who could not believe their luck, on the head of the, no doubt, still shaking Henry Tudor. He was, illegally in every sense, the new king and he spent the rest of his life worrying about that.

He ordered, in a fit of spite, that Richard be stripped of his armour and slung naked over the back of a horse, his hands dangling down one side, his feet the other and they were roped together. A herald, either Blanc Sanglier or Norroy, led the animal from the field, but not before some anonymous footsoldier stabbed the king in the buttocks in what today is sometimes called by archaeologists an 'insult injury'.

Richard's corpse did indeed pass over Bow Bridge in Leicester and was displayed naked for two days on the riverbank nearby. Then he was buried, his hands still tied, without shroud or coffin, in a hastily dug hole that was too small for him, in the choir of Grey Friars. His head was forced to one side to fit.

Richard III was the last king of England to die in battle. He was also the last of the Plantagenets. In fact, until recently, and certainly when Olivier made his film, 1485 was considered the end of the Middle Ages and the beginning of the modern period. We now believe that such neat beginnings and endings do not work. Richard began many new ideas that the Tudors continued and they in turn, harked back to much that was Ricardian or pre-Ricardian, if only to promote the idea that they were not Johnny-come-latelies, but were part of an ancient tradition.

Chapter 14

Beneath Swaledale

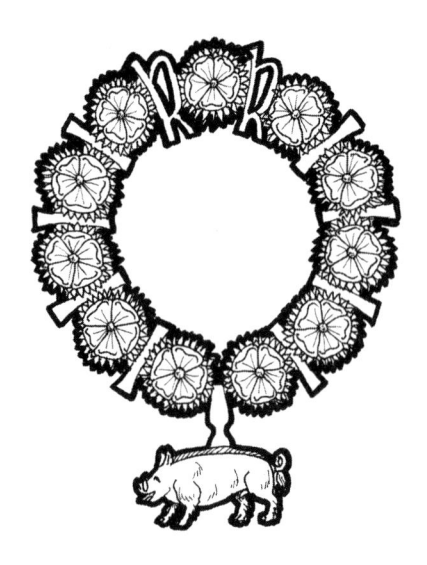

The Yorkist collar of the suns in splendour taken from a tomb destroyed by fire in 1997.

In March 2014, Philippa Langley, co-founder of the *Looking For Richard* project, wrote, 'We have searched for Richard and found him. It is now time to honour him.'

The wounds to Richard's skull told a clear picture of how he had died, but not who delivered the blows. A number of men claimed this 'honour' and one of them was knighted for his services by a grateful Henry VII. The position of the body implied that the ex-king had been buried quickly, perhaps in a grave prepared for somebody else and probably not by the priests of the Grey Friars, who would surely have placed him in a shroud and coffin with all the solemnity due to a king of England. Whereas Richard himself honoured his enemies – Hastings was buried in St George's Chapel, Windsor; Henry VI was disinterred from Chertsey and reburied in Westminster Abbey – Richard himself had no grave marker for ten years. In 1495, Henry VII reluctantly allowed a canopy, probably a simple table tomb, to be placed over the grave. There was no ceremonial reburial. Likewise, whereas Richard set up a chantry for the men killed at Towton, it was not until 1511 that a similar one was built near Bosworth, not by Henry Tudor, but his son, Henry VIII.

Based on the skeleton, the University of Leicester's experts concluded that the king was 'white [?], male, slender, gracile (almost feminine)'. Straight away, a new mythology was born. Richard may not have been a hunch-backed monster, but he was a little on the girly side! This ignores the fact of course that he had killed William Brandon single-handedly and battered John Cheney off his horse. We know from the disinterred body of Cheney that he stood 6ft 8in, a giant today as he was then! '[Richard's] natural height,' the experts continued, 'was 5 feet 8 inches (1.72m), a little taller than the average, but scoliosis … could have reduced this by up to a foot (0.3m).' This odd conclusion was challenged by modern sufferers from scoliosis who were able to prove, just by standing there, that this was nonsense. 'Scoliosis,' said the experts, 'may also have placed additional strain on his heart and lungs and caused him pain.' Depending on how we read various contemporary accounts of Richard's habit of gnawing his lip and playing with his rings and dagger-hilt, this may be true. Alternatively, they may be examples of anxiety, which would not be surprising in a man with Richard's lifestyle.

His diet was high-protein and expensive, with large quantities of seafood and this became more obvious in the last years of his life. In other words, he ate better as king than he did as Duke of Gloucester, which should not surprise us at all. He had the usual poor teeth of most people at the time and suffered from the roundworm parasite, again a very common condition.

Putting to rest the Tudor nonsense of deformity was an important step in the direction of truth, but those who had spent years trying to find the king's body now had to decide what to do with it.

Diehard Ricardians were in no doubt. As king, Richard should have been buried at Westminster Abbey or St George's Chapel. Had he won Bosworth, this is presumably what would have happened. Hard core supporters went further and said that the Tudor usurpers should be turfed out of their tombs (Henry VII especially) and Richard laid to rest in their place. The problem with that is; where would it end? Henry IV, who had usurped Richard II's crown and almost certainly had him murdered, would be another candidate. So would Edward IV, who had forced Henry VI off the throne and probably had him murdered too. Sensibilities and practicalities would not let this happen.

If not Westminster Abbey, how about York Minster? We know that Richard had had his son invested as Prince of Wales here, that he intended to set up a college of a hundred priests in its cloisters. And if he did not always see eye to eye with the Bishop, that was inevitable when churchmen got involved in politics and bishops of York, like kings, come and go.

What about any of Richard's Northern castles? Middleham, where his son was born and died and where he himself had lived twice during his life? Or Sheriff Hutton, where he had intended, perhaps, to establish the Council of the North (see Epilogue)? Or Sandal, where his father had been killed? If not the North, then how about Fotheringhay, the traditional burial place of the Plantagenets, their restored tombs still in place in the local church?

The media put forward all these ideas and more, as arguments raged back and forth, but the bottom line was that the funding provided to look for Richard in the first place was provided by the University of Leicester and they had the final say. And Leicester city could make much of the Richard legends – the Blue Boar inn, the spur and head striking Bow Bridge, the prophetic old crone. It was far from ideal for those who genuinely wanted to honour Richard, but it would have to do.

The king's re-interment, heavily covered by the media, took place in March 2015. A handsome booklet was produced which charted the events. Called 'the last journey of the last Plantagenet', the funeral cortege left the university buildings at 11am on Sunday, the 22nd and reached Fenn Lance Farm near the village of Stoke Golding at 1.05pm. In the fields here a number of finds have recently been discovered, including, in 2009, the silver-gilt boar badge that almost certainly belonged to one of the men charging behind Richard at Bosworth. Here too is Crown Hill, where it is likely that Henry Tudor was unofficially crowned with the circlet banged off Richard's helmet. The procession then moved to Dadlington, burial place of many of the fallen in battle and on to Sutton Cheney, where Richard may have camped on the previous night.

A service was held by the Bishop of Leicester for invited guests and the cortege moved on to Market Bosworth by mid-afternoon. From there, the procession followed what must have been Richard's approximate route out of Leicester on 21 August 1485, through Newbold Verdon and Desford to Bow Bridge in the city itself. Here, on the brightly painted Victorian replacement of the bridge that Richard would have known, a short ceremony was held during which the coffin, draped in the royal arms of the fifteenth century, was transferred to a horse-drawn hearse. Two attendants, wearing replica plate armour of the 1480s, rode behind it.

Inside the city, changed beyond all recognition since Richard's day, the cortege followed a rough circle, the streets lined with Yorkist supporters, the historically minded and the just plain curious. It was a rather dull day, the 'clouds that lowered' on Richard's house, lowering still. It followed the High Street, then turned at Gallowtree Gate, along Halford Street and back onto Belvoir Street before completing the circle along Pocklington's Walk to the Richard III Centre at St Martin's, across the square from the cathedral. All this was filmed by various television camera crews and was shown on giant screens at Jubilee Square and the Church Tower in the city.

The cathedral of St Martin's was originally a Norman church and the king's remains lay less than 100 yards away in the Grey Friars for over 500 years. From 1982, a memorial tablet to Richard stood in the chancel which, on that Sunday, would be replaced by the new tomb. The official reception of the body was marked in the evening by a service of compline, one of the trickier problems for the organizers. Richard, of course, was Catholic, as was the whole of Europe in 1485 and, in Richard's case, a particularly devout one. Yet, here he was, being re-buried in an Anglican cathedral. Experts pointed out that the king himself once owned a copy of an English Bible, but that did not remotely make him a Lollard, as the first Protestants were known in England. The powers that be decided that since the Anglican faith is now the official denomination of the state, it was right and proper for the king to be buried in that particular piece of consecrated ground. Compline was a nod in the direction of fifteenth-century Catholicism.

For three days, Richard's coffin, decorated with heraldry and white roses, stood above ground while visitors came to pay their respects. Five hundred and thirty years earlier, their ancestors may have stood by Bow Bridge gawping at the king's naked body on the banks of the Soar, so that Henry Tudor could be sure that everybody knew that his enemy was really dead.

Various services were held in the cathedral on Monday, Tuesday and Wednesday and the re-interment ceremony took place in the late morning of Thursday, 26 March. The tomb, a black slab bearing Richard's name and dates, along with the royal coat of arms and topped by a slab of Swaledale marble from Yorkshire was displayed to the public the next day and on the Friday there was a special peal of bells rung for Richard III.

Leicester was determined to capitalize on the king while affording him what dignity it could. The cathedral was festooned with flowers all week and on Friday, the 27th, 8,000 flames were lit on candles around the cathedral gardens and Jubilee Square, with fireworks exploding into the night sky in the form of a crown over the Richard III Centre. Saturday, the 21st was King Richard III Day, a family friendly hands-on display, complete with talks on the king and the finding of his body. There was a Ricardian art exhibition at the Guildhall and walking tours of the city's historic landmarks. Philippa Langley spoke about the *Looking For Richard* project and a number of local drama groups got involved too. The Tyrsby Players staged a trial of Richard at the Jewry Wall Museum, in which the murder of the princes was the charge. In nearby Newbold Verdon, there was a fifteenth-century banquet and Medieval dancing, reflecting the gaiety, if not of Richard's court, certainly of his brother Edward's.

Along the procession route, local schoolchildren formed guards of honour and played music. Re-enactors were not forgotten either. Throughout the week it was possible to meet Sir Robert and Lady Chamberlain, staunch Yorkists who remained loyal to Richard to the end. There were falconry displays, arms and armour talks, book signings (archaeologist Richard Buckley with his hot-off-the-press *The King Under the Car Park*) and a literary conference discussing the complexities of writing about *Richard and His Times* (I wish I had been there!).

Dr Nicole Fayard talked about the *'Other' Richards*, the fictionalised accounts of the man that have appeared over the centuries and *Richard III in Fact and Fiction – who should we believe*? starred many of the people whose works appear in the bibliography of this book – David Baldwin, John Ashdown-Hill, Peter Hammond, Joanna Hickman and Alison Weir.

They showed Ian McKellen's 1995 filmed version of the Shakespeare play which is a fascinating take on the original. Set in a Fascist 1930s, the white boar badge is manipulated into a swastika. McKellen has Hitler hair and a toothbrush moustache. The Woodvilles are played by Americans, all Hollywood brashness and vulgarity. Most of the fighting at Bosworth takes place in the empty shell of Battersea Power Station. When I saw this version in the cinema, forty years on from my visit to Olivier's Richard at the old Majestic in Macclesfield, I wondered how McKellen was going to deal with the 'A horse! A horse!' bit in a 1930s world of tanks and bombers. The answer was brilliant – or corny – take your pick! At the height of the battle, his jeep breaks down, so naturally, he calls for his four-legged friend instead – the old ways are best!

I am sorry that I missed all the events of this week in Leicester, but the talk I would most like to have heard was that delivered by Dr Philip Shaw in the Central Library. Called *The King's Speech*, it dealt with the 'dialect and written practices of Richard III'. How much closer can we get to the real man than to understand exactly what he *sounded* like?

A block of Swaledale marble and, over the body itself, a sprinkling of soil from Middleham. In the end, these were the only links with his beloved North that Richard III was allowed.

'Now,' as US Secretary of State Edwin Stanton said in 1865 of another murdered leader, Abraham Lincoln, 'he belongs to the angels.'

Epilogue

The Angel of the North?

Arms of John de la Pole, Richard's heir and leader of the Council of the North, Richard's legacy which lasted for a century and a half.

'Richard,' says historian Amy Licence, 'is well known for having been a Northerner.' This simple line raises all sorts of questions, not only about Richard Plantagenet himself but about what 'the North' actually was. Today, we are used to vague notions of the North/South divide, in which the South is usually seen as rich, 'posh' and 'soft' by the North and the North condemned as rough, poor and uncivilized by the South. There have been various attempts by recent governments to redress the economic imbalance, in an effort to encourage London businesses northward. The problem with these realignments is that they do not always make sense; the transference of the Tower of London armouries, for instance, to Leeds was a particularly peculiar move in some people's eyes. The North became the nation's industrial power house in terms of textiles, coal, iron and steel and shipbuilding in the eighteenth and nineteenth centuries, but it never made armour. Much of this was imported anyway, from Spain, Italy and Germany; the only English armoury was based at Greenwich in London under Henry VIII.

In the fifteenth century, the North was perceived as a wild and dangerous place. At a time when regional dialects were far stronger than today, Northerners spoke what was virtually a foreign language. Margaret of Anjou's Lancastrians in 1455 and Richard's Yorkists, brought south in the disturbed summer of 1483, would have been incomprehensible to Londoners.

What makes Richard a Northerner is his deliberate decision to live and work north of the River Trent. The Plantagenets, like all kings of England, were peripatetic; they moved from royal castle to royal castle and foisted themselves on other people's castles and monasteries from time to time, at no expense (it must be noted) to themselves. London was England's capital from 1066, replacing Winchester, and although the Plantagenets had residences in the Tower, Windsor and Placentia, these were strung along the Thames and not focused in one place. 'The government' was wherever the king was. So Henry VI, Edward IV and Richard III all travelled extensively and took their courts with them, including the great seals of office, a sizeable retinue of armed retainers and half the contents of the Treasury, including the Crown jewels. They called councils and parliaments wherever they went – we have come across them at Coventry and Carlisle in this book – in a way that would be unthinkable today.

But Richard was different. When he was given various Neville lands in 1471 and added more by marrying Anne three years later, he effectively shifted his power base to the north of the Trent. True, he held Anne's own birthplace of Warwick and other acres south of the river, but increasingly his focus became Middleham, Sheriff Hutton, York and Sandal. If things had gone differently in 1483, if Richard had not become king at all, there is every reason to believe that he would have made the North his permanent home, a palatinate alongside, but loyal to, his brother Edward in the South.

The most obvious evidence for this is Richard's creation of the Council of the North. This began in the 1470s out of Richard's genuine concern for 'good governance' of the people he now found himself responsible for. He heard petitions from high and low alike, he played Solomon in an enormous variety of disputes. He used his quite considerable knowledge of the law to carry out fair arbitration that won hearts and minds. The York city records contain the names of some of the men who were members of this Council: Baron Greystoke; Francis Lovell (an honorary Northerner!); Lord Scrope of Bolton and Lord Scrope of Masham; Sir William Parre; Sir James Harrington; Sir Richard Nele; the lawyers Miles Metcalfe and Richard Pygott as well as justices of Assize for the Northern circuit. James Tyrell, Richard Ratcliffe and Ralph Assheton were on hand to talk to key people on behalf of the duke and to take swift action when necessary. John Kendall, Richard's secretary, wrote down all the details.

Throughout the North, as elsewhere, ordinary people were at the mercy of unscrupulous landlords who had complete powers of eviction. In an illiterate age, 'paperwork' did not exist for the common man and most tenants held land by ancient custom and precedent that was not written down anywhere. The Council of the North stepped in in these situations, carrying out the fair government that in theory went hand in hand with landholding privilege. Richard was Duke of Gloucester and held half a dozen other titles too, but on his own initiatives and via the Council, he gained the reputation of a fair lord. From 1484 onwards, Richard, now king, began to favour Sheriff Hutton rather than Middleham or Sandal, as the headquarters of the Council. He actually set the organization up at York in July of that year.

As Richard assumed the duties of king, inevitably his personal control of the Council lessened and he appointed John de la Pole, Earl of Lincoln, his heir on the death of Edward of Middleham, as Lord President '*per consilium regis*' (for the Council of the King). Even so, it was Richard's instructions that were followed to the letter and Lincoln seems to have been as loyal to him as Richard had been to Edward IV. The Council promoted harmony and peace after so many years of unquiet. It issued subpoenas, enforcing attendance at court, delivered summations and punished where necessary.

Clarence's son, the Earl of Warwick, though still a boy, joined the Council. This, as we have seen, was the normal pattern for the sons of the aristocracy and good practice for the future. The fact that Henry VII imprisoned the boy and eventually executed him on flimsy grounds does not detract from what might have been. Lincoln's brother-in-law, Lord Morley, joined too and if all this smacks of nepotism today, it was how things worked in the fifteenth century. The tragedy is that family ties all too often meant nothing at all in terms of loyalty. In many ways, the most important member of the Council was Henry Percy, the Earl of Northumberland. As Lord of the North, Richard had to keep this man sweet or overthrow him. The latter course would mean *another* civil war north of the Trent and Richard wisely avoided that, giving powers and deference to Percy when appropriate. Northumberland retained the Warden-Generalship of the Scottish Marches and the captaincy of Berwick (even though it was Richard who would actually take the place for him in 1482). Percy was Sheriff of Northumberland for life and his income from his northern estates rivalled those of Gloucester. Even so, Percy was a petulant and tricky ally. While quite prepared to preside over the execution of Rivers, Grey and Vaughan at Pontefract in 1483, his hanging back off the field of battle at Bosworth was every bit as much an act of treachery as the work of the Stanleys.

Richard's generosity is abundant everywhere. In terms of Northerners, he gave titles and huge cash payments to Richard Ratcliffe, Thomas Lord Stanley, Sir John Conyers, Sir Richard Tunstall and Sir Thomas Burgh. Robert Brackenbury was given grants equalling an income of £400 (almost £7 million today) a year. John Kendall got £450 a year and became a King's Councillor. And while, inevitably, it is the great and famous whose details have survived, it is highly likely that Richard was also giving promotion, power and handouts to much more lowly men from the North. Seven members of the Metcalfe family from Wensleydale received annuities, for example.

All this, of course, was noted with contempt by the Croyland continuator (whoever he was, he was not from the North!); not only was Richard spending money hand-over-fist, he was giving it to men from north of the Trent. Historian Anthony

Cheetham goes further, perhaps, in explaining the continuator's annoyance – '[The Council] replaced the King's age-old dependence on feudal chieftains with a modern, streamlined replica of the parent Council at Westminster.' The Tudors, although little concerned with the North under Henry VII, continued the tradition.

When Richard became king, he was keen to keep the Council as it was and not let it fall into Northumberland's hands. The king kept the title of Warden of the West March, based in Carlisle, with Lord Dacre as his number two.

Under the Tudors, things changed. Northumberland was given his head, at least until rebels killed him, and he became, briefly, Lord of the North. Henry VIII had no interest in shires far from his own sphere, but he reconstituted the Council in 1525 under nominal control of his illegitimate son Henry Fitzroy. It became a royal institution five years later, but was sharply reduced in status after it failed to prevent the rising known as the Pilgrimage of Grace, a general Northern uprising against Henry VIII's religious policies and dissolution of the monasteries.

So dangerous had the North become by Elizabeth's reign, culminating in the Rebellion of the North, again on religious grounds, in 1569, that the queen's cousin, Lord Huntingdon, was put in charge of it and after him, Lord Burghley. In 1628, Charles I put his unpopular minister Thomas Wentworth, Earl of Strafford, in control. He was attainted and executed in 1641. The Long Parliament, a group of smug, self-satisfied Puritans finally turfed out by Oliver Cromwell, abolished the Council soon afterwards, but by then the country was so hopelessly divided in a civil war infinitely more pernicious than the Wars of the Roses and the Council had perhaps become an irrelevance.

Sheriff Hutton may have been intended as the Council's base, but it may never have met there. At Sandal, however, a new tower, complete with bakehouse and brewhouse, was built in October 1484 and 2,000 marks a year were set aside for the group, whose treasurer was, by then, John Davney. The regulations of the Council were set out by Richard in July of that year. Personal interests were to be taken into account; if a Council member's own estates were involved, he could not take part in discussions or decisions. The Council had to meet quarterly, at York or elsewhere as dictated and Lincoln had to be present, along with at least two justices of the peace. A particular target was 'all riots, forcible entries, distress takings, variance, debates and other misbehaviours against our laws and peace'. Punishment for many crimes was imprisonment – 'for we will that our castles be our gaol'. The Council's job was to put down insurrection, which is probably why Henry VIII was incensed about the failure to deal with the Pilgrimage of Grace. It had the right to arbitrate in property disputes and all decisions were officially and automatically in the king's name. The fact that there was no similar organization set up in either Wales or Ireland (where the Yorkists were popular) may simply be that Richard ran out of time. Alternatively, he may only have been interested in the North itself.

We know that Richard gave grants, jobs and other handouts to the Church and to individuals across the North. He also employed huge numbers of people, providing for the workers and their families, in the various castles he lived in. Nowhere is this more obvious than at Middleham, where the Duke of Gloucester created two markets in the town and an annual fair. In a rural community prone to long winters and bad weather, sheep farming and simple crop rotation had their limitations. By employing staff, as cooks, scullions, grooms and general labourers, Richard was giving locals a vital lifeline.

The accounts of Middleham from August 1471 to October 1473 give a useful example. Richard Conyers was the accountant and the figures relate to forty-nine men and one woman in the duke's service. Each of them held an indenture (a duplicate document with a tooth-like edge, the other half held by Richard) as proof of their contract. Payment was made twice a year, at Easter and Michaelmas, and the jobs were for life, removing the threat of being a 'masterless man' which haunted thousands before and after Richard's time. John Conyers, one of four family members at Middleham, received an annual fee of £20 (around £16,500 today). He was a knight, but the squire Thomas Turnstall received £33 6s 8d (£28,000 today). The lowest paid was Richard Hardwyk, for whom no rank is listed, on £1 6s 8d. The only woman in the list is Alice Burgh, gentlewoman, whose brother William worked at Middleham too. She received £6 13s 4d (£5,500), the same as her brother (feminists, please note!), but her role is unclear. She had been a nurse to Prince Edward, but Philip Hammond conjectures that she may also have been the mother of one of Richard's illegitimate children.

William Burgh's indenture contract has survived and he was duty bound 'well and convenably [appropriately] horsed and harnessed [in armour] shall be ready to ride, come and go with, toward and for the said Duke [Gloucester] as well in time of peace as of war'. The income was to come from the farms of Middleham and Sleightholme nearby and Richard was entitled to a third of any loot Burgh obtained during periods of warfare. This was 1474, only three years after Barnet and Tewkesbury and nobody imagined such a thing in England as a permanent and lasting peace.

We should be wary of seeing Richard as a modern ruler, a liberal anxious to engage in democracy and give power to his people. He was a man of his times, deeply religious, fiercely loyal, something of a Puritan perhaps before society had invented Puritans. He was a risk taker, as all men were in the risky fifteenth century. He was a scholar and a soldier, a husband, a father, a brother, a duke and a king. He had no hesitation in ordering the execution of enemies – men like him were, after all, role models for Machiavelli's *The Prince* written in 1515. Richard was brought up in a treacherous, dysfunctional family from which, in the end, there was no escape.

The North loved him. At Easter time in the year after Bosworth, Francis Lovell and the Earl of Lincoln raised a rebellion in the North. With a deep irony,

Henry VII sent the Earl of Northumberland to put it down. This rising fizzled out, the citizens of York being as difficult as possible and refusing to appoint to their city any of the men suggested by the new king. Three years later, however, faced with a punishing new tax, the men of Yorkshire went on the rampage; the 'rude and rustical people' as Henry called them. Again, Northumberland was ordered to sort them out, but many of his retinue deserted him at Thirsk as he had deserted Richard four years earlier. He was dragged from his horse and hacked to death. Most people north of the Trent cheered; even Henry VII reinstituted the Council of the North and took a whopping £10,000 (at least £7 million today) from Northumberland's estate. Richard was avenged. William Stanley, too, fell from grace. While his brother Thomas became Earl of Derby, William, who had, after all, saved Henry Tudor's life at Bosworth, was accused of plotting treason on behalf of the pretender Perkin Warbeck and was beheaded on 5 February 1495.

As for Henry himself, the North was unimpressed. York put on pageants for him, going through the motions in a way they would not have dreamt of for Richard. For Gloucester and his wife, all the stops were pulled out, everybody cheered. Henry was, in Paul Murray Kendall's words, 'the unadventurous adventurer'. His one claim to fame was perhaps giving rise to Elizabeth, the 'Gloriana' who presided over a golden age which, in itself, has recently come under scrutiny to reveal a far more tarnished side. 'Seldom has a man', Kendall writes, 'or a monarch, been given so much credit for being somebody's grandfather.'

Kendall paints a romantic picture of the Duke of Gloucester, lean, slight, perpetually worried as he portrays him, riding alone in the Dales, galloping across the moors. The North is the place of big skies, of glorious beauty and, after the bustle in London, and even the scurry of York and Middleham, it is a place of peace. The scars of Victorian industry, so exciting in its own day and so unplanned, are fading now. The sheep graze still, as they did in Richard's day over the graves of the men who fought and died for him.

This was the land he loved. *This* was the land he made his own.

Appendix I
Richard's Places in the North

Although Richard III held estates all over England and, as king, could be said to hold Calais as well, this section concentrates on his properties north of the Trent. It takes a feat of imagination now to picture the North as it would have been in Richard's day. Forget the cities and towns, ignore the motorways. Follow the 'B' roads and a little of what Richard knew becomes visible. In his day, even major towns were tiny by comparison with their modern counterparts. On the other hand, once important centres like Selaby, the birthplace of Robert Brackenbury or Coverham Abbey, perhaps the last resting place of Edward of Middleham, have all but disappeared.

There were virtually no hedges in Richard's North and far less arable land than there is today. There was no tarmac, just mud roads frozen to ice in winter and awash with floods after rain. Signposts were non-existent and no spotter-planes ever flew over battlefields!

The following is an alphabetical list.

Barnard Castle

Eleventh-century castle ruins at the heart of the town overlooking the River Tees. Originally the property of the Balliol family who became kings of Scotland, it passed to Richard as part of the Neville estate forfeited in 1471. Buildings in the Inner Ward, the Round Tower and the Mortham Tower were all enlarged and improved during his tenure as lord of the estate. The boar, which was his badge, can still be seen on the lintel of a window in the great chamber. The Brackenbury Tower, a twelfth-century addition near the gateway, is named after Sir Robert Brackenbury who was Constable of the Tower of London, as well as Barnard Castle, and died with Richard at Bosworth.

Richard intended to set up a college for priests here, but the plan seems to have been abandoned, perhaps in favour of York. The town's church, St Mary's, has Ricardian links too, including another carved boar and stone heads of Richard and Edward IV.

Excellent guidebook and friendly staff make this a worthwhile place to visit and the vicar is especially helpful.
English Heritage
Phone: 01833 638212
Website: www.english-heritage.org.uk/visit/places/barnard-castle

Berwick-on-Tweed

Town at the mouth of the River Tweed, disputed by England and Scotland. Richard laid siege to it in his Scots campaign of 1482, although fighting was minimal. Ever since then, Berwick has been resolutely English. The current town fortifications, with arrowhead bastions and flanking-fire walls were not there in Richard's day, but are Elizabethan earthworks built after a neutrality agreement between England and Scotland in 1551. At the time, Richard was criticized for not ransacking the town, which was the usual perk an attacking commander gave to his men.

Website: www.visitnorthumberland.com/berwick-upon-tweed

Bowes Castle

Eleventh-century castle ruins built by a nephew of Alan Rufus, who also owned Middleham, Richmond and Sheriff Hutton as the Honour of Richmond. The castle stood on the site of a Roman fort and passed to Richard as part of the Neville estates in 1471. The building seems to have been run down by the 1320s and there is little evidence of re-building.

By comparison with other northern castles, Bowes is a little disappointing. Run by English Heritage with an excellent guidebook, it is an unmanned site for visitors to wander at their will.

No phone number as it is unmanned, free entry during 'reasonable daylight hours'. Website: www.english-heritage.org.uk/visit/places/bowes-castle

Carlisle

Town at the confluence of the Rivers Calder, Petteril and Eden, the place was Luguvallium under the Romans towards the western end of Hadrian's Wall. There was a Norman castle here in the 1080s which has been enlarged and extended. Edward I held two parliaments in the town and it became Richard's in connection with his role as Warden of the Western Marches under his brother Edward in the 1470s.

Website: https://www.visitcumbria.com/car/carlisle

Conisbrough

Eleventh-century castle ruins on the site of a Saxon burgh. It was originally held by the Earl of Surrey and Sussex, William de Warenne, to protect the Don Valley.

It became a Plantagenet fortress in the twelfth century and was perhaps the birthplace of Richard of York, Richard's father, in 1411.

Owned and run by English Heritage with an excellent guidebook.

Website: www.english-heritage.org.uk/visit/places/conisbrough-castle.

Coverham

Abbey and parish church near Middleham and *very* difficult to find via narrow, country lanes. It was a Praemonstratensian building belonging to the monastic Order of the White Canons, founded elsewhere in 1190 and set up at Coverham twenty years later. It was often attacked by the Scots on their raids into northern England and may conceivably be the burial place of Richard's son, Edward of Middleham. The abbey was dissolved along with hundreds of others by Henry VIII in 1536 and is now on private land, difficult to see and impossible to reach.

Durham

City on the River Wear founded, according to tradition, by St Cuthbert, one of Richard's favourite Northern saints. A castle was built there by the Normans, but it was as a religious centre founded by the monks of Lindisfarne that Dunelm (Durham) became famous. The tombs of Cuthbert and Bede attracted pilgrims from all over the world and the cathedral's bishops were appointed by 'Divine Providence' as opposed to 'Divine Permission'. Their powers were immense, from raising armies to striking their own coins, and they carried the title of prince bishops. William Dudley was bishop during Richard's Lordship of the North, replaced by John Sherwood in the first year of his reign.

The cathedral and city are bursting with historical sites and references and are a tangible reminder of the power of the Medieval Church.

Website: www.thisisdurham.com

Edinburgh

Capital of Scotland on the Firth of Forth. Originally Din Eidyn, the stronghold of the Celtic Gododdyn tribe, it was a royal fortress from the twelfth century, and James III, Richard's contemporary, called it 'the principal burgh of our kingdom'. The castle was formidable, built on its massive granite formation and when Richard entered the city with an army in 1482, the citizens surrendered, but the castle did not. As with Berwick, he was criticized for not destroying the place, but sixty years later, Henry VIII's troops showed no such mercy. The orders ran in 1544:

> 'Put all to fire and sword, burn Edinburgh, so razed and defaced when you have sacked and gotten what ye can of it, as there may remains forever a perpetual memory of the vengeance of God lightened upon [them] for their falsehood and disloyalty.'

Most Englishmen felt the same in 1482.

Edinburgh has a lot more to recommend it today!

Website: www.edinburgh.org

Gainsborough

Lincolnshire town on the Trent at the southern limit of the North as it was understood in Richard's day and technically the last venue of the royal progress he undertook in the summer of 1483. 'The capital that never was', it was the headquarters of Cnut, the Viking king of England, during his raids in 1013–16. Thomas Burgh was Lord of the Manor from 1455 and, in one of the possibly spurious places linked with Richard, he may have stayed in the Old Hall which still stands.

Website: www.vistoruk.com/gainsborough

Middleham

Castle in Wensleydale which was the favourite residence of both Richard Neville, Earl of Warwick and Richard III. A settlement since Roman times, the original castle, close to the existing one, was built by Alan Rufus and is today called William's Hill. The stone version was begun in 1190 and, under the Nevilles and Richard, it was converted from a fortress to a comfortable family home.

Richard spent part of his teenaged years here and it was the home of the duke and his wife, Anne (the Earl of Warwick's daughter). Their son, Edward, was born and died in the castle, but is buried elsewhere. The town had an annual fair on St Alkelda's Day and two market places. The Middleham Jewel and various artefacts date from Richard's residence at the castle, but the 1996 statue to the king in the keep has not found general favour. Sculptor Linda Thompson explained the heraldic significance of the boar at Richard's feet and the suns and roses of York, as well as the demon and basilisk in a nod to Shakespeare. She sums up her explanation with 'the sculpture illustrates the heavy burden which history has heaped upon this Northern king'. Edward IV set up a leper colony nearby in fields now used by the horses of the Middleham Trainers' Association.

The castle is run by English Heritage with friendly staff and an excellent guidebook, but car parking in the town can be difficult and the roads are narrow.

Website: www.english-heritage.org.uk/visit/places/middleham-castle

Newark

Castle and town on the River Trent in Nottinghamshire, the traditional boundary of North and South in Medieval England. Henry I gave a charter to the bishop of Lincoln to build a castle on the site of an earlier settlement – 'Know ye that I have granted to Alexander, Bishop of Lincoln, that he may make a ditch and rampart of his fishpond of Niwerc upon the Fosseway …' There was a mint here in the twelfth century and King John ate his last meal at the castle before dying of dysentery.

A re-enactment group regularly displays the moves of the battle of Stoke Field, fought nearby two years after Bosworth, in which Richard's heir, John de la Pole, was killed and from which his supporter Francis, Viscount Lovell, disappeared for ever. The casualties at Stoke were probably higher than at Bosworth, but it will remain forever the forgotten battle.

Website: www.visit-newark.co.uk

Nottingham Castle

Cathedral town overlooking the River Leen which, in Celtic times, was called Tig Guocobauc, the place of caves, which still riddle the sandstone outcrop on which the castle was built in 1068. The markets and walls followed in the next two centuries to make Nottingham a thriving centre of textiles and lacemaking. Forever associated with the semi-mythical outlaw Robin Hood and the corrupt local government of the county sheriff, by Richard's day, the town had a reputation for religious sculptures made from alabaster and was granted self-government in 1449. The castle was exempt from this and it was here that Richard learnt of the death of his son, Edward, in spring 1484. After that, he referred to Nottingham as his 'castle of care'. It was from here that he rode out on the Bosworth campaign.

The castle is run by Nottingham City Council.

Website: www.nottinghamcastle.org.uk

Penrith

Castle and town in Cumberland (today's Cumbria) which featured prominently in the defences of the Western Marches, of which Richard was lord. A Roman fort, Vareda, stood nearby, guarding the legionary road between Carlisle and Manchester.

The castle was a late development, built between 1399 and 1470 and so would only just have been completed when Richard was Lord of the North. Its main purpose was to repel raids by the Scots. Ralph Neville of Raby built the major towers and the Penrith estates netted the family about £350 (£2.3 million today) a year. Richard used the castle as a base for his 1482 campaign against the Scots and his lordship included the Forest of Cumberland.

Website: www.english-heritage.org.uk/visit/places/penrith-castle

Pontefract

Castle and town in West Yorkshire, begun in 1070 by Ilbert de Lacy. It passed through a number of hands before John of Gaunt, Duke of Lancaster, enlarged and improved it in the 1350s. Richard II was murdered here, possibly in the underground cellars still open to the public on certain days and, under Richard III's orders, Rivers, Gray and Vaughan, adherents of the Woodvilles, were executed here. Before that, Richard's father, Richard of York, and his brother, Edmund of Rutland, were buried, possibly in the town.

The castle has an excellent café and shop with friendly staff and a good guide book, run by Wakefield Museums and Castles.

Website: www.pontefractcastle.co.uk

Raby Castle

Castle in today's County Durham, held by the Neville family from the thirteenth century. Ralph Neville was the first Baron Raby and the castle was enlarged and fortified by subsequent generations. Cecily Neville, 'Proud Cis' who was Richard's mother, was born here in 1415. Surviving Medieval parts of the castle are the servants' hall and the old kitchen, built in 1360 and the chapel (1364-67) which, like Ludlow, was once separate from the rest of the building. The portrait of Cecily Neville dates from restoration in 1901.

Today renowned for its classical art collection, Raby is in the private hands of the Vane family, Barons Barnard, who are descended from the Nevilles. It is open to the public and has extensive grounds, a good guidebook and tearoom in the old stable block.

Website: www.raby.co.uk/raby-castle

Richmond

Richmond stands on the left bank of the River Swale, north-west of York. St Mary's church below the castle on the steep, cobbled hill, is today the regimental museum of the Green Howards. The centre of the honour of Richmond, both town and castle came to prominence as a result of Henry Tudor, Earl of Richmond, winning at Bosworth in August 1485 and being crowned Henry VII.

The castle was originally Norman, but much of the later stonework dates from the reign of Henry I who also adapted Scarborough, Bowes and Newcastle. The keep, huge and square, was completed by 1171 and was originally part of the gatehouse.

Website: www.english-heritage.org.uk/visit/places/richmond-castle

Sandal Castle

Castle overlooking the River Calder and the site of the battle of Wakefield. The fortress is ruined and conservation work has recently been carried out. It was a principal stronghold of Richard's father, Richard of York, and the castle from which he went to his death. Richard III may have organized meetings of the Council of the North here in the last year of his life.
Run by Wakefield Council.

Website: www.wakefield.gov.uk/events-and-culture/castles/sandal-castle

Scarborough

Town and castle on the North Yorkshire coast. Now and for many years a tourist resort, it was originally a Viking settlement built on the site of a Roman lighthouse. The castle was built by Henry II, who gave charters to the town. It was held in the fourteenth century by Piers Gaveston, the favourite of Edward II. The famous Scarborough Fair, of folksong fame, was set up under a royal charter in 1253, running from Assumption Day (15 August) to Michaelmas (29 September).

Richard's connection lay in the fishing village's use as a naval base. As Lord High Admiral, his job was to maintain the fleet for use against French threats and piracy in the North Sea and the Channel. Richard III House, on the seafront, is first mentioned in the seventeenth century and probably has no actual links with the king. In 1910, for example, it was the local headquarters of the Seamen's Mission.

Website: https://www.discoveryorkshirecoast.com/scarborough

Selaby

Hall and hamlet in County Durham, the home of Robert Brackenbury, steward of Barnard Castle, Constable of the Tower of London and supporter of Richard. The Hall is in private hands and dates from the mid-seventeenth century but it may be on the site of an older building, Brackenbury's residence.

Interestingly, in the context of Richard's horse, White Surrey perhaps being of Arab stock (White Syria), one of the earliest recorded Arabs imported to Britain was the Selaby Turk, owned by the Marshall family who owned Selaby Hall. Is it too fanciful to see some sort of horse-breeding continuation over the centuries here?

Sheriff Hutton

Castle and village north-east of York, the settlement is mentioned in Domesday and featured in the twelfth-century civil war between Stephen and Matilda. It became part of the Neville 'empire' and passed to the crown (Edward IV) in 1480. Richard's niece, Elizabeth of York and Edward, Earl of Warwick, the son of Clarence, lived here briefly and it is possible that Richard intended it as a headquarters of the Council of the North. Today the castle is on private land and although the village is welcoming and friendly (with an excellent deli and coffee shop) access to the castle itself is not possible.

The twelfth-century church of St Helen and Holy Cross was extended in the fourteenth and fifteenth centuries and an alabaster tomb in the chancel was believed (and apparently still is, by the church authorities!) to be the grave of Richard's son, Edward of Middleham. It is much more likely to be that of a son of Ralph Neville, Earl of Westmoreland.

Skipton-in-Craven

Castle and town on the River Aire, called 'in-Craven' to distinguish it from another Skipton (sheep town) on the River Swale. The castle was built in 1090 by Robert de Romille and it was enlarged and strengthened over the years to repel raids from Scotland. The town that grew up traded in sheep and woollens and boasts one of the oldest mills in Yorkshire, in continual use since 1310.

The castle was the stronghold of John 'Black face' Clifford, killed at Towton in 1461 fighting for Henry VI. Much of what we see today is Tudor, a comfortable residence rather than a fortress. There is a very comprehensive tour leaflet for visitors, although Richard seems to have had little to do with the place. A number of re-enactor groups bring Skipton alive in the summer months.

Staindrop

Village near Raby and Barnard Castle in County Durham. The Saxon church of St Mary has alabaster monuments of the Neville family. Ralph Neville, 1st Earl of Westmoreland, lies in noble splendour, complete with fourteenth-century armour, between his two wives, neither of whom is actually buried there. There are two thirteenth-century female tombs in the aisle, but there is dispute over whose they are. The Medieval font has the Neville coat of arms carved onto one of its facets. Once royal (the manor belonged to King Cnut), Staindrop was passed into the control of the Bishops of Durham.

Towton

Battlefield of 1461 between the villages of Towton and Saxton above the Cock Beck, now a small stream. Fought in a freak snowstorm in March, Towton was a resounding victory for Edward of York who became Edward IV as a result. The field today is much as it was in the fifteenth century, allowing for new hedges, and a stone cross, which may have been part of Richard's chantry build in the 1480s, still marks the line of the Lancastrian advance. The Cock Beck at the bottom of Bloody Meadow where most of the slaughter took place is on private farmland and spotter planes regularly pass overhead, possibly looking out for illegal metal detecting. Signs explaining the battle are very good, but also carry a warning that police patrol the area at night.

Wakefield

Battle of 1460 below Richard of York's castle at Sandal Magna and south of the River Calder. The field today is partly covered by a modern housing estate and linking roads. The area nearest to the castle is still largely open, but the hedges of enclosed fields have changed the general appearance. The wooded area in which the Lancastrians may have deployed has now gone, as has the deer park which was certainly there in Tudor times and possibly earlier.

A Victorian monument marking the spot where Richard of York was killed is almost certainly in the wrong place (in what is now a primary school playground) and no mention of any earlier marker exists.

Website: www.battlefieldsofbritain.co.uk/battle_wakefield

York

City on the River Ouse that had once been Eboracum, the base of the Roman VI Legion. It is the seat of the bishops of York, the second highest See in the country and has often been regarded as the capital of the North. Richard was very popular in the city, attending Mass and other solemnities in the Minster and handling all sorts of domestic issues concerning the city's administration. He intended to set up a college of priests one hundred strong here and gave generously to both the Minster and the city.

Alone of English towns, the aldermen of York lamented publicly the death of Richard 'piteously slain and murdered' at Bosworth, risking the wrath of Henry VII.

York is bristling with history including the Richard III Experience at Monk Bar. In the interests of twenty-first-century balance, there is a Henry VII Experience at Micklegate Bar, where the heads of Richard's father and brother were once on display.

Website: www.visityork.org

Appendix II

The Murders of Richard III

Arms of William Shakespeare. If Richard had won Bosworth, Shakespeare wouldn't have had a coat of arms at all!

Many readers of this book will not be that familiar with the work of Tudor apologists like Edward Hall, Polydore Vergil, Thomas More and Ralph Holinshed. They will, however, be familiar with at least some of the prolific work of William Shakespeare, who used all or most of the above as his sources to write *The Tragedy of King Richard the Third*. It is the Shakespeare version, with its deliciously Machiavellian, hunch-backed, black-clothed cripple that still informs most people's views, despite three centuries of attempts to put the record straight.

In Act V, Scene III of the play, on the night before Bosworth, Richard is troubled by the appearance of the ghosts of those he has supposedly murdered. It is a brilliant dramatic convention, spoiled a little by the positive appearance of those same ghosts to Henry Tudor (which is often left out of recent productions as being too repetitive).

Let us see how accurate Shakespeare was in his condemnation of the king.

Prince Edward, son to Henry the Sixth

'Let me sit heavy on thy soul tomorrow!
Think, how thou stab'dest me in my prime of youth
At Tewkesbury: despair, therefore and die!'

As we have seen, Edward, Prince of Wales, was almost certainly killed in the headlong retreat by the Lancastrians, running north through the town after their front collapsed. The legend of Richard's personal dispatch of Edward is pure Lancastrian/Tudor propaganda, rather as the Yorkist propaganda had Lord Clifford personally murdering Edmund, Duke of Rutland, at Wakefield. Richard did, of course, condemn men to death after the battle in his legitimate role as Constable of England. Edward was not among them.

Henry the Sixth

> *'When I was mortal, my anointed body*
> *By thee was punched full of deadly holes:*
> *Think on the Tower and me: despair and die!'*

There is some dispute about whether Richard of Gloucester was present in London when Henry died, but if he was, he was one among an estimated 50,000 others, hundreds of whom had access to the Tower. Henry had been a constant thorn in the Yorkist side for years. His constant imprisonments and escapes merely added to his own confusion and misery. He died within hours of Edward IV's arrival in London on 21 May 1471 and was almost certainly killed by guards acting on the king's orders. When Henry's body was re-interred in November 1910, there was said to be a bloodstain on the skull which *could* indicate execution by axe, the traditional means of dispatch of a king.

Clarence

> *'Let me sit heavy on thy soul tomorrow!*
> *I, that was wash'd to death with fulsome wine,*
> *Poor Clarence, by thy guile betrayed to death!*
> *Tomorrow in the battle think on me,*
> *And fall thy edgeless sword: despair and die.'*

'Poor Clarence' was perfectly happy to betray his own brothers, Edward and Richard, with the connivance of the Earl of Warwick and it is a bit rich of Shakespeare to call the kettle black. It is true that he and Richard quarrelled over acquisition of the Neville estates and that, as adults, the brothers were not as close as they had been as children. Even so, Clarence was found guilty of treason by a lawfully constituted court and his murder, if it was not an actual execution, was almost certainly ordered by his brother Edward, not his brother Richard. Circumstantial evidence has Richard bitterly upset over Clarence's death which may have kept him even more resolutely in the North after it.

Rivers, Grey and Vaughan

> Rivers: *'Let me sit heavy on thy soul tomorrow,*
> *Rivers, that died at Pomfret! Despair and die!'*
> Grey: *'Think upon Grey and let thy soul despair!'*
> Vaughan: *'Think upon Vaughan, and with guilty fear*
> *Let fall thy lance: despair and die!'*

Those three, in Richard's eyes, were traitors. They had connived with the hated Woodville family to control the new king, Edward V, whereas the princes' father's will had stipulated that it was their uncle Richard who was to be their Protector. Execution may seem harsh, but the whole experience of Richard's life was that leaving enemies alive was dangerous. There is considerable evidence to suggest that there was an attempted ambush on Richard and Buckingham by these men and if that was the case, the execution decision was perfectly justified. They may even have faced a formal trial at Pontefract under the Earl of Northumberland.

Hastings

> *'Bloody and guilty, guiltily awake*
> *And in a bloody battle end thy days!*
> *Think on Lord Hastings: despair and die!'*

The whole Hastings episode, involving strawberries, witchcraft and Jane Shore is excellent melodrama, but how much of it is true we have discussed in Chapter 10. The fact is that Hastings had turned against Richard and treason against the king, as in the cases of Clarence, Rivers, Grey and Vaughan above, could only be punished by death. The lack of trial in Hastings' case implies that Richard was going beyond the bounds of legality here, but again, we must bear in mind the fact that the Constable of England was not bound to provide one and tensions at the time ran high.

The Two Young Princes

> *'Dream on thy cousins [nephews] smother'd in the Tower:*
> *Let us be lead within thy bosom, Richard,*
> *And weigh thee down to ruin, shame and death*
> *Thy nephews' souls bid thee despair and die!'*

This is the big one! The crime of child murder which will forever colour our view of Richard III. It is discussed in detail in Chapter 11, but the bottom line is, despite the bodies discovered in 1674, there is no hard evidence that the princes died young at all, either in the Tower or anywhere else. Politically, Richard stood to gain, but so did Henry Tudor and even Harry Buckingham.

Lady Anne

> 'Richard, thy wife, that wretched Anne, thy wife,
> That never slept a quiet hour with thee,
> Now fills thy sleep with perturbations:
> Tomorrow in the battle think on me,
> And fall thy edgeless sword: despair and die.'

Other than the princes, this is the saddest accusation made against Richard, that he had Anne poisoned to enable him to make a dynastic marriage with Elizabeth, his niece (the future wife of Henry VII). There is no evidence at all that the couple were unhappy and both were devastated by the early death of their son, Edward of Middleham. Anne almost certainly died of tuberculosis, a common killer, on 16 March 1485. Richard's negotiations to marry either a Portuguese or a Spanish princess after her death (not, note, Elizabeth of York) may seem cynical to twenty-first-century eyes, but it was normal royal practice in the fifteenth.

Buckingham

> 'The first was I that help'd thee to the crown;
> The last was I that felt thy tyranny;
> O, in the battle think on Buckingham,
> And die in terror of thy guiltiness.
> Dream on, dream on, of bloody deeds and death:
> Fainting, despair; despairing, yield thy breath!'

Harry Stafford, Duke of Buckingham, was a traitor, pure and simple. Like many men in the Wars of the Roses, including Warwick and Clarence, he changed sides with the wind of politics and was caught out. Mounting an armed insurrection against a king was the surest way of dying in the fifteenth century.

> 'Methought', whispers Richard after he wakes up screaming, 'the
>   souls of all that that I had murder'd
> Came to my tent: and every one did threat
> Tomorrow's vengeance on the head of Richard.'

Incidentally, those same souls, in the Shakespeare version, were wasting their time heaping praise and success on Henry Tudor who was to 'beget a happy race of kings'. All his life, Henry was plagued by doubt and insecurity, aware of just how lucky he had been at Bosworth. Like Anne, he died of tuberculosis in April 1509. His eldest surviving son, Henry VIII, destroyed the Catholic church and innumerable lives in the process, before dying, possibly of syphilis, in January 1547. *His* eldest son, Edward VI, barely made it to his sixteenth birthday before tuberculosis, exacerbated by measles, killed him. Henry's daughter Mary died of ovarian cancer in the November of 1558, a bitter and vengeful woman. Her sister Elizabeth lived longer than any of them, but not before both she and her sister had burned hundreds of Protestants and Catholics between them in the name of religion. Bronchopneumonia finished Elizabeth in March 1603. Unlike the Plantagenets, the Tudors targeted and executed women with an almost reckless glee (including two of Henry VIII's queens). The reign of Elizabeth was the first in history in which the extensive use of torture was sanctioned by the queen herself. So much for Shakespeare's 'happy race of kings'.

Richard, of course, *did* die in the battle, as the ghosts predicted, but it had nothing to do with their doom and gloom. That was all about bad timing and bad luck.

Select Bibliography

Allen Brown, R., *English Castles,* Boydell Press, 2004
Ashdown-Hill, John, *The Mythology of Richard III*, Amberley, 2016
Baldwin, David, *Richard III,* Amberley, 2013
Brewer, Clifford, *The Death of Kings,* Abson Books, 2005
Carson, Annette, *Richard III: The Maligned King*, History Press, 2008
Cheetham, Anthony, *The Life and Times of Richard III,* BCA, 1972
Gravett, Christopher, *Bosworth 1485,* Osprey, 1999
Guest, Ken and Denise, *British Battles,* Harper Collins, 1996
Hammond, P.W., *Food and Feast in Medieval England*, Alan Sutton, 1993
Hammond, Peter, *The Children of Richard III,* Fonthill, 2018
Hancock, Peter, *Richard III and the Murder in the Tower*, History Press, 2011
Hardy, Robert, (Intro), *The Battle of Tewkesbury 1471,* Tewkesbury Medieval Festival 2011
Hicks, Michael, *Richard III*, Tempus, 2003
Jones, Michael K., *Bosworth 1485: Psychology of a Battle*, History Press, 2010
Kendall, Paul Murray, *Richard the Third,* George Allen and Unwin, 1955
Laughey, Philippa and Jones, Michael, *The Search for Richard III,* John Murray, 2013
Lewis, Matthew, *The Survival of the Princes in the Tower*, History Press, 2017
Lewis, Matthew, *Richard, Duke of York, King by Right*, Amberley, 2017
Licence, Amy, *Cecily Neville, Mother of Kings,* Amberley, 2014
McLachlan, Sean, *Medieval Handgonnes*, Osprey, 2010
Mortimer, Ian, *The Time Traveller's Guide to Medieval England,* Vintage, 2009
Orme, Nicholas, *Medieval Children,* Yale University Press, 2001
Penn, Thomas, *The Brothers York*, Allen Lane, 2019
Penn, Thomas, *Winter King: the Dawn of Tudor England*, Penguin, 2012
Pollard, A.J., *Richard III and the Princes in the Tower*, Alan Sutton, 1991
Ross, Charles, *Richard III*, Yale University Press, 1999
Santiuste, David, *Edward IV and the Wars of the Roses*, Pen and Sword, 2017
Skidmore, Chris, *Richard III: Brother, Protector, King*, Weidenfeld and Nicholson, 2017
Skinner, Julia and Sackett, Eliza, *British Castles (Francis Frith Collection),* Bounty, 2006
Weir, Alison, *Britain's Royal Families,* Pimlico, 2002

Weir, Alison, *The Princes in the Tower*, Pimlico, 1994
Young and Adair, *Hastings to Culloden,* G. Bell & Sons, 1964

Pamphlets/Guides
Hislop, Michael, *Barnard Castle, Bowes Castle and Egglestone Abbey,* English Heritage
Innes-Smith, Robert, *Raby Castle,* Jarrold Publishing, 2019
Kenyon, John R., *Middleham Castle,* English Heritage
Pembrill, Colin, *Fotheringhay Church and its Royal Associations,* Friends of Fotheringhay Church
Roberts, Ian, *The Medieval Cellar at Pontefract Castle,* West Yorkshire Archaeological Services
King Richard Reinterment, 21–29 March 2015

Index

Albany, Alexander, Duke of 97-9
Anne, Queen *see* Anne Neville
Argentein, Dr John 115, 116, 119

Battles
    Agincourt 4, 7, 12, 37, 95
    Barnet 64-72, 81-4, 94, 136, 140, 153
    Blore Heath 22, 23, 32, 33
    Bosworth viii, x, 16, 35, 50, 51, 53, 76, 90, 114, 115, 117, 133-46, 151, 153-5, 159, 161, 164, 165, 169
    Ludford Bridge 21, 23, 24, 26, 32, 35, 44, 105
    Mortimer's Cross 39-41, 48
    St Albans 20, 30, 33, 37, 41, 44, 45, 48, 55, 68, 71, 103
    Tewkesbury 72-8, 83, 94, 95, 98, 104, 105, 126, 140, 153, 165
    Wakefield 21-39, 41, 44, 45, 47, 64, 110, 111, 161, 166
Baynard's Castle, London 27, 28, 44, 52, 106, 108, 112
Berwick 63, 65, 96, 98, 99, 151, 156, 158
Blanc Sanglier 128, 143
Bourchier, Thomas, Archbishop of Canterbury 108, 113
Brackenbury, Robert 120, 134, 136, 141, 151, 155, 162
Brandon, William 142, 145
Bruges 43, 44, 51, 52, 90
Buckingham, Anne, Duchess of 24, 27, 44
Buckingham, Henry Stafford, Duke of 79, 102, 103, 105, 106, 108, 113, 114, 117, 121, 124, 125, 130, 131, 133, 167, 168
Buckingham, Humphrey Stafford, Duke of 26, 27

Burgh, Alice 78, 153
Burgundy, Philip, Duke of 42, 43, 51, 65, 66, 94, 95, 105

Calais 22-4, 26, 52, 63, 67, 68, 78, 82, 99, 101, 117, 155
Cambridge, Richard, Earl of 1, 3, 4
Canterbury 52, 87, 90
Carlisle 81, 82, 87, 97, 98, 152, 156, 160
Castles
    Bamburgh 63, 94, 96
    Barnard Castle 2, 7, 8, 82, 87-9, 93, 96, 118, 154, 162, 163
    Bowes 52, 156, 161
    Conisbrough 1-5, 32, 156
    Fotheringhay 13-17, 19, 64, 94, 97, 98, 110, 145
    Ludlow 13, 15, 16, 18-24, 28-30, 63, 68, 100-102
    Middleham 30, 55-63, 65-8, 81-92, 96, 100, 103, 105, 130, 135, 145, 148, 150, 151, 153, 154, 156-9
    Pontefract 4, 5, 31, 32, 35, 38, 45, 51, 65, 68, 69, 84, 103, 108-11, 130, 151, 160, 167
    Raby 7-17, 61, 120, 134, 160, 163
    Sandal 2, 20, 26, 31-6, 41, 45, 60, 69, 91, 92, 108, 130, 145, 150-2, 161, 163
    Warwick 21, 57, 58, 67, 82, 95, 104
    Windsor 13, 95, 100, 107, 124, 125, 127, 136, 144, 150
Catesby, William 50, 91, 106, 141
Cato, Angelo, Archbishop of Vienne 103
Chronicles
    Annales Rerum Anglicorum 33, 38
    Chronicle of Tewkesbury Abbey 75

Croyland Chronicle 40, 67, 76, 83, 99, 100, 102-105, 110, 114-17, 129, 135, 138, 151, 152
De Occupatione Regni Anglie Per Ricardum Tertium Libellus 103
English Chronicle 33, 38
Great Chronicle of London 115, 118, 138
Gregory's Chronicle 35, 49
History of the Earls of Warwick (Rous Roll) 104, 118, 127, 135
John Benet's Chronicle 33
Recueil des Croniques et anciennes istoires de la Grant Bretagne 33
Register of Abbot Whethamstede 33, 38, 42
Charles VII of France 43
Cheney, John 142, 145
Chester 28, 63
Clarence, George, Duke of 15, 18-20, 23, 27, 29, 38, 42, 44, 51-4, 56, 58, 63, 65-9, 72, 75-8, 80, 82, 83, 94-7, 118, 126, 127, 135, 167, 168
Clifford, Lord Henry 30, 47
Council of the North 60, 61, 85, 89, 91, 92, 108, 130, 134, 141, 145, 149, 150, 152, 154, 161, 162
Coventry 20, 21, 23, 24, 32, 45, 69, 128, 131, 150
Coverham Abbey 89, 155, 156

Dacre, Lord 30, 50, 58, 84, 152
De Waurin, Jean 33, 35
Denham, John 48, 49
Dighton, John 118, 120, 121
Dintingdale 47
Doncaster 2, 32
Durham 61, 63, 87, 91, 92, 123, 129, 157, 160, 162, 163

Edinburgh 98, 99, 158-9
Edward III 1, 4, 7, 8, 29, 44, 53, 54, 102, 121, 130

Edward IV 4, 5, 14, 15, 18, 19, 22-4, 26, 27, 29, 30, 35, 38-40, 42, 44, 45, 47-56, 59, 62-72, 74-84, 95-107, 113, 114, 116, 122, 124, 126, 128, 138, 145, 147, 150, 151, 155, 159, 162, 163, 166
Edward of Middleham 85, 86, 90, 91, 105, 116, 124, 127-30, 135, 151, 153, 155, 157, 158, 159, 162, 168
Edward V 68, 78, 95, 100-103, 105-108, 114-20, 122, 167
Edward, Prince of Wales 19, 30, 41, 72, 75, 82, 104, 126, 165-6

Fabyan, Robert 15, 138
Falstoff Place, Southwark 27-9, 39, 42
Falstoff, Sir John 13, 28
Fauconberg, Lord William 13, 27, 47, 48, 69, 75
Ferrybridge 45, 47
Forest, Miles 89, 118, 120-2
Frederick III, Holy Roman Emperor 92

Gainsborough 130, 158
Grafton Regis, Northants 56, 102
Great Council 19, 20, 83, 95, 101-104, 106, 108, 128, 129, 151, 152
Grey, Richard 102, 103, 108, 110, 111, 130, 151, 167
Greystoke, Baron 30, 58, 84, 97, 129, 150

Hall, Edward 25, 36, 165
Harrington, James 141, 150
Harrington, Thomas 32, 37
Hastings, William, Lord 50, 53, 67, 68, 70, 71, 73-5, 79, 91, 101, 105-107, 114, 124-6, 129, 130, 134, 144, 167
Henry IV 1, 4, 5, 7, 145
Henry V 4, 5, 7, 11-13, 19, 28, 40
Henry VI (play) 16, 25, 37, 38, 47, 49, 75
Henry VI 12, 13, 15, 16, 19, 20, 23-7, 29, 30, 39-41, 43, 44, 47, 50, 51, 54, 68, 69, 72, 75, 76, 82, 96, 138, 144, 145, 150, 163, 165, 166

Henry VII 68, 76, 79, 82, 91, 92, 94, 104, 108, 112-18, 121, 128, 130-8, 140-7, 151, 152, 154, 161, 164, 165, 168, 169
Henry VIII 16, 50, 52, 81, 90, 117, 121, 144, 149, 152, 157, 158, 169
Holinshed, Raphael 36, 165

James III of Scotland 93-5, 97-9, 128, 157

Kendall, John 129, 150, 151
Kirby Muxloe 50, 107

Leicester xii, xiii, 20, 61, 62, 119, 128, 131, 138, 142-4, 146-8
Leland, John 50, 51, 124
Lincoln 130, 131
Lincoln, John de la Pole, Earl of Lincoln 61, 92, 113, 150, 151, 159
Looking for Richard (Film) xi
Looking for Richard (Project) xii-xiii
Louis XI of France 43, 55, 63, 65-6, 82, 94, 103, 128
Lovell, Viscount Francis 58, 91, 92, 97, 108, 113, 126, 136, 150, 153, 159

Mancini, Dominic 96, 102-105, 108, 110, 112, 114-17
Margaret Beaufort 72, 82, 113, 116, 121, 130, 131
Margaret of Anjou 15, 20, 22-4, 26, 29, 30, 33, 36, 37, 40-5, 51-3, 63, 68, 69, 72, 74, 75, 82, 93, 96, 101, 149
Martyn, Alice 42, 43, 78
Maximilian I 62, 117
Metcalfe, James 59, 85, 151
Metcalfe, Miles 129, 150, 151
Micklegate Bar, York 39, 51, 59, 129, 164
Milford Haven 136-7
Minster Lovell 116, 126
Montagu, John Neville, Marquess of 33, 64, 66, 68, 69, 71
More, Thomas 16, 79, 89, 107, 108, 117-21, 126, 165

Morton, John, Bishop of Ely 106-108, 118, 126, 130, 131, 134
Mowbray, Anne 95, 115

Neville, Anne 59-61, 72, 78, 79, 82, 83, 85-7, 90, 91, 95, 104, 113, 116, 124, 127-30, 135, 150, 158
Neville, Cecily 8, 10-16, 19, 21, 23, 24, 27-9, 39, 42-4, 69, 82, 85, 86, 91, 94, 96, 99, 106, 128, 160
Neville, George, Bishop of Exeter 44, 49, 59, 64, 66
Neville, Isobel 59, 67, 78, 95, 135
Neville, Richard, Earl of Warwick 20, 22, 23, 26, 27, 29, 30, 40-5, 47, 51, 54, 55, 57, 59, 60, 63, 64-9, 71, 72, 77, 80, 81, 83-5, 95, 127, 159
Newark 67, 159
Norfolk, John Howard, Duke of 75, 81, 95, 106, 113-15, 124, 131, 136, 138, 141
Northampton 26, 27, 30, 32, 102
Northumberland, Henry Percy, Earl of 30, 66, 77, 112, 151, 152
Nottingham 67, 69, 128, 135, 136, 138, 159

Oxford 126
Oxford, John de Vere, Earl of 70, 71, 137, 140, 141

Parre, Thomas 32, 37, 39
Paston family 14, 28, 29, 51
Penrith 81, 160
Pickering, James 32, 37, 39
Picquigny, Treaty of 94, 97
Placentia, palace of (Greenwich) 53, 65, 115, 124, 125, 150
Plantagenet, John of Gloucester 78, 79, 130
Plantagenet, Katherine 79

Rivers
  Aire 45, 47, 81, 162
  Avon 57, 82, 127
  Calder 25, 37, 38, 156, 161, 163

Cock 48-50, 163
Corve 21
Don 1, 2, 156
Eamont 81
Nene 13, 26
Ouse 90, 91, 164
Severn 72, 74, 83, 126
Soar 128, 138, 147
Swale 82, 161, 162
Swilgate 74
Tarn 22
Tees 82, 88, 89, 155
Teme 21, 23
Trent 78, 80, 84, 110, 111, 150, 151, 154, 155, 158, 159
Tweed 98, 156
Ure 56
Ratcliffe, Richard 91, 92, 103, 108, 134, 150, 151
Richard II 1, 4, 7, 29, 30, 110, 160
Richard III
  Birth 14, 16
  Early Childhood 5, 18-23, 25, 27, 29, 42, 33, 51, 52, 53, 54
  Childhood at Middleham 56-9, 61, 63-5
  Barnet 70-2
  Tewkesbury 72-6
  Admiral 65, 81, 82, 95, 101, 161
  Scotland 93-9, 156
  Marriage 82-4, 86, 87, 90, 91
  Lordship of the North 77-92, 96, 153, 156, 157, 158, 160-4
  Duke of Gloucester 66-9, 89, 93, 94, 96, 100, 102-108, 112
  Coronation 85, 113, 117
  Royal Progress 116, 123-32, 159
  Reign 40, 41, 48, 51, 59, 61-3, 133, 135, 136
  The Princes 28, 115-22
  Bosworth 14, 16, 35, 128, 133-43
  Reburial 119, 144-8
  Legacy 92, 146, 149-54
Richard III (Film) viii-x, 82

Richard III (play) 53, 59, 75, 80, 84, 95, 101, 106, 108, 110, 116, 117, 120, 122, 130, 131, 135, 147, 165-9
Richard III Society xii, 78
Richmond, Henry Tudor, Earl of
  see Henry VII
Richmond, Yorkshire 63, 65, 81, 82, 85, 156, 161
Rivers, Anthony Woodville, Earl 101, 103, 108, 110, 111, 130, 151, 160, 167
Rivers, Lady Jacquetta 44
Rivers, Richard Woodville, Earl 56, 66-8, 131
Rotherham 2
Rotherham, Thomas, Archbishop of York 106, 129, 134
Rous, John 16, 104, 118, 127, 128, 130, 135
Russell, John, Bishop of Lincoln 104, 115
Rutland, Edmund, Duke of 14, 18, 19, 22-4, 26, 29, 30, 34, 36, 37, 39, 42, 45, 51, 94, 110, 160, 166

Salisbury, Thomas Neville, Earl of 20, 37, 39
Saxton 47, 48, 50, 163
Scarborough 81, 161, 162
Scrope of Bolton, Lord 58, 59, 61, 84, 150
Scrope of Masham, Lord 4, 58, 84, 98, 150
Selaby 120, 134, 153, 162
Shakespeare, William xii, xiii, 13, 25, 28, 36, 37, 63, 82, 92, 102, 103, 126, 141, 158
Sheriff Hutton 55-63, 81, 86, 89-91, 103, 121, 130, 135, 145, 150-2, 156, 162
Shore, Jane 42, 79, 105, 107, 167
Skipton-in-Craven 81, 162-3
Somerset, Edmund Beaufort, Duke of 15, 33, 38, 41, 48-50, 70, 71, 73, 74
St George's Chapel, Windsor 54, 76, 100, 107, 124, 144, 145
St Paul's Cathedral, London 15, 20, 30, 44, 58, 72, 76, 105, 108, 120
Staindrop 7, 11, 12, 94, 163

Stanley, George, Lord Strange 14, 129, 138
Stanley, Lord Thomas 68, 91, 92, 99, 106, 113, 121, 129, 131, 136, 138, 141, 142, 151
Stanley, Sir William 14, 75, 97, 137, 138, 141, 142, 151, 154
Stillington, Robert, Bishop of Bath and Wells 106, 114
Stony Stratford 102, 105, 118

Titulus Regius 44, 112, 114
Tower of London 26, 28, 32, 52, 68, 69, 75, 84, 89, 95, 98, 101, 102, 105-108, 111, 115-21, 124, 126, 127, 130, 134, 149, 150, 162, 166, 167
Trollope, Andrew 23, 35, 48, 49, 50
Tudor, Jasper, Earl of Pembroke 72
Tyrell, James 84, 117, 118, 120, 150

Utrecht 43, 44, 47, 51

Vaughan, Thomas 102, 103, 110, 111, 130, 151, 160, 167
Vergil, Polydore 37, 104, 138, 165
Von Poppelau, Nicholas 62, 92

Wakefield 2, 69, 91, 108, 160, 163
Warbeck, Perkin 117, 154
Warwick the Kingmaker *see* Neville, Richard, Earl of Warwick
Warwick, Edward, Earl of 108, 124, 129, 130, 162
Wenlock, John 48, 49, 52, 74
Westminster Abbey, London 43, 44, 68, 83, 105, 113, 115, 119, 144, 145
Westminster Palace, London 13, 30, 95, 135, 152
Westmoreland, Ralph Neville, Earl of 5, 7, 8, 12, 58, 82, 162, 163
White Surrey 141, 142, 162
Woodville, Elizabeth 35, 56, 65, 78, 82, 105, 106

York 7, 30, 39, 40, 45, 49-51, 59, 66, 67, 69, 78, 82, 85-7, 89, 90, 92, 96, 98, 102, 105, 117, 120, 129, 130, 135, 145, 150-2, 154, 155, 161, 162, 164
York, Richard, Duke of (Prince) 105-107, 119-21
York, Richard, Duke of 1, 2, 5, 13-15, 18-20, 22-6, 28-39, 41-5, 59, 64, 94, 102, 110, 157, 160, 161, 163, 164